D1029293

MAIN LINE TO OBLIVION

KENNIKAT PRESS

NATIONAL UNIVERSITY PUBLICATIONS

SERIES IN AMERICAN STUDIES

Under the General Editorial Supervision of
JAMES P. SHENTON
Professor of History, Columbia University

ROBERT B. CARSON

MAIN LINE TO OBLIVION

**THE DISINTEGRATION OF NEW YORK RAILROADS
IN THE TWENTIETH CENTURY**

NATIONAL UNIVERSITY PUBLICATIONS
KENNIKAT PRESS
Port Washington, N.Y. // London

Library of Congress Catalog Card Number 75-139352
ISBN 0-8046-9003-0

Manufactured in the United States of America

Published by
Kennikat Press
Port Washington, N.Y./London

To The Memory of My Father,
A Very Special Kind of Businessman

PREFACE

Each attempt at an interpretive study develops its own unique history as it meanders along the twists and turns of its author's mind, and, for some readers, the story of the effort's genesis and maturity may be of interest. This one began a good many years ago in Dr. Harry Pierce's course in American economic history, a graduate class which met weekly in the dusty fourth floor seminar rooms of Syracuse University's Maxwell Hall. It resulted from the chance suggestion of Professor Pierce that not much attention had been paid by economic historians to American railroad history in the twentieth century. Some of the ideas that follow first appeared in a research paper for Pierce's seminar. Eventually, that paper grew into a doctoral dissertation, written, sometimes it seemed in blood, under the demanding but stimulating direction of Dr. Pierce. The author can only hope that at least a small fraction of that teacher's commitment to meticulous detail and his breadth of knowledge about American railroad and business history is captured in the following work.

From research paper to published manuscript, however, there has been the accumulation of many other debts, some intellectual and some of a more personal kind. The discovery of Gabriel Kolko's *Triumph of Conservatism* at a very early period in my study was crucial, for Professor Kolko's analysis of the Progressive Era provided for this writer a means to organize his own half-developed ideas on railroad and government relations. The publication of Kolko's controversial *Railroads and Regulation, 1877-1916,* somewhat later in my labors, was also helpful, for while it only slightly overlapped my own research it convinced me that I was on the right track in my study of twentieth-century railroad affairs. The intellectual debt to Dr. Kolko will be evident to all who are familiar with his work.

Professor Martin Sklar of Northern Illinois University, through many hours of discussion, further sharpened my understanding of government and corporate relations in America. Professor Daniel Fine of Indiana (Pennsylvania) State University contributed mightily to my perception of political processes in the United States. Dr. Louis Salkever, now chairman of the Department of Economics at the State University of New York at Albany and Dr. Sanford Gordon of State University College, Oneonta, New York, were understanding department chairmen, and a would-be author in the academic world is very much in need of sympathy from his department head. To Dr. David DeGrood of the University of Bridgeport, I owe a special gratitude for the encouragement he offered when I periodically became depressed with the manuscript's development and considered "forgetting it all." Mrs. Susan DeJoy, my typist, also deserves special recognition for struggling patiently with my scribbling and for working diligently to meet deadlines.

There has also been "institutional" help. Mr. Harry Eddy of the Association of American Railroads in Washington, D.C. provided much useful material that could not be obtained elsewhere. The librarians of Syracuse University and the State University Colleges at New Paltz and Oneonta, New York, labored to get obscure books, periodicals, and official records through inter-library loans. During the last stages of the manuscript's development, the State University of New York Research Foundation provided some much needed and greatly appreciated financial aid in the form of a faculty fellowship.

An unrepayable debt is owed my wife, Marjorie Gale Carson, not just for wifely duties such as steady encouragement and keeping the kids out of their father's way when necessary, but for the contribution of her own skills in the preparation of the railroad maps in the appendix.

TABLE OF CONTENTS

MAIN LINE TO OBLIVION

INTRODUCTION

The era of railroad building in the nineteenth century has long preoccupied chroniclers of American railroads and economic historians almost to the complete exclusion of studying twentieth-century developments. The result has been to produce a not wholly inaccurate impression that American railroad history ends about 1900. The reasons for this disproportionate study are not surprising. American historians have generally represented the nineteenth-century building of railroads as an indispensable technological step in American economic development and have advanced a fairly substantial body of theory to support this position. These "indispensability theories" have variously emphasized that railroads were an essential component of social overhead capital that tied the nation together commercially or that railroad construction provided crucial stimulation to capital formation and expanded investment in related industries.

This emphasis upon the railroad's role as a stimulant to capital formation, which has enjoyed wide support among economic and business historians, is well illustrated in Leland Jenks' 1944 study, "Railroads as an Economic Force in American History."[1] Building on the then popular economic growth theories of the economist Joseph Schumpeter, Jenks saw the railroads as the single most important force in American economic development. Through the work of the railroad promoter, capital was accumulated not just within the railroad industry but also in other related industries. He concluded:

> ...The conviction that the railroad could run anywhere at a profit put fresh spurs to American ingenuity and opened closed paddocks of potential enterprise.

3

Innovations are the work of enterprisers. For the railroad as an idea, the role of entrepreneurship was pretty much identical with promotion.... Each railway project involved the sanguine judgement of enterprising individuals and groups in particular local situations that a certain line could be of direct or indirect pecuniary advantage to themselves. It was linked to specific plans for town promotion and real estate speculation, to combinations for contracting services and supplies and for exploitation of resources, in anticipation of the actual movement of traffic by rail. The railway projector became an exemplification of business organization, of the ability of man to master his environment.[2]

More recently, W. W. Rostow and others have given new life to the "indispensability thesis" by pointing out that the whole process of economic development depends upon both the accumulation of capital and the creation of a commercial infrastructure. In Rostow's economic stage approach to the history of American development, the railroads were the crucial first step in these directions. However, neither Rostow's nor Jenks' interpretations are especially innovative, since nineteenth-century observers of railroad building usually had held the same views.[3] There have been some quite recent efforts to "revise" these interpretations of the role played by railroads in the nineteenth century, but the indispensability arguments nevertheless remain well entrenched in contemporary studies of the economic development of the United States.[4]

Quite irrespective of well-developed theories on railroads' contribution to economic growth, railroads in the nineteenth century have also attracted the historian's attention because they provided a business history with a full measure of vitality and excess. The personal financial extravagances of Gould, Vanderbilt, Drew and others were never to be matched again. The rate wars and the stories of farmers and merchants struggling against powerful railroad interests, from the point of view of historical interpretation, were an integral part of nineteenth-century America. The railroads characterized an age and they drew appropriate attention.

There was to be no similar central role for railroads in the nation's twentieth-century economic development, as interest in new industries and new economic problems thrust railroads aside. The diminished role was, of course, not simply an illusion. There was abundant evidence that the technology, the finances, and the corporate organization of railroads had a dwindling impact on the business of America.

The downward slide of railroad fortunes in the twentieth century has been neither swift nor altogether continuous. As Table 1 shows, the peak of railroad building was reached in 1916, when operating first trackage or mainline attained approximately 254,000 miles.[5] By 1966, the American railroad network had declined to less than 212,000 miles, and the general impression among rail management and government officials was that the end of this contraction was not yet in sight.[6] The reduction in rail operations was also observable in other ways. By the 1960's, many former passenger-carrying roads had discontinued service, and all had greatly reduced passenger operations. Meanwhile, the frequency of freight service and the

TABLE 1

RAILROAD MAINLINE MILEAGE IN THE UNITED STATES
SELECTED YEARS 1830-1960 [a]

Year	Mileage
1830	27
1840	2,818
1850	9,021
1860	30,626
1870	57,922
1880	93,296
1890	160,544
1900	194,321
1910	243,107
1916 (peak year)	254,250
1920	252,844
1930	249,052
1940	233,670
1950	223,779
1960	217,552

[a] U.S. Bureau of the Census, *Historical Statistics of the United States, Colonial Times to 1957* (Washington, D. C., U. S. Government Printing Office, 1960), p. 427 and Interstate Commerce Commission, *Transportation Statistics* (selected years).

maintenance of allied railroad enterprises such as ticket and baggage agencies and less-than-carload freight had been drastically curtailed.[7]

Less apparent than the physical contraction of rail operations has been the parallel reduction of the network into fewer and fewer corporate properties. The disappearance of some railroad companies, of course, reflected the abandonment of all their operations; however, most lost their identity initially through merger and consolidation. In New York State, about half of the seventy separate railroad corporations operating in 1900 had disappeared through merger by 1964.[8]

The twentieth-century changes in the railroad network, both the reduction in the railroad plant and the integration of properties into fewer corporate entities, have been largely ignored by business and economic historians.[9] Relying on a plethora of more or less uneven statistical studies produced by labor and transportation economists and students of public regulation, economic historians have tended to generalize twentieth-century changes in the railroad network as the result of "neutral" technological developments and uninspired government regulation, which made railroads poor competitors with other modes of transportation.[10] Such an explanation of developments in the industry after 1900 is deceptive in its simplicity and apparent logic — a kind of converse of the indispensability thesis. If railroads grew because they were technologically essential to economic development, then their decline can be explained as a function of their technological obsolescence. This approach, however, really doesn't answer many questions. It fails to explain why certain lines were abandoned and others are still operated or why some roads were absorbed in mergers and others were not. It provides no insight to the development of railroad corporate policy except to suggest that it must have been formed "willy-nilly" in reaction to exogenous technological and regulatory developments over which the railroads had no control.[11]

In the following analysis, using New York railroads as a focal point, the physical contraction of the network and the integration of corporate properties are not viewed as simply neutral results of technological change and government policy but as interconnected features of a rational corporate policy that has been developing since the era of railroad expansion ended.

Specifically, abandonment and consolidation have been employed as methods of dealing with the chronic railroad problem of excess capacity.

The economic concept of "excess capacity," of course, refers to the degree of underutilization of plant and equipment that a nation, an industry, or a firm might suffer. A high degree of excess capacity necessarily indicates a relatively poor economic use of productive facilities. While the concept has received increased attention in recent years from economists concerned with problems of economic growth, it has been most inadequately developed as a statistical device. The calculation, in mathematical terms, of excess capacity in the railroad industry or for any particular railroad has not been attempted and would be a most difficult undertaking. However, this is not to say that the underutilization of plant and equipment in the railroad industry has not been recognized as a serious problem.

For the purposes of this study, no mathematical precision is attempted in defining or using the concept of excess capacity. Rather, it is used loosely to describe the quite obvious, but unmeasured, underutilization of the network in general and most railroads in particular. While industry, government, and financial leaders may not always have called this problem "excess capacity," and may have had no way of measuring its intensity, they have shown, since the late years of the nineteenth century, that they were aware that the American railroad network was constructed to carry more traffic than in fact it was able to originate.[12]

By the last decade of the nineteenth century, railroads had literally penetrated every corner of the American countryside, with the eastern states having by far the highest intensity of rail trackage. Local boosters of municipalities or even self-respecting crossroads were quick to point out the present and future economic benefits of their rail connections. However, the frenzied constructions of the seventies, eighties, and nineties, viewed not as immediately profitable speculative achievements, but in the calmer circumstances of earning an operating profit, had produced in most areas of the nation too intensive a distribution of rail service for the actual traffic available.

When railroads, or for that matter any industry, employs existing plant and equipment in such a way that additional business can only be profitably handled by expanded investment, excess capacity naturally does not exist. However, American railroads did not enjoy the bliss of this happy state of economic affairs. Instead, the existence of excess capacity within the industry tended to create chronic price instability and the periodic appearance of aggressive competition.

Since most of the expenses of a railroad were fixed costs for plant and equipment which had to be paid even if revenues fell to zero, railroads, if they desired or were compelled, could reduce rates quite radically—to that point where total revenue at least covered variable operating costs and left at least some portion of income to be applied against fixed costs. While it could be expected that rates might fall in times of business recession as each railroad sought to gain a larger share of a dwindling market, the chronic underutilization of the railroad plant in times of comparative business prosperity meant persistent price instability. Railroad operators who believed that rate reductions or rebates would have the effect of increasing their business and revenues without increasing fixed costs might at any time resolve to lower rates. Quite naturally, such actions by any one railroad evoked similar actions from competitiors so that the earnings of all might fall appreciably. As a result, the closing decades of the century were characterized by a series of bitter rate wars within the industry.

Although it was widely held that the normal expansion of business would eventually provide adequate earnings for all railroad properties, railroad leaders began to understand that in the meantime an orderly market had to be maintained. Successively in the closing decades of the nineteenth century, as the economic crisis of the railroads deepened, the operators tried pools and traffic associations and finally mergers and intercorporate control in efforts to create market stability and eliminate competition. Meanwhile, the Interstate Commerce Commission, also having accepted the view that competition among railroads was "destructive," implicitly supported in its rate policies and other regulative activities the industry's own economic outlook. This interpretation of the commission's early policy toward the railroads has been ably examined in Gabriel Kolko's recent *Railroads and Regulation, 1887-1916*.[13] Kolko contends that the creation of the I.C.C. in 1887, and successive acts broadening its power were both philosophically and politically consistent with the prevailing opinion of rail leaders.

The need for "security, stability, and predictability" had been demonstrated by the high costs of internecine competion in the 1880's. In fact, Kolko points out, the market conditions for railroads at this time had become decidedly more competitive, whereas the period of trunk and transcontinental railroad building, 1860-1875, had tended to exhibit more monopolistic characteristics.

The railroad managements, therefore, had attempted a number of schemes to eliminate the costlier excesses of rebating and preferential ratesetting which this competion stimulated. Meanwhile, much Federal encouragement to the creation of railroad pools was also offered. For example, Joseph Nimmo, Secretary of the Interior, had been especially enthusiastic in discussions with the transcontinental railroad operators about the Iowa Pool. Kolko holds that few rail leaders opposed the passage of a federal regulatory law, and the actual passage of the Interstate Commerce Act in 1887 was not seen initially as a threat. In fact, the greatest disability of the act was its timidity. Unable to set rates, the I.C.C. looked hopefully to the railroads to solve their rate competition, again utilizing pools; but, in the late 1880's, the pooling agreements broke down. At this point, the railroads turned directly to the Federal government, agitating for greater regulation, while simultaneously attempting to resolve the problem through an increase of mergers and consolidations. Overall, according to Kolko, the movement for regulation was generated by the recognition by government and the rail industry of the need to control competition. This interpretation, he argues quite correctly, offers a decided improvement over the conventional analysis that has represented regulation as a response to monopolistic tendencies in the rail industry and, therefore, implied the anti-railroad bias of all federal regulation.

Kolko's study, however, focuses almost entirely on government-business relations in policy-making rather than examining what this meant in terms of the rail network or the structure of rail operations. Moreover, he does not go much beyond 1916, and many of his observations on the coalescence of government and railroad interests are, as we shall see, even more appropriate to events after World War I.

The railroads soon found that the mere elimination of competition, even with I.C.C. help, was not enough to solve the problem of excess capacity. The expected natural increase in

railroad business in the twentieth century, which was supposed
to economically justify the existing railroad network, did not
take place, and the rise of competitive transportation modes,
shifts in the structure of consumer demand, and changes in
the spatial distribution of economic activity caused a considerable increase in underutilization of the railroad network.
Without hope of making some lines ever pay out, railroads
again turned to the Interstate Commerce Commission, this
time for approval to abandon portions or, in a few cases, all
of their operations. By the mid-twentieth century, a fairly
recognizable trend in railroad policy had emerged. Consolidation
and abandonment were the means by which the rail network
could be reduced to eliminate excess capacity. Consolidation,
of course, was no longer needed to suppress competition in
the highly regulated industry. Rather, it now served as a prelude to obtaining later "economies" through the abandonment
of duplicating trackage and service.

The following study of New York's railroad network in the
twentieth century attempts to examine in detail how this railroad
policy developed and what its effects have been upon the railroad facilities of the state. Although the operation of railroads
in the United States has varied, and differing geographic, economic, legal and corporate conditions have produced some
regional uniqueness, New York's experience is generally symp-
tomatic of the national railroad situation and especially in-
structive with regard to eastern railroads. Because state political units rarely conform to the limits of corporate rail operation, the study is not rigorous in its geographic limitation,
and the story of changes in New York's railroad network is
developed against an examination of national and regional
patterns.

After a survey of the dimensions of the network at the
beginning of the century, five arbitrary periods have been
selected as a frame for analysis: 1) the end of the era of building, 1900-1916; 2) federal control and operations under the
Transportation Act of 1920, 1917-1929; 3) the depression, 1929-
1940; 4) the wartime prosperity and the post-war decline,
1941-1957; and 5) after the Transportation Act of 1958.

I

THE RAILROAD NETWORK AT THE CLOSE OF THE NINETEENTH CENTURY

The selection of the beginning of the twentieth century as the starting point for a study of the decline of American railroads, and of New York railroads in particular, is in many respects arbitrary and probably reflects as much literary license as it does any clear historical demarcation. The net additions to trackage in New York, although slight compared to the 30 percent expansion of the national rail network between 1900 and 1916, nevertheless continued until 1914, and total investment, employment and earnings steadily advanced until the 1930's. However, looking deeper than these statistical measures, it is apparent that the end of the old century and the coming of the new roughly approximates a significant benchmark in the development of the railroad industry.

The approach of the new century had evoked almost childish excitement among Americans, and among the business community the anticipation had been especially great. The nation seemed to be finally recovering from the long depression of the nineties and the resurgence of industrial development along with the growing economic expansion of the nation into world markets seemed to augur the coming of a new epoch of economic progress. Looking back over the year just ended, the New York *Times* financial editor described 1899 as " . . . a wonderful year . . . a veritable *annua mirabilis*," with even greater gains expected for 1900.[1] Noting the protracted depression in rail earnings, the *Times* offered that the future now looked much brighter, with the growth of overseas trade and a boom in agricultural prices pointing the way to higher rail revenues. However, among most railroad leaders, an appraisal of the new century was more guarded and conservative. The "Railroad Era" of American history, despite the fact there were additional lines to be built and fortunes to be made, seemed to have closed sometime shortly after the panic of 1893. The gloom hung somewhat heavier over eastern railroads than over those in the western states, for in east or what was called the Trunk Line Territory, the crisis of the 1890's had been profoundly sobering.

In a sense the change was caught in the 1900 report of the New York Board of Railroad Commissioners. Reporting on the prospects for New York railroads in the twentieth century, the commissioners speculated that there would need to be important changes in the economic organization of the industry. For one thing, they noted, " ... it would seem that for some time at least there will be perhaps but little new steam building in the state except for connecting or terminal lines." Moreover, companies would have to "address themselves to the problem of improving earnings on already operating lines."[2] From the point of view of the New York Railroad Commissioners, the era of building was over and the new century should mark a maturing of corporate policy so that the existing railroad plant could become more efficient and profitable.

The commissioners' views on the changes in the railroad industry appear to have coincided with the general outlook of railroad leadership in the east. Actually, eastern railroads had demonstrated an increasingly cautious attitude toward new railroad constuction since well before the turn of the century. Railroad construction had not rebounded after the panic of 1893, and, as the following table illustrates, construction in New York, which had been slowing down since the eighties, added only about seventy miles to the state's network between 1895 and 1900. Meanwhile, other less apparent, conservative shifts in business policy were also under way among eastern railroads during the closing years of the nineteenth century; however, the full development of these new corporate policies did not take place until after 1900.

TABLE 2

RAILROAD MAINLINE MILEAGE IN NEW YORK STATE
SELECTED YEARS 1835-1964 [a]

Year	Miles of Mainline	Year	Miles of Mainline
1835	350 (est.)	1905	8,274
1845	700 (est.)	1910	8,512
1855	2,432	1915	8,473
1860	2,682	1920	8,390
1865	2,821	1925	8,442
1870	3,973	1930	8,310
1875	5,499	1935	8,187
1880	5,957	1940	7,739
1885	7,311	1945	7,607
1890	7,895	1950	7,493
1895	8,032	1955	7,373
1900	8,099	1960	6,463
		1964	5,883

[a] Calculated from U.S. Interstate Commerce Commission, *Statistics of Railways in the United States*, miscellaneous years, 1890-1953, and *Transport Statistics of the United States*, 1954-1965.

The Railroad Map of 1900

In 1900, New York State had a railroad network of 8,099 miles of first or mainline tracks and approximately 15,000 miles of tracks of all kinds.[3] Even a cursory study of the physical patterns of the state's railroad routes, as obtained from Map 1 (see Appendix), shows that virtually every area of the state had well developed railroad connections. Only in the Adirondack and the Catskill Mountains was there a sparse distribution of lines; yet, even in these remote and relatively unpopulated areas of the state, there were several important operating routes. Virtually all large villages had direct railroad connections, and, excluding the Adirondacks and Catskills, no place in the state was more than fifteen miles from a rail line. The saturation of mainline trackage to land area in New York was one of the greatest in the United States, only exceeded by Connecticut, Massachusetts, New Jersey, Pennsylvania, Illinois, Indiana and Ohio.

In all, seventy-one railroad companies, the survivors and successors of over eight hundred steam railroad charters issued in New York, were operating in 1900.[4] However, the railroad network was dominated by a few very large railroads. The twelve largest lines accounted for over 80 percent of mainline mileage, and excluding ten companies which were essentially switching or terminal operations, the remaining roads were mostly very small, usually wholly dependent upon the larger companies for their business and in some cases owned or controlled by the large roads.

The most prominent feature of the physical pattern and the corporate organization of New York railroads was the dominant role of the two large "trunk line" carriers in the state, the New York Central and the Erie. These two roads accounted for most of the east-west, cross-state traffic between New York City and the mid-west. Of the two, the Central was clearly the strongest in 1900. It operated over 2500 miles of track in New York, and its 450-mile mainline from New York City to Buffalo, with connections from Buffalo to Chicago over its subsidiary, the Lake Shore and Michigan Southern, was clearly the best trunk route from the eastern seaboard to the mid-west. The Central also enjoyed the lowest operational and maintainence cost per mile of any eastern railroad.[5] Moreover, its mainline, paralleling the transportation route pioneered by the Erie Canal, serviced the state's most populous and fastest growing urban centers, while its lateral or branch lines also entered thriving areas. Such cities as New York, Yonkers, Schenectady, Amsterdam, Watertown, Syracuse, Rochester, and Buffalo, along mainline routes of the Central, had more than doubled their population between 1880 and 1900.[6]

The Erie Railroad had been New York's first long railroad, and, despite its generally poor route through the southern tier of New York State, it had surpassed the Central as a freight carrier until the mid-1880's.[7] Its main cross-state route ran through comparatively small cities in southern New York, and of these only Binghamton, with a population of 39,647 in 1900, and Jamestown, with 22,892 people, had experienced any significant population growth in the closing years of the century.[8] The Erie route into Buffalo was indirect and an afterthought to the original construction of the road. Its line to Rochester was really only a spur, and it did not reach Syracuse,

Utica, or Albany at all. In the 1870's and 1880's, the Erie and the New York Central had been involved in a number of competitive rate conflicts, but by 1900, the Central's economic power and technical superiority made the Erie a weak second trunk line in New York. In fact, the Erie had gone into bankruptcy following the panic of 1893 and had been reorganized in 1895 by the New York Central's banker, J.P. Morgan. Morgan, as was his custom, retained power over the road's management and financial affairs.

Although the other two eastern trunk lines, the Pennsylvania and the Baltimore and Ohio, seemed of little consequence with regard to the New York Railroad Map of 1900, these two lines, nonetheless, had a considerable impact on the structure of the New York railroad network. The B & O, with its through-route to Chicago from Baltimore, the most southerly and longest of the trunks, owned and operated no property in New York; and the Pennsylvania controlled in New York only the northern extremities (Elmira to Lake Ontario) of the Northern Central, although it did acquire access to New York City and purchased control of the Long Island Railroad and the Western New York and Pennsylvania before 1900 ended. In the seventies and eighties, all four trunks had been engaged in the brutal competition of trying to maintain a position in the east-west overhead traffic, and the actions of the Pennsylvania and the B & O had directly affected the rates and service of New York roads. The trunks remained potential competitors and their rivalry, especially the rivalry between the stronger Pennsylvania and New York Central roads, which had contributed so much to the financial instability of the eastern railroads in the nineteenth century, was to be a central feature of eastern railroad policy after 1900.

New York State south of Lake Ontario and the Adirondack Mountains was interlaced with a dozen or more lateral or feeder trunks. Generally these roads ran in a north-south direction through the rural midlands of the state, connecting with one or both of New York's through lines. A number of these railroads were quite long with fairly well developed spurs and branches of their own. The Delaware and Hudson, the Delaware Lackawana and Western, the Lehigh Valley, the New York Ontario and Western and the New York portion of the Pennsylvania Railroad system (the Western New York

and Pennsylvania and the North Central) were all over 300
miles long.[9]

Characteristically, most of these longer lateral roads were
important coal carriers. The Pennsylvania Railroad properties,
along with the smaller Pittsburgh Shawmut and Northern, the
Buffalo Rochester and Pittsburgh, and the New York and
Pennsylvania carried coal from Pennsylvania's western bituminous
region, and the other large feeders tapped the anthracite fields
around Scranton and Carbondale, Pennsylvania. During the
last two decades of the nineteenth century, the anthracite
business had more than doubled, and coal had come to dominate the affairs of the larger railroads. Eight of New York's
large railroads depended upon coal for about half of their total
freight tonnage in 1900. The Lehigh Valley, the Lackawanna,
the Delaware and Hudson, and the Erie were, in that order,
the most important anthracite carriers in New York and each
owned or controlled sizeable coal properties of their own,
assuring themselves a continuing foothold in the coal traffic.
Of less importance was the New York Ontario and Western
which had a less developed connection to the anthracite fields.[10]
Nevertheless, the NYO & W gained 70 percent of its freight
from coal. The New York Central like many of the smaller
railroads, had no direct connection with the coal region and its
movement of coal came exclusively from trans-shipment received from other roads.

The lateral roads were also important carriers of agricultural
products. More than 25 percent of all freight originated in New
York by such roads as the Delaware Lackawanna and Western,
the Delaware and Hudson, the Lehigh Valley, the New York
and Pennsylvania, the Pittsburgh Shawmut and Northern, the
Ogdensburg and Lake Champlain and the New York Chicago
and St. Louis was agricultural products.[11]

About thirty of New York's railroads, excluding those which
were primarily switching operations, operated routes of less
than twenty-five miles. These roads were little more than short
spurs connecting with the longer lateral or trunk lines. Usually
they had been built with local incentive and capital to connect
communities with the longer roads which had for one reason or
another passed them by. Most of these spurs depended upon
agricultural commodities for their earnings. Such lines as the
Kanonah and Prattsburg, the Dansville and Mount Morris and

the Buffalo Arcade and Attica earned most of their revenue from agricultural goods. In other cases, these roads depended upon a single industry, mine, or mill to originate enough traffic to keep the road going. A few of the roads, such as the Unadilla Valley and the Ulster and Delaware managed a precarious existence as connecting lines between larger roads. Most of the small roads had only one or two engines and a few pieces of rolling stock. Their contribution to total freight flow in New York was probably even smaller than the modest amount of trackage they operated might indicate. An indication of the small scale of operations of these roads may be seen in a comparison of the Kanonah and Prattsburg, which carried less than 15,000 tons of freight of all kinds in 1900, while the New York Central originated over 10 million tons in New York State.

As noted before, the larger railroads quite dominated the New York railroad network, and, primarily these roads relied upon the long distance movement of certain commodities for the bulk of their earnings, coal from Pennsylvania to the larger New York cities or the east-west overhead movement of machine tools, grain and certain consumer goods. However, there was also an important regional or local character to the New York rail network in 1900 which was not so obvious and is much more difficult to evaluate. For one thing, the rail network performed the important task of tying outlying small villages and communities to larger villages and cities. Passenger service, which in one form or another was offered by most New York railroads, had created considerable local labor mobility. By the close of the century, the prospects for an expanded commuter traffic had led to the planning and building of new suburban and interurban electric railroads. In a few cases, steam railroads themselves were building electric trolley operations since their feasability had been demonstrated by the railroads' own local passenger service.[12]

Many commodities were also moved by rail over comparatively short distances from industries and communities surrounding urban centers to distribution or processing centers in the cities. The very important shipment of milk from rural collecting points to milk plants in cities is, perhaps, the best example of this type of regional or local freight movement; however, other commodities such as mine or lumber products were similarly moved short distances to processing centers.

Although, in the aggregate, these local passenger and commodity movements earned only a comparatively small portion of total railroad income, these operations were vitally important to the communities served. Indeed, most villages in 1900, however precarious their economic condition, existed only because of their railroad connections. As we shall see, it was this regional or local aspect of railroad operation that was most substantially changed in later years.

While a cursory study of the general pattern and distribution of rail lines and traffic gives some important insights, an understanding of the overall condition of the New York rail network at the close of the century requires an examination of the financial and corporate structure of the railroads. To obtain this understanding it is necessary to look back in some detail over the era of railroad building in New York, for the methods of finance and organization that were employed left an indelible mark on rail operations in the twentieth century.

The Problems of Excessive Capitalization and Excess Capacity

As anticipated, railroad earnings for 1900 were sharply up, a decided improvement over the depths reached in the mid and late 1890's. Freight tonnage carried by New York roads increased by eight percent over the year before, and, largely on the basis of this gain, railroads reported a handsome 14 percent rise in net income.[13] But despite such recent gains, New York railroads, like most in the nation, were in serious trouble. Evident in their balance sheets and income statements, regardless of the recent brightening of business conditions, were enormous problems of excessive capitalization and excess capacity, the legacies of the era of speculative building.[14]

In New York State, capitalization per mile of mainline of steam railroads was over $80,000.[15] Although this measure of capital investment had serious limitations since it failed to give any appreciation of the quality either of the trackage or the capital invested, it was a frequently used measurement and about the only device available for comparative judgement of railroads' capital structures. Whatever its shortcomings, the relative over-capitalization of New York roads is apparent in that the national average for capitalization per mile of track was only $51,000.[16]

Most New York roads labored under a large funded debt whose fixed maintenance charges cut heavily into earnings. Interest payments by the Erie, despite its recent reorganization by J.P. Morgan, amounted to about 65 percent of net earnings. For the Lehigh Valley, the New York Central and the Lake Shore, respectively, payments were 59, 42, and 23 percent of net earnings. The burdens of these fixed charges were great enough to place a number of roads under the constant threat of bankruptcy and receivership. A general decline in business activity, even if the decline were not too great, could mean financial failure. Even in the improved business conditions of 1900, few roads were able to make large dividend payments. In fact, total dividend payments increased only about $1 million over 1899 and the average return was a scant 2.5 percent. Of those roads in New York earning more than $1 million in gross revenues, only about half managed to pay any dividends.

A calculation of the degree of excess capacity or under-utilization in the New York railroad network of 1900 is a good deal more difficult to arrive at than a measurement of capitalization problems. As early as the 1870's, several railroad trade journals and a number of important monographs had produced fairly elaborate accounting techniques for measuring capitalization and earning relationships.[17] However, the problem of excess capacity had been less diligently studied before the closing years of the century. To be sure, government, railroad, and financial leaders had been aware since the 1870's that in certain areas and over certain routes, the American railroad network evidenced too intensive a distribution of service to be justified by the available traffic. It was well known that this meant for some roads periodic reversion to highly competitive rate-making practices and that for others it simply produced very low earnings even in the absence of rate wars and competition. As a rule, until the protracted economic depression of the 1890's, observers had successfully explained away such difficulties as being only temporary. In the anticipated natural expansion of business, it was argued, virtually all railroads were to enjoy a more intensive and economic

utilization of their facilities. While excess capacity was a problem, it had been mostly seen as a transitional difficulty, to be
endured until the nation grew to the scale of its railroad
network.

Excessive capitalization and excess capacity were, of course,
the by-products of the highly speculative era of building following the Civil War. Throughout the United States, railroads
were laid down without much regard for the routes they were
to operate or for the costs of construction. The availability
of government aid and foreign capital and the belief that a
railroad eventually could be made to run almost anywhere at
a profit had meant the construction of most American railroads without much planning.

During the sixties and seventies, a number of proposals
had been offered which would have made much of the new
railroad building, particularly the western roads, purely public
enterprise.[18] These proposals, like other plans which would have
imposed rigorous public controls on the intensity and distribution of the building of new railroad enterprises, were never
accepted. While Congress retained some loose controls over
the transcontinentals' use of awarded lands, the Federal authorities developed no "national railroad policy." Railroads,
much more than the canals and turnpikes before them, were
a function of private planning and private prerogatives. As
Carter Goodrich has observed: "...the era of national subsidy was characterized by the settled convictions that the Federal
government was not to be entrusted with the construction or
operation of internal improvements."[19] Such a decision was to
have important ramifications in the twentieth century when the
American railroad network was complete and when the bills
for the era of *laissez faire* began to fall due. For the time
being, however, it meant that the private promoters could determine the intensity and distribution of railroad operations
according to their own profit-seeking instincts.

The acceleration in railroad building considerably exceeded
the rate of real national economic growth. The increase in
trackage between 1865 and 1900 was about 700 percent for the
country.[20] Gross National Product, meanwhile, grew by only
400 percent.[21] Even considering the favorable relative shifts
from other transportantion modes to railroads and the generally
accelerated rate of industrial and external commercial activity,
the new building outdistanced increases in demand.

In looking at the pattern of railroad building during the seventies and eighties, it is apparent that even profit-seeking in the ordinary market sense was frequently absent as a "planning" device. In the western states, where it was assumed traffic demand would develop as the railroads opened new areas, there could be little hope for immediate operational profit. Even in the eastern states, where population and commercial patterns were well established, much of the new construction was rationalized on the grounds that practically any building would pay out as the expansive mood of America continued. However, immediate profits flowed from construction itself and from promotional stock-jobbing, so that frequently track was laid down and operated with little or no concern for traffic demand, real or imagined. Most of the railroad building was accomplished in three spurts of speculative construction, 1867-1873, 1878-1883, and 1891-1893, each ending in financial panic and recession.

During these years, New York railroads had compiled an especially inglorious financial record. For example, the Erie Railroad had seen its capitalization grow from $17 million to over $77 million between 1868 and 1872 as its notorious directors, Drew, Gould, and Fisk poured Erie stock onto the market for the sole purpose of speculation and without any significant increase in real investment. The result, of course, was that the Erie was permanently weakened. The New York Central had undertaken similar adventures in 1868, when its directors authorized the cleaning of its treasury and a vast increase in the road's bonded debt to scrape together a scandalous 80 percent dividend payment to its shareholders.[22]

Meanwhile, most of the lateral roads in New York were built during the speculative construction of the 1870's and 1880's, when New York railroad trackage more than doubled, and to an even greater degree reflected the mood of loose financial operations. Much of this building had been encouraged by the legislature's passage of the General Bonding Law of 1869 which permitted local government units to issue debt instruments for the purpose of acquiring railroad securities.[23] The act provided general legislation for what specific legislation had from time to time permitted. The effect of the act was to encourage the building of several dozen little roads through the hinterlands of the state. Municipalities interested in procuring railroads to stimulate their economic development made substantial contributions to railroad promoters through the subscription of railroad stocks. Clearly, communities that might never have gained railroad service were able under the General Bonding Law to entice railroads to their locations. Harry Pierce points out that municipal debts of $27 million for railroad construction were outstanding by 1875.[24] Moreover, the state made donations of another $1,182,000 to particular roads during this period.[25]

The state authorities saw no particular need for the construction of additional cross-state routes, nor did the General Bonding Law and state financial aid in the 1870's encourage the building of such lines. Instead, state and local aid led to the building of fairly short lines which meandered across the state too frequently in search of capital funds rather than traffic. By the time the depression of 1884-1885 halted this building spree, New York had developed an extremely extensive railroad network through most of the state.

Initially, most of these lateral lines depended upon the shipment of agricultural products for the bulk of their earnings. However, in the closing decades of the nineteenth century, New York State began to undergo a severe rural depopulation, and about half of the towns which received railroad facilities after the Civil War reported population declines, giving rise to the wry observation that once the railroad was built to a small town, the people got on the train and left. The revolution in American agriculture in the later years of the century was to see New York State decline as a major farm producer as the corn, wheat and grazing lands of the west were opened by railroads.[26] Relatively few eastern producers could compete with cheap western products. Instead of opening local produce to new markets and stimulating new industry as the railroad promoters of the 1870's had claimed, many New York agricultural communities found that railroad building elsewhere had eliminated many of the advantages of their own rail connections. While railroads were still crucial to the economies of rural communities in New York, they had not provided the promised economic growth. The loss of population and the decline in the shipment of agricultural commodities and agricultural machinery, meanwhile, brought increased operating problems to many of the little speculative roads.

The panic and depression of 1873 and the depression of 1884-1885 caused the collapse of a number of the small railroads. Some were abandoned outright. A few retained their identity and continued to operate, but most were eventually grafted onto the established trunk carriers, the Central and the Erie, or became integral parts of such large lateral lines as the Delaware and Hudson, the Delaware Lackawanna and Western, the Lehigh Valley, the New York Ontario and Western, the Baltimore and Ohio, the Rutland, and the Pennsylvania. While some of the speculative constructions of the seventies and eighties were to become important originators or carriers of traffic, in the main, this building had produced more trackage than could be put to economic use. The excess capacity of the industry naturally tended to generate a high degree of rate and service competition. In the case of the longer lateral roads involved in anthracite coal traffic, the saturation of rail routes from New York cities to Pennsylvania coal fields caused great instability in coal commodity rates and set off a number of rate wars among the coal roads.

The developments in New York were only a fragment of what was happening nationally, and the activities of American railroad promoters provoked vigorous complaints that builders had little concern for real operating problems. Speaking for English investors in 1884, the *Railway News* cited an example of these promotional activities:

> The fact that the accounts of this company (the New York Central Railroad) for the year 1882 showed that there was a deficit of $1.5 million on the payment of 8 percent dividend — which was nevertheless punctually declared and distributed quarter by quarter — has undoubtedly done much to injure the credit of the lines with a large class of investors. People in this country are so accustomed to the accurate division of profits of a concern among the shareholders that the idea of payment of a "regular" dividend out of fluctuating revenues naturally appears heretical. [27]

A year before, the American *Bankers Magazine* had observed that the preoccupation with rail promotion had caused "Unusual squandering" of our capital and had actually restricted economic expansion. The magazine observed on the eve of a major panic and recession:

> The investments in railroads ... exceeds that in government bonds or banks ... A few men comparatively manage

a very large portion of the capital thus invested. Every year brings out the unwelcome fact more clearly that railroad officials are using their place and power rather to advance their own interests rather than the companies they represent...
Of course not all railroads are managed in this way, but too many are—so many indeed that throughout the year the feeling of uncertainty with respect to them has been rapidly increasing....

The future of American railroads is not an altogether cheerful one. A shadow is thrown over the entire railroad property of the country.[28]

In 1885, Henry Poor, the well-known analyst of railroad securities, concluded that most of the recent building spree had been ill-advised, producing such "redundant properties" as the West Shore and the Nickel Plate (New York Chicago and St. Louis). "Of the 40,000 miles of road built in the five years ending with 1883," Poor observed, "no small part was built on speculation, and for that matter, paralleled already existing lines."[29] In writing this, Poor was especially concerned about the promotional struggles which had produced the West Shore and threatened all out civil war between the New York Central and the Pennsylvania.

Looking at the national railroad network, with what he felt to be its excessive building and enormous over-capitalization, Poor yet hoped that the natural expansion of rail traffic would justify such excesses. He observed:

The country is now at its lowest depths so far as the railroads are concerned. The evil done, the remedy must now be applied. It is not the case for the sponge. Now competing lines must await the steady and certain increase of the general business of the country; the competing ones must be taken up by the lines they parallel, and used as side tracks.... It is to be remembered that the rates of interest paid by the railroad companies on bonds equal 6, 7, or 8 percent.... (These bonds will be replaced by those) bearing 3-1/2, 4 or 5 percent, the reduction in rates incurring wholly to the benefit of the shareholders.[30]

The burdens of excessive capitalization and excess capacity could not be long ignored, and beginning in the mid 1880's and into the early 1890's, a number of major financial reorganizations were effected to wring a good deal of the "water" from certain roads' bloated capital structures and to integrate some of the speculative roads into larger, better organized systems.[31] The guiding force behind these financial reorganizations was the shrewd mind of J.P. Morgan, who early recognized the prospects for self-destruction which had been built into the American railroad system.[32] Morgan, a crucial figure in the following study, first entered the field of railroad reorganization in the wake of the panic and depression of 1884-85 with the reordering of the West Shore's shattered financial structure and its absorption into Vanderbilt's New York Central. However, his greatest achievements in financial reorganization came after the panic of 1893 when one-quarter of the nation's railroad trackage, representing a capitalization of over $2,000,000,000, went into receivership.[33] Morgan directly participated in half a dozen important reorganizations, including those of the Erie, the Reading and the Northern Pacific; but, his influence was, by 1893, even greater than these undertakings would indicate. Morgan virtually dominated the reorganization movement, either through his banking house's actual financial dealings with various railroads or the powerful "moral suasion" he was able to wield over other financial houses and practically all of rail management.[34] The nature and extent of this type of financial power is an essential problem of this study and is examined in some detail in the following chapters.

Early Attempts to Limit Competition

The continuing business crisis after 1893 soon demonstrated that mere financial reorganization of the rail network was not enough. Simply overhauling the capital structure of operating railroads, at least within the limits acceptable to rail managers and their bankers, could not insulate the industry from the growing crisis. In the face of falling revenues, railroads had again resorted to rate-cutting and other competitive devices. In the east, the Pennsylvania and the New York Central had shown some ability to adapt to the general business depression; but, few other eastern roads were as strong and the entire industry appeared on the verge of collapse. To many rail leaders, the situation called for immediate and united corporate action. No longer could the periodic occurence of rate wars and the associated collapse of weaker railroads be tolerated. The specific action selected by the industry was to construct, both formally and informally, a high degree of intercorporate integration. In terms of economic analysis, such a policy was a quite logical response to the chronic dilemmas of excess capacity and competition. In fact, corporate integration, in one form or another, was to remain the keystone of industry policy in the twentieth century.

American railroads always had been marked by a tendency toward corporate merger and integration. During the early years of railroad building, with vision and construction handicapped by capital deficiencies and technological primitiveness, most roads were short inter-city operations which usually competed unfavorably with alternative methods of transportation. The eventual "end-to-end" merger of many of these small roads into longer systems during the sixties and seventies was essential to railroads' development as an important transportation industry.[35]

These "end-to-end" mergers led to the building of a truly national railroad network; but, they also had the effect of encouraging railroad competition. In the east, as noted in the preceeding section, each of the trunk carriers, the New York Central, the Erie, the Pennsylvania, and the Baltimore and Ohio, were interested in increasing their share of east-west

TABLE 3

RAILROADS OVER ONE THOUSAND MILES IN LENGTH,
NUMBER AND PERCENTAGE OF UNITED STATES MILEAGE
1867-1910[a]

Year	Number of Roads	Percentage of U.S. Mileage
1867	1	7
1877	11	20
1887	28	44
1896	44	57
1900	48	60
1910	54	67

[a] William Z. Ripley, *Railroads-Finance and Organization* (New York: Longmans Green and Company, 1914), p. 458.

traffic. Improving their market position meant the acquisition or construction of routes which would extend their operations further into the mid-west or give them desired feeder lines for the generation of traffic. The procedure followed by these roads in acquiring new properties was simply to obtain a long enough mainline with sufficient feeders or friendly connections to make the cost of constructing parallel or directly competitive routes prohibitive. Ironically, as the eastern trunks expanded in corporate size, reducing the number of separate railroad units in the market by mergers and consolidations, greater competition developed between them as they gradually invaded each other's "territory." By increasing their feeder connections and through the improvement of overhead service, competition began to emerge on both long and short haul service.

While the earlier merger attempts usually had sought only to improve a particular firm's market position through the savings and efficiency of a single integrated management and the assurity of friendly traffic connections, consolidations and other efforts to end competition after the panic of 1893 were aimed at producing order for the entire industry. Corporate policies began to take on the form of deliberately halting all types of rivalry and the setting up of cooperative spheres of influence in the railroad network. While formal mergers were still employed, new forces of control, such as majority stock ownership or long term leases were common techniques for controlling competition.[36] However, of more consequence was the increasingly obvious effectiveness of management in establishing informal inter-firm agreement on operations, traffic and rates which might maintain business peace in railroad operations.[37]

The combination and cooperation efforts after 1893 were facilitated by two new developments in the railroad industry— the growing intervention of the federal government in railroad affairs and the rise of banker influence.[38] Both of these events were to leave a deep and permanent mark on American railroads' corporate and management structure.

Pressure for federal regulation in railroad affairs had been building for a long time. The short-lived peace agreements of the seventies and eighties had frequently provided for the pooling of traffic as well as the maintenance of rates, often discriminatory rates. Although the pools usually collapsed from internal weaknesses, they attracted increased opposition from

shippers and the public. While many government officials at
both state and federal levels saw little that was undesirable in
these agreements, the more obnoxious aspects of the pools,
especially the discriminatory rates, clearly invited government
intervention — first by the state legislatures and then by Congress.

The passage of the Commerce Act of 1887 destroyed the pooling agreements and prohibited discriminatory rate making.*
Although the act marked a sharp break with past federal attitudes toward the railroads, it evoked few condemnations from
railroad leaders. To many, the act tended to sanction the
growth of industrywide cooperation, the logic being that if the
I.C.C. was to "maintain" reasonable rates and service, this
was nothing more than what the railroads had been seeking to
establish themselves.[39] The Commission had been created with
virtually no enforcement powers, and, as a result, it seemed that
enforcement of the act depended upon considerable voluntary
cooperation by the railroads. Most rail operators certainly saw
no immediate threat in the Commission.[40] If the act posed any
problems, it was the problem of finding a way around the anti-
business implications of too literal an interpretation of the
legislation.

The technique arrived at for controlling this potential intervention in corporate affairs was the "traffic association." The
object of such privately organized associations was to develop
a measure of intercorporate control over rate setting and service
which met, at least overtly, the specifications of the Commerce
Act of 1887. In 1889, the western railroads, acting under the
leadership and inspiration of J.P. Morgan, had experimented
with the traffic association concept in the creation of the Interstate Commerce Railway Association. Hiring the Hon. Aldace
F. Walker away from the Interstate Commerce Commission to
head this new agency was a rather obvious attempt to give it

---

* The general enactments under the Interstate Commerce Act of 1887 were:
  1 — that all rates must be "just and reasonable." Unjust and Unreasonable
       rates were unlawful.
  2 — personal discrimination in rating was unlawful. That is it was unlawful to
       charge more for one person for like service that is charged of others.
  3 — No preferential treatment may be accorded one person not accorded others.
  4 — Short haul traffic "under substantially similar conditions and circumstances"
       cannot command greater compensation than long haul movement over the
       same line.
  5 — Pooling was prohibited.
  6 — The Interstate Commerce Commission was established to administer the act.

respectability.[41] By the beginning of 1891, however, the agency, which had sought little more than the maintenance of uniform rates and performed the public relations function of presenting a better image of rail leadership, had collapsed and was replaced by the Western Traffic Association.[42] The new organization, through a number of round-about techniques began to perform additional functions as a traffic pool. While such activities clearly violated the literal intent of the Commerce Act, most railroad leaders believed that they were within the bounds which the I.C.C. had established in practice.[43]

Three years after the formation of the Western Association, the idea was introduced in the east. Its champions there, as in the west, were J. P. Morgan and his banking and railroad associates. The foundation for the eastern association was laid on April 27, 1894, when the old arch-rivals, the Pennsylvania and the Central, jointly signed a traffic agreement announcing an end to their long standing warfare. Typical of the existing attitude toward the Interstate Commerce Commission and fully aware that the Commission was virtually impotent in imposing peace among the railroads, the document noted:

> It is believed to be for the general interest of the Public, as well as the parties hereto . . . to secure uniform and reasonable rates.

> Where it is the intent of the Interstate Commerce Act that the rates for transportation traffic by railroads and the facilities offered in connection therewith should be reasonable, uniform and stable, it is therefore deemed wise and proper that the following contract should be entered into between the said parties, and such mutual relations established for the government of the business as will promote these interests.[44]

The agreement elicited five major conditions: 1) that the parties act in harmony in setting rates, "dealing firmly and justly with other lines," 2) that no agreement be made with other companies which would endanger this agreement, 3) that there would be no invasion of each other's area, 4) that no attempt be employed through lateral lines, perhaps under one party's control, to influence rates, and 5) that the public service of the parties "be as uniform in character as possible."[45] The plan tried to avoid the I.C.C.'s possible opposition to pooling by "freezing" the existing division of traffic between the roads.

Certainly the maintenance of uniform rates and service, it was hoped, would lead to this result.

The desire of eastern rail managements for peace was sincere. The Baltimore and Ohio directors proposed the *ad hoc* creation of a commission staffed by representatives of the eastern trunk lines, to set and administer rates. The minutes of their board meeting of October 16, 1895, recommended:

> In undertaking this task it was admitted that the only way to correct the evil of rate cutting was to take the power of rate making out of the hands of the different companies, and to place it in the absolute control of a commission, in which commission shall also be vested the power to control and curtail the soliciting of freight and passenger agencies which has become so numerous, expensive and discouraging.[46]

That the Baltimore and Ohio directors had not considered the I.C.C. an appropriate body to handle these proposed functions testifies to management's attitude toward the regulatory agency. Such views were based more in the companies' indifference to the Commission than in fear. Nevertheless, the prohibitions against pooling in the Interstate Commerce Act remained distinct threats to the creation of a private regulatory commission, and eastern railroads began to lobby in 1895 for the passage of legislation which would permit "enlightened" pooling.[47]

The bill, however, was lost, and most eastern roads saw their only hope for maintaining peace in joining the New York Central-Pennsylvania reapproachment. The agreement of 1894 eventually led to the creation of the Joint Traffic Association in 1895.[48] Thirty-two roads joined as signatories to the general conditions set forth in the Central-Pennsylvania agreement.[49]

Although it is easy to impugn management's motives in the introduction and operation of the traffic association concept, it should be pointed out that much evidence could support any claim on their part that these agreements were both legal and consistent with the early policy of government regulations in the industry. First of all, there was a substantial body of corporate legal opinion that held that railroads were not liable to the Sherman Act of 1890 since the Commerce Act of 1887 really excepted them from the later act's provisions. If the alleged pooling activities of the traffic association were in violation of the Commerce Act, railroads held, then it remained for the I.C.C. to initiate action against them and none had been forthcoming. Moreover, when private shipping interests had brought suit against the Trans-Missouri Freight Association, a smaller regional agency of the Western Traffic Association, two lower court decisions that upheld the railroad contention that the Sherman Act's restrictions on "restraint of trade" were not applicable. However, in 1897, to the shock and surprise of rail leaders, the Supreme Court struck down the Trans-Missouri Association under the provisions of the Sherman Act. The next year, on October 24, 1898, the court similarly declared the Joint Traffic Association illegal.[50]

The two adverse court decisions, of course, were not the end of the matter so far as the railroads were concerned. The traffic association concept had worked fairly well through the hard times of the mid 1890's. After a brief flare-up of rate-cutting in 1893 and 1894, a large measure of price stability was finally obtained. Nor were railroads convinced that the Trans-Missouri decision reflected a radical change in federal regulatory attitude toward the industry. It simply remained for new devices to be discovered and employed that would produce the necessary checks upon disruptive competition, devices that were acceptable within the emerging framework of regulatory policy.

A second force contributing to greater intercorporate agreement in the 1890's was the rise of banker influence over railroad affairs;[51] and, as noted before, the key personality in this development was J. P. Morgan.[52] Morgan had served as banker for the Vanderbilts and the Central since the 1870's. Through the eighties and early nineties he had strengthened his ties with the Central by handling several important issues of bonds and in aiding in several mergers.[53] Meanwhile, through Drexel and Company, a Morgan firm in Philadelphia, he had established banking connections with the Pennsylvania system.[54] Unlike the Central, however, the Pennsylvania retained greater independence from banker control. A third eastern trunk, the Erie, came under Morgan influence in 1893, when J. P. Morgan and Company reorganized the railroad's shattered capital structure and Morgan men were placed on the Board of Directors.

John Pierpont Morgan stands out among those business leaders of the late nineteenth century who have been termed, and not without some perverse sense of affection, as "Robber

Barons." His business instincts were not the rapacious drives of such contemporaries as Jay Gould, Commodore Vanderbilt, or Jim Fisk. And, he had an eminently broader vision in business affairs than such geniuses as Andrew Carnegie, John D. Rockefeller, or Henry Ford. He was a moderately well-educated and cultured man who saw business as a noble calling, not as simple legal thievery. Morgan, both in his personal and business style and in his social and economic philosophy stands as an archetype of the American businessman, a model that remained durable well into the twentieth century and which even now is not altogether obsolete in America. As much as any man, Morgan was responsible for the development of a new business philosophy which grew up out of the jungle of *laissez faire*. Morgan's influence upon America between the 1880's and World War I is towering. He dominated in steel, coal, farm machines, international and domestic banking, and railroads. Twice American Presidents had to seek his personal aid to deal with financial panics, undertakings, it might be added, which were not without special economic benefit to Morgan himself. However, it was really in railroads that Morgan earned his first great successes and that he left his most lasting impact.

Morgan's economic philosophy advocated a kind of "noncompetitive capitalism." Rejecting competition as a wasteful immature stage in the development of the economy, Morgan urged that collaboration by industrial and financial men of wisdom on matters affecting the market would assure both profits for the owners of capital and satisfaction for consumers and workers.[56] Morgan sought stability and security for business decision-making, and competition posed a threat to both these conditions. In July 1885, Morgan had been instrumental in bringing peace in the eastern rate wars between the New York Central and the Pennsylvania. The two roads had engaged in battles since the mid 1870's, periodically ceasing the engagements with peace agreements or simple exhaustion. However, matters reached their worst in 1883, when William Vanderbilt and the Central, with $5,000,000 in aid from Andrew Carnegie, began to build the South Pennsylvania Railroad, a direct parallel to the Pennsylvania mainline from Reading to Pittsburgh. The Pennsylvania retaliated by attempting to obtain the bonds of the bankrupt West Shore which paralleled the Central from New

York to Buffalo. The prospect for all-out civil war was very real, and to Morgan, such competitive bloodletting was foolishness.

Inviting Chauncey Depew of the Central and President George Roberts and Frank Thompson of the Pennsylvania for a cruise on his yacht, the *Corsair,* Morgan was able to impose his will in the well-known "Corsair Compact."[58] As a result of the informal agreement between these two giants, the New York Central ceased the building of the South Pennsylvania and the Pennsylvania ended its interest in the West Shore. The latter road was later reorganized by Drexel, Morgan and Company and leased by the New York Central.

The "Corsair Compact" proved insufficient to halt a renewal of the rate wars in the east; but it had brought a measure of intercorporate agreement between the Pennsylvania and the Central upon which later peacemaking ventures could be based.

The passage of the Interstate Commerce Act of 1887, as noted earlier, supplied the impetus for further experimentation by Morgan with the suppression of competition. Now his economic theories about non-competitive capitalism could be interpreted as having official sanction so long as the Commerce Act was viewed as a legislative effort to bring peace and harmony to American railroads. While it is not entirely clear what Morgan's personal attitude to the act was, he used it as a pretext for furthering intercorporate agreement. Using his personal prestige and his enormous financial power, Morgan had compelled the forging of the Inter-State Commerce Railway Association. His connections with the New York Central and the Pennsylvania had led to the traffic agreement between these two roads in 1894, and his influence among the other eastern roads precipitated the formation of the Joint Traffic Association. All of these undertakings, of course, failed, either because the courts refused to sustain them or because rail leadership lacked Morgan's singlemindedness; however, Morgan had laid a basis for future intercorporate agreements that would prove more durable. Undeterred by the failures of the early 1890's, Morgan's efforts would prove more successful in the new century.

Morgan and his fellow bankers saw the problems quite clearly, in fact, much more clearly than has been generally admitted. Naturally, as a successful banker, Morgan sensed profit, both immediate and long term, in the extensive financial reorgani-

zation and integration of the American railroad network. But,
the preservation of profit depended also on the economic preservation of the railroads themselves. To Morgan, this meant
the control of railroad competition which he correctly understood was a constant threat posed by the excess capacity within
the industry. The financial community's resulting efforts to
build a few strong railroad stems that cooperatively dominated
the whole network have often been misunderstood as simple
power plays based on nothing more than a brazen effort to
exploit consumers and shippers. In fact, stability rather than
exploitation was the goal. Regardless of how uneconomic such
a policy was to be in fact, in theory at least, it was a logical
and rational response for the time and circumstances. Morgan's
program has, of course, been modified by the railroads, and
by forces beyond the railroads' control since the close of the
nineteenth century, but, as the following study labors to show, it
has not been abandoned.

II

THE END OF RAILROAD COMPETITION, 1900-1916

Attempts to reduce competition virtually dominated eastern railroad corporate policy from the beginning of the century up to World War I, and, in general, the efforts must be counted as successful for there was no return to the rate wars of the seventies, eighties and nineties. While some observers still contended that the problem of excess capacity would eventually disappear as the national expansion of business raised all railroad earnings, there was no sign in this period that excess capacity was dwindling or that railroads were eager to return to earlier competitive habits. Variously, the railroads tried formal market agreements, coordination with public regulation authorities, corporate consolidation and informal corporate leadership by the larger trunks as devices to limit industry competition. To a surprising extent, railroads found a source of aid in federal regulation. Although the motives were mixed, the outcome of corporate policies and the actions of legislative and regulatory authorities unmistakably led in the same direction — to create a large measure of stabilization in rail operations through either external or internal controls.

Community of Interest

The striking down of the Joint Traffic Association in 1898 seemed to indicate that all privately created pools or traffic agreements among separate companies would be held illegal. This undoubtedly moved Morgan and other bankers, as well

35

as rail management, to see the need of perfecting other methods
of controlling competition which did not violate prevailing
interpretations of the Interstate Commerce Act or the Sherman
Act. The technique selected to maintain intercorporate harmony
was to create formal and informal combinations within the
industry through banker sponsored financial integration.[1] Within
three years of the Joint Traffic Association ruling, one-eighth
of the mileage of American railroads was effectively brought
under the control of other railroad companies by the use of
such devices as merger, lease, stock control (either direct or
indirect through holding companies) and by the interchange of
directors.[2] The latter device had special favor with the bankers,
who, using their financial connections with a number of roads,
might force upon separate lines similar directors.[3] In this way,
a high degree of central management was obtained without
actual corporate consolidation which might have invited more
governmental scrutiny under the Sherman Act. The effect of all
these types of combination techniques produced by 1905 a situation, according to William Z. Ripley, in which a majority of
the boards of directors of eastern railroads which controlled
all rail connections into New York, Philadelphia and Boston
"might be selected from a list of 39 persons."[4] Such combinations, of course, promised considerable profit to Morgan
and other banking interests   through the anticipated rise of
security prices and through fees received for any refinancing
or reorganizing programs.

In the east, the striking down of the Joint Traffic Association initially produced gloom and confusion among rail leaders.
Briefly, Frank Thompson of the Pennsylvania urged that management consider operating the association surreptitiously and informally, but the obvious illegality and the prospect of court
action against the participating roads quickly ended this discussion.[5] Nevertheless, the return to the old anarchy of rate
cutting could not be accepted. John Cowen and Oscar Murray,
the receivers of the B & O, announced their own plan on
December 20, 1898. In a letter to Martin Knapp, Chairman
of the I.C.C., the receivers admitted that the B & O and the
other trunk lines had maintained joint agreements, and they
observed that now that the Supreme Court had applied the
anti-trust acts to railroads there was a need for an impartial
agency to maintain rail rates and, thus, insulate the industry

from catastrophic rate wars. Cowen and Murray nominated the I.C.C. for the job, observing:

> The I.C.C. not only commands the respect of the railroad carriers for its impartiality, but also in its powers to investigate complaints of illegal rate cutting, and to put a stop to all illegal practices, for surpassing any association which the carriers have even created by agreements between themselves.

> We see no reason why the Commission should refuse its aid to the carriers in an effort to prevent competition from taking the form of illegal concessions through secret rates, drawbacks, rebates, and other devices; and we see no reason why carriers should not seek the aid of the Commission in such an effort by reporting to the Commission any departure from published rates.[6]

The reaction of the other roads to the B & O proposal was swift and unfavorable. The servile tone of the letter seemed bad enough to Morgan and the Central and Pennsylvania leaders, but the suggestion that the I.C.C. now accede to power previously held by the railroads themselves was thoroughly unacceptable. To date, the Commission had exercised only moderate authority in railroad operations, and most railroad men were content with that state of affairs. They were not yet willing to make it the final arbiter on rates nor did they wish to give any more "legitimacy" to the agency.

Through the winter and spring of 1899, eastern rail leaders circulated a number of memorandums and working papers aimed at dealing with the Pondora's Box that the B & O receivers had opened. By summer an idea which supposedly originated in the Pennsylvania's board rooms, but bore the unmistakable imprint of J. P. Morgan, began to gain support. The proposal, ostensibly authored by A. J. Cassatt, president of the Pennsylvania and a close personal friend of J. P. Morgan, called for the creation of a "Community of Interest" between the Pennsylvania and the Central in the east.[7] Cassatt urged that these two trunks create a final solution in the east by jointly purchasing control of the troublesome independent carriers, those that tended to spark price competition or in other ways create instability. Such a plan assured rate leadership for the Central and the Pennsylvania and, by reducing roads outside the community of interest to subservience, created a virtual "duopoly" in eastern railroad transportation.

The community of interest plan clearly had Morgan approval, if not Morgan inspiration, as a new technique for
creating non-competitive stability, for he and his financial connections played a key role in its initiation and development.
The community of interest activities of the Central and the
Pennsylvania began with their joint acquisition of control of
the Chesapeake and Ohio Railroad. The Chesapeake and Ohio
had only recently been reorganized by Drexel, Morgan and
Company, and that financial house as was Morgan's style,
retained control through key directorships. The Central and
the Pennsylvania together paid $8,175,000, each taking 25 per-
cent of the Chesapeake and Ohio stock. Half of the payment
went directly to J. P. Morgan and Company which handled
the arrangements. The Pennsylvania was permitted to assume
leadership in the corporate policies of the road since its line
more directly affected Pennsylvania properties.[8]

Between 1900 and 1901, the Pennsylvania acquired 39 percent of the stock of the Norfolk and Western, another southern
bituminous carrier which along with its Chesapeake and Ohio
holdings virtually assured the Pennsylvania domination over
bituminous coal movement.[9] The Pennsylvania next moved
against the Baltimore and Ohio. By shifting some of its banking
business to the Baltimore and Ohio bankers, Kuhn, Loeb and
Company, the Pennsylvania began to exert power over the
Baltimore and Ohio's financial affairs.[10] The shift by the
Pennsylvania of its banking business to Kuhn, Loeb and Company and also to Speyer and Company apparently had the
approval of Morgan, who showed decreasing interest in southern
railroad affairs and was much more interested in northern roads
related to the New York Central. Moreover, connections between Kuhn, Loeb and Morgan's financial houses were cordial.

By 1902, the Pennsylvania had acquired 40 percent of the
Baltimore and Ohio's stock,[11] an investment in the securities
of its trunk rival amounting to $65,000,000 and giving the
Pennsylvania enough authority in the road's corporate affairs
to place its Fourth Vice President, Leonor P. Loree, in the
presidency.

In a masterful understatement and exposition of the community of interest policies, President Cassatt explained the
Pennsylvania's acquisition of the Baltimore and Ohio to his
board of directors:

For the purpose of enabling closer relations with other trunk lines, it had seemed wise to acquire an interest in some of the railways reaching the seaboard and unite them with the other shareholders who control these properties, in supporting a conservative policy of management. It was hoped in this way to secure reasonable and stable rates and prevent the unjust discrimination which inevitably resulted from conflicts between the railways and between rival communities, and that aside from the indirect benefits thus sought to be gained it was believed that these holdings would, as investments, be directly profitable.[12]

By the end of 1902, the Pennsylvania had spent over $110,000,000 in acquiring stocks of eastern railroads which had been allocated to it by arrangements under the community of interest.[13] The arrangements with the New York Central, which had permitted the Pennsylvania to increase its power over roads to the south of its mainline, were even durable enough to permit the Pennsylvania to "invade" New York State without retribution from the Central. In 1900, the Pennsylvania acquired the controlling interest in the Long Island Railroad.[14] In 1904, contracts were let to commence the construction of the Hudson River tubes to give the Pennsylvania direct access to the New York City market.[15] The Pennsylvania, meanwhile, had acquired access to Buffalo in 1900 when it purchased control of the struggling Western New York and Pennsylvania Railway, a line with two spurs running southward from Buffalo and Rochester through the Pennsylvania oil fields to Mahoningtown, just north of Pittsburgh.[16] By taking 97 percent of the stock and 91 percent of the bonds of the old "oil road," now largely dependent on coal, the Pennsylvania had assumed a property that never was to pay its fixed charges and, through the circuitous route that it operated, did not pose much threat to the Central's rich overhead traffic west of Buffalo.[17]

While the stock of the Western New York was really worthless in terms of market value, the Pennsylvania paid about $9.00 per share. With the bonds, this totaled $6,000,000. In the next two decades another $28,000,000 was spent on improving the property. Briefly, the road seemed to have some promise as a coal carrier, but, overall, the investment by the Pennsylvania was ill-chosen.

While the Pennsylvania was mostly concerned with increasing its control over the southern coal carriers and making con-

nections into New York City, the New York Central had been
strengthening its position over New York to Chicago traffic
and had begun to penetrate the Pennsylvania anthracite region.
In maintaining its position as a trunk line, the Central had
been in much better shape than the Pennsylvania at the beginning of the community of interest. First of all, the only
potential threat to traffic crossing New York State, the Erie,
was a virtual captive of the Central. Morgan financial interests
had reorganized the Erie after its collapse in 1893 and had retained control of its management. As bankers for the Central
and as important stockholders, the Morgan camp could be
counted upon to support coordination between the Central and
the Erie. In fact, Morgan maintained financial associations
with practically all New York roads which had direct traffic
interchange with the Central. With regard to obtaining friendly
connections or pacifying potential competitors, the Central did
not have to resort to purchasing stocks of other roads. Thus,
its activities under the community of interest were less ambitious
than those of the Pennsylvania.

The only complete acquisitions through stock purchases by the
Central at this time were the Lake Shore, the Michigan Central,
the "Big Four," and the Lake Erie and Western, and these
were really "family deals," with the Vanderbilts exchanging
personal holdings for New York Central stock or cash.[18]
Neither these actions nor the ninety-nine year leasing of the
Boston and Albany, which assured the Central connections
with New England, were good examples of community of
interest in operation.[19]

The Central's purchase of anthracite roads' securities provides a better illustration of the workings of community of
interest. Through the Lake Shore, from 1901 to 1904, the Central joined with the Baltimore and Ohio (under Pennsylvania
Railroad control) to purchase jointly, 49 percent of the Philadelphia and Reading stock.[20] Earlier, the Lake Shore had
joined with three roads directly under Morgan's financial control, the Erie, the Lackawanna, and the Jersey Central, to
purchase 20 percent of the Lehigh Valley's outstanding stock.
The Lake Shore took about two-fifths of this purchase.[21] This
invasion of the Pennsylvania anthracite region was part of a
long developing Morgan plan, and, there is much evidence to
suggest that the anthracite coal situation was a basic feature of
Morgan's sponsorship of the community of interest.[22]

Since 1874, eight railroad companies had more or less dominated the Pennsylvania anthracite coal fields around the Hazel-
ton-Wilkes Barre-Scranton area—the Erie, the Pennsylvania,
the Lehigh Valley, the Reading, the Delaware and Hudson, the
Delaware Lackawanna and Western, the New York Ontario
and Western, and the Jersey Central.[23] The anthracite industry
had begun rather inauspiciously about fifty years before; however, not until there developed a wider use of coal burning
stoves and furnaces and a general public acceptance of the
new fuel did the industry thrive. In 1840, production had been
only 864,000 tons. By 1867, it had grown to over 13,000,000
tons and by 1904, anthracite coal production stood at more
than 57,000,000 tons.[24] The sudden upsurge in demand for
"hard" coal after the Civil War brought chaos to the Pennsylvania coal fields. Without state regulation of any kind, even
to protect the state's pet canal projects, the carriers developed
their own concept of stabilization in the form of controlling,
by purchase, lease or other means, the coal mines.[25] The
Delaware and Hudson, the Lehigh Valley, and the Reading
were already entrenched by the time the Pennsylvania Railroad
arrived upon the scene in 1873. The Pennsylvania officially
"regretted" the practice of buying out or crushing the independent coal operators but its directors justified such actions
by asserting:

> The policy of the state of Pennsylvania has led to the
> absorption, either directly or indirectly, of nearly all of the
> best anthracite coal properties in the state, by all of the
> carrying companies leading from that coal region to the
> seaboard . . . . These purchases were being made quietly but
> rapidly by other railway companies . . . . To prevent such a
> result, and to obtain some of this traffic for its railroad, the
> Pennsylvania Railroad Company was compelled to follow
> the example of the other railroad companies by securing, in
> the vicinity of its lines, the control of coal lands that would
> continue to supply transportation for them.[26]

Competition among the carriers was keen during the seventies
and eighties. The seasonal fluctuations in coal demand and the
high degree of competition among the carriers served to create
much price instability. With characteristic opposition to such a
situation, J. P. Morgan entered upon the anthracite scene. In
1898, Morgan and Company reorganized the Lehigh Valley

Railroad, long a casualty of the coal wars and in receivership since 1893.[27] Over the next few years, Morgan interests developed alliances with the Delaware and Hudson, the Lackawanna, the Jersey Central, and the Reading.[28] With existing financial connections to the Erie and the Pennsylvania, Morgan banking interests were the strongest financial group involved in the coal region, and Morgan moved quickly to bring peace to the anthracite roads.

Coal not directly owned by the railroad companies nor controlled through wholly owned coal companies was to be controlled by forcing the independent operators to sign long-term agreements with the carriers. This was a first step toward peace because the independents had been able to set the railroads against one another by forcing rate reductions. The number of independent operators was small but they were large enough and the carriers disorganized enough to force either favorable rate reductions or rebates. The success of Morgan's moves are seen in Ripley's calculations that, in the decade after 1900, the eight coal carriers were able to increase their direct coal production holdings from 62 percent to 90 percent of coal output, and they were able to gain control of three-quarters of the

TABLE 4

SHARES IN ANTHRACITE TRAFFIC BY MAJOR CARRIERS,
SELECTED YEARS, 1899-1911
(in percentages)[a]

Road	1899	1902	1908	1911
Reading	20.70	18.94	19.45	18.96
Lehigh V.	15.22	14.84	16.66	18.02
Jersey Central	11.77	11.63	13.14	13.18
DL. & W.	13.33	16.51	15.60	14.11
D. & H.	8.81	9.91	9.99	10.30
Penn.	11.46	8.37	9.31	9.28
Erie	10.64	12.22	11.52	12.58
NYO. & W.	3.68	5.22	4.33	3.57
DS. & S.	3.45	2.36	—	—

[a]*Financial Review*, 1903 (New York: William B. Dana Company, 1908), p. 38, and *Financial Review*, 1912, (New York: William B. Dana Company, 1912), p. 60.

mines.[29] The coal carriers enforced rigid price agreement and after 1899 maintained an informal but consistent proportioning of hard coal transportation.[30] In the face of seasonal fluctuations, labor difficulties and expanding demand, the coal co-operativeness survived for nearly two decades.

After bringing peace to the operations of the coal roads, which doubled the earnings of the anthracite carriers between 1897 and 1907, Morgan's next step was to integrate the coal cooperation into the community of interest. The plan called for the parceling of the anthracite coal business to the New York Central and the awarding of bituminous traffic to the Pennsylvania. The Central's movement into the anthracite region, with apparent Pennsylvania agreement, and the Pennsylvania's extension of power over the Norfolk and Western and the Chesapeake and Ohio were pivotal to the plan's success.[31] As might be expected, the plan did not receive wide publicity from either railroad's management. However, a Philadelphia Press reporter observed in 1903:

Both the Pennsylvania and the Vanderbilts have worked in harmony for the past few years and the bond is closer now than ever before. The latest deal gives to the Vanderbilt-Cassatt-Morgan interests all the roads east of the Mississippi River with the exception of a few minor roads.... There are a few anthracite roads to be secured but it is believed that the Vanderbilt-Morgan interest is so great that there is no fear of any outside parties securing control.[32]

Complaints about the growing corporate integration in the east, however, had been infrequent during the early years of community of interest. In 1900, for example, the New York Board of Railroad Commissioners reported that, despite the evidence of collusion among the roads in setting rates during the year, it had received but one complaint. Apparently accepting the integration of corporate policies as inevitable and possibly desirable, the Board noted:

The tendency toward consolidation of interests in railroad properties continues. This tendency, extending as it does over the country, may render of little importance the legislation by Congress of "pooling." How the interests of the public may ultimately be affected is conjectural, but, so far as this State is concerned, this board has power to enforce recommendations through the courts.... It is notable, however, that for several years past complaints as to freight rates have been comparatively infrequent, and usually have involved very small matters.[33]

One further example of the New York Central-Pennsylvania duopoly over eastern railroad affairs was their successful destruction of a "fifth" trunk system which was attempted in the east. This system, planned by George Gould, who had been putting together rail properties in the mid-west, was based upon the combination of some unconnected ownings he held in Ohio, West Virginia, Virginia, and Pennsylvania.[34] Gould controlled the Wabash, which gave him connections to Buffalo and Toledo; and, from Toledo, his Wheeling and Lake Erie Railroad reached Wheeling, West Virginia. However, between Wheeling and Cumberland, Maryland, there was a 100-mile break in the line before connections could be made with his Western Maryland into Baltimore. Gould's projected system would have been about 1000 miles in length, and, while not being an exceptionally good route, it would have created a new trunkline outside the sphere of influence of the community of interest. Gould had no connections with the Morgan camp and his antagonism to the Vanderbilts was a family affair of long standing.

Gould's plan received considerable support from Andrew Carnegie, who had been irritated by the community of interest's opposition to rebating and who over the years had used his economic power against the Pennsylvania on a number of occasions.[35] With the help of Carnegie, who promised to route one-quarter of his coal, iron ore, and steel traffic over Gould's road, the Wabash-Pittsburgh Railroad Terminal Company was built to connect Wheeling and Pittsburgh. The 50-mile road opened on June 19, 1904.[36] The Pennsylvania, directly and through its control of the Baltimore and Ohio, refused to interchange traffic with the Gould properties. The Central promised similar support to the Pennsylvania's opposition to the new line. Earlier, when Gould had begun construction of the road, the Pennsylvania had retaliated by breakings its association with Gould's Western Union Company and had eventually torn down the Western Union's telegraph poles along its mainline.[37] The economic pressure created by the Central and the Pennsylvania presented serious hardships for Gould. In all, he spent nearly $45,000,000 or $750,000 per mile, to gain access to Pittsburgh. However, his arrangements with Carnegie never materialized as Carnegie sold his interests in steel, and the new United States Steel Corporation, a Morgan inspired creation, began friendlier relations with the Pennsylvania and the Baltimore and Ohio.[38] Suffering from a shortage of capital, Gould was unable to close the gap in his proposed trunk line between Pittsburgh and the northernmost extension of his Western Maryland at Connellsville, Pennsylvania, and the threat of a fifth system disappeared in the gathering clouds of depression in 1907. The destruction of the Gould system, of course, had been the kind of situation that the community of interest had been created for.

The community of interest's apparently successful operations and a general rise in business prosperity brought a new respectability to railroad securities. With the bitter experience of the seventies, eighties, and early nineties fading and faith in railroad securities returning in the financial community, there was a steady advance in security prices. Although there was only a comparatively moderate increase in the stock price of the Central and the Pennsylvania by mid 1902 as compared to mid 1890, the smaller roads made substantial advances. During this period the B & O stock had risen from 15 to 99, the Erie from 12 to 25, and the DL & W from 157 to 286. Even the struggling little New York, Ontario and Western advanced from 15 to 43, while the Buffalo, Rochester and Pittsburgh skyrocketed from 28 to 125. There was hopeful talk along Wall Street that this was a permanent trend and that the older insanity of railroad finance had been replaced by a new conservatism; however, the ending of the community of interest in 1906 and the depression of 1907 threatened this optimism. By mid 1907, the Baltimore and Ohio stock fell thirty points, the New York Central tumbled fifty points, and the Pennsylvania's stock fell by forty; however, the stocks quickly regained much of this loss. Moreover, even in the depths of the depression of 1907, security prices remained higher than July 1898.[39]

While the community of interest had been quite effective in maintaining published rates among eastern railroads and had brought considerable stability to the traffic division among the roads, the problem of rebates still hung heavily over the east.[40]

Large shippers were able to command refunds on shipping
fees and, while intercorporate harmony among eastern railroads tended to discourage much rebating, it has been estimated
that rebates were still taking as much as 10 percent of total
railroad gross revenues.[41] Shortly after the formation of the
community of interest, President Cassatt of the Pennsylvania,
with the help of the New York Central, and presumably with
the agreement and encouragement of Morgan, began agitation
for an end to rebating.[42]

In 1903, with the passage of the Elkins Act, which amended
the Interstate Commerce Act to make any deviation from the
published rates *ipso facto* evidence of wrongdoing (rather than
waiting for time-consuming court action), the rebating problem
was largely solved. The passage of the act provided the railroads with legal protection from the pressures of shippers seeking rebates, and it marked the beginning of railroad dependence
upon Interstate Commerce Law for protection from competition.

For two decades after the formation of the community of
interest arrangements, the railroads fought for an amendment
to the Interstate Commerce Act that would have permitted
pooling. With the apparent destruction of rate competition
among common carriers, a development aided by the passage
of the Interstate Commerce Act, the Elkins Act, and eventually
by the Hepburn Act, pooling seemed justifiable to both rail
leaders and to some members of the I.C.C.[43] However, not
until after 1920, was this authority informally granted to the
railroads.

Meanwhile, the growth of corporate power and cooperativeness among eastern railroads, paralleling similar developments
in the western states, made lurid reading for the general public.
With greater attention focused on rail operations after passage
of the Elkins Act in 1903, the public calm which had sur-
rounded the formation of community of interest was broken.
The *Baltimore Herald* measured the growing public concern
in 1903, when reporting the New York Central and Baltimore
and Ohio acquisition of the Reading:

> Another community of interest tending toward the increas-
> ing consolidation of trunk line railroads has been con-
> solidated.... The New York Central and the Pennsylvania
> have in the past few years come close together on a working
> basis. Recently they secured control of the Manhattan Ele-

vated in New York City. They are both interested in the construction of a tunnel under New York, which is an alleged Pennsylvania scheme. The Pennsylvania under the interstate commerce laws, applying to railroads, could not become a purchaser of the Reading, as they are parallel lines. The Baltimore and Ohio is not a competitor, therefore, the B & O could become and was made the ostensible purchaser.

The B & O, however, is in partnership with the Pennsylvania and New York Central. It is a three cornered deal and a big step toward a financial combination of all trunk lines in the country.[44]

The reporter further noted that such combinations were little concerned with the "Public Interest" in the development of "Community of Interest."

The pressure for greater railroad legislation after 1903 came in varying degrees from virtually all parties interested in the railroads. A wide variety of opinion supported plans for additional regulation. The interested public and many small shippers still flirted with visions of reconstructing intercorporate rate competition. The large shippers wanted greater I.C.C. power over rate setting and, presumably, lower rates.[45] Many of the rail leaders thought the passage of the Elkins Act had been enough, but others such as Cassatt, desired the broadening of I.C.C. power over rates, arguing that stable rates would benefit intercorporate planning in the industry. Other rail leaders, threatened by the growing, ambitious and unpredictable state regulatory agencies, frankly desired a strong uniform regulation at the national level which would insulate them from the capriciousness of the state commissions. Revealing the financial community's view on railroad regulation, the *Wall Street Journal* observed that "the foremost railroad men of the country are at this time working in harmony...for the federal regulation of rates."[46] The writer, moreover, believed that such a development would greatly improve the railroad situation.

Meanwhile, the federal government had begun proceedings in 1902 against the Northern Securities Company — the Harriman-Hill combination — and in 1904 the holding company was dissolved and holding companies declared illegal means of obtaining monopoly control. On March 7, 1906, Congress ordered the I.C.C. to investigate rail discrimination in the east as an outgrowth of the Pennsylvania's and New York Central's activities

in the destruction of George Gould's proposed system.[47] Three
months later the *New York Times* reported that the I.C.C.
was requesting all "interested parties" to appear before it during
hearings on "the problem of railroad monopoly."[48]

The End of Community of Interest

While it was clear by early 1906 that some form of railroad
regulatory legislation would pass the current Congress, it was by
no means certain what this legislation would be — either in intent or form. Even after passage, there was some confusion as
to whether the Hepburn Act was a victory or a defeat for any
one side. The new act provided that: 1) the Interstate Commerce Commission authority be broadened to include related
rail activities (terminal facilities, etc.), 2) railroads submit income accounting reports, 3) the Interstate Commerce Commission could set maximum rates, 4) railroads were prohibited from
shipping certain commodities (i.e. coal) that they had ownership
interests in unless they were used in common carrier activities,
5) orders of the Interstate Commerce Commission were effective
as directed by the commission, and 6) that the Interstate Commerce Commission be increased to seven members to handle
the additional workload.

By giving the I.C.C. power to set standardized rates, any
lingering notions about resuscitating railroad price competition
should have been finally destroyed. By giving the rate setting
powers to the commission, the act, theoretically at least, weakened the corporations' capacity to determine their own pricing.
For itself, the I.C.C. later observed:

> The Hepburn Act of 1906 marked the beginning of effective
> Federal railway regulation. It was written with knowledge of
> the main defects in the original (I.C.C.) act which had been
> clearly demonstrated by the decisions of the courts, and of the
> recommendations which had repeatedly been voiced in the
> annual reports of the Commission.
>
> The outstanding addition to regulation ... was the definite
> authority given the Commission to prescribe maximum rates,
> regulations or practices for the future. It provided that such
> orders were to be effective as determined by the Commission
> with the burden on the carriers to test the validity of the
> order before the courts.[49] *

---

* American historians have tended to look at the passage of the Hepburn Act
as an ending to the more obnoxious activities of American railroads. As a

Paralleling the passage of the Hepburn Act, the New York legislators replaced the old Railroad Commission with the more vigorous Public Service Commission. As one observer noted: "For many years the old railroad commission had been an utter nonentity, abjectly subservient to the powerful railroad and trolley companies."[50] From the outset, the Public Service Commission proceeded to act as a complement to federal legislation. Whereas federal regulatory authority was aimed principally at the problems of rates and service, the Public Service Commission was particularly concerned with the financial activities of railroads under its jurisdiction.[51] This approach varied from the actions of the commissions of many other states and posed a real threat to roads operating in New York.

Reacting to the Hepburn Act and to the newly created New York Public Service Commission, the eastern railroads moved between 1906 and 1908 to mollify their critics. Correspondence among eastern railroad executives referred frequently to the need for creating a better public image.[52] Several planned mergers were quickly abandoned as the legal staffs of eastern railroads perceived that certain aspects of public policy implicit in the Northern Securities case could be turned against eastern railroad combination, even though eastern consolidation had been accomplished by means other than holding companies.

In November, 1906, the Pennsylvania and the Central ended their Chesapeake and Ohio agreement, the initial stock purchase of the community of interest agreement.[53] The two roads developed some minor disagreement as to the disposition of the Chesapeake and Ohio stock. The original agreement stipulated that both the Pennsylvania and the Central had the right of first refusal. While the Pennsylvania wanted the Central to take its shares, believing that few charges of monopolistic intent

result, the act has been hailed as an important watershed in American business history. However, after 1906, railroads did not cease in their intercorporate, non-competitive actions and rail management continued on their earlier policy path. Historians, like Faulkner (Harold U. Faulkner, *The Decline of Laissez Faire* (New York: Holt, Rinehart, Winston, 1962), pp. 197-199 and 202-208), while essentially correct in their maintenance that Federal authority to regulate rates, pools, rebates, etc. grew from 1903 to 1910 and that the courts ceased to be railroad protectors, erroneously infer that this handicapped the railroads in maintaining non-competitive arrangements. The Interstate Commerce Commission clearly did not yet act as the manager of American railroads. Moreover, although it remains for another study, it seems quite possible that internal controls were encouraged by the increased authority of the Interstate Commerce Commission.

could be leveled against it by such an action, the Central declined.[54] Both roads disposed of their holdings gradually to keep the stock price high. The Pennsylvania also sold about half its investment in the Baltimore and Ohio, retaining about a 20 percent interest.[55] Similarly, it reduced its ownings in the Norfolk and Western to about 20 percent.[56]

The New York Central had been less active under the community of interest arrangement than the Pennsylvania. Its interest in the Chesapeake and Ohio had not been very great and the decision to dispose of these ownings had little effect on Central policy, for the original investment in the road had been based upon the need to support the Pennsylvania. Only the Lehigh Valley, of roads under New York Central control, might have qualified as "monopolization through ownership of a competing carrier," and the Central and the other Morgan roads, the Erie, the Lackawanna, and the Reading sold most of their Lehigh Valley stocks in 1908. Control of the road, however, was little changed, as J. P. Morgan and Company assumed most of the ownings.[57] Meanwhile, the Central retained its holdings of Reading, New Haven, and Rutland stocks as well as its ownings in several smaller roads acquired after 1900.[58]

The actions taken by the two leading eastern trunks signaled an end to the formal arrangements of community of interest, and the division of eastern railroads into two great corporate properties was, for the time being, abandoned. The effect, however, was not to restore the earlier competitive situation, nor did it bring any serious change to the corporate harmony of eastern railroads. The ending of community of interest was accomplished largely as it began, quitely and will little public notice. Even the manifestations of public outrage, which had been important in the passage of the Hepburn Act and which had threatened the railroads with more rigorous regulation, died away. Nevertheless, some noteworthy scars from the Hepburn Act and the ending of community of interest remained.

First, and most important, the schemes for the private regulation of rates and service, a critical part of Morgan's earlier proposals, from which the community of interest idea developed, were destroyed by the Hepburn Act. Morgan's plan for enlightened private regulation, where great corporate empires were ruled by businessmen of vision, was replaced by the fact of greater external government control. The goals of both private and governmental regulation may have been the same, even the results may have been identical; but, for many railroad leaders the Hepburn Act had gone too far. Conservative bankers and rail managers, some of whom might have supported some broadening of Interstate Commerce Commission powers, became wary of the Commission as time passed. President Cassatt of the Pennsylvania, who had been foremost among eastern railroad spokesmen in supporting the expansion of public regulation, had died on December 28, 1906.[59] Cassatt, a close friend of Morgan and familiar with the perspectives of eastern bankers, had formally introduced the community of interest proposal, had worked for the passage of the Elkins Act, and had favored portions of the Hepburn Act. Without Cassatt to champion greater government and business integration over regulatory functions, the attitude of the industry took on greater hostility toward federal regulation, or at least toward certain actions of the Interstate Commerce Commission.[60]

In 1911, after the passage the year before of the Mann-Elkins Act, which gave the Commission the power to revise rates through suspension of rate changes and placed the burden of justifying rate changes on the railroads, a leading financial publication evinced the attitudes of much of the railroad community in protesting:

> In the railroad field, entirely new conditions were imposed by the amendment of the Inter-State Commerce Law . . . . This vested the Interstate Commerce Commission with new and almost autocratic powers over the affairs of the roads. It placed the railroad carrying interest, with its enormous investment of $18,000,000,000, completely at the mercy of this body of seven men. The Commission had never in the past shown the slightest regard for railroad interests, but it was hoped that with increased powers and responsibility it would now become conservative and proceed in a judicial and judicious manner. Unfortunately, such hopes were quickly dashed.[61]

The writer was particularly distressed by the recent decision of the Commission to disallow a rate increase.[62] While the rate decision had sparked the comments, the article continued on to attack government interference in business in general, setting forth the position that government interference was uneconomic and "against the public interest."[63] The argument, somewhat excessively shrill in this case, would be heard again and again as the industry protested specific Commission decisions. However, the sharpness of such attacks on the Commission should not be over-emphasized, for opposition to regulation was usually on particular questions not with the philosophic principle of regulation itself.

While attacks upon the Commission and public regulation in general were offered for the public's consumption, railroads were still able to secure favorable legislation. In the Mann-Elkins Act, a Commerce Court with powers to suspend or stay Commission orders was created, and the court soon proved to have decided pro-railroad sentiments. Although the court was abolished by Congress in 1913, neither this action nor unfavorable rate decisions by the Commission thoroughly destroyed the hopes of many railroad leaders that public policy could be redirected to lines more beneficial to the railroads.[64]

President Samuel Rea of the Pennsylvania observed in 1914:

> I believe in regulation by Commission, and I urge, therefore, that we do not encourage destruction of such regulation, but rather its conservation, by adopting it, as we have banking regulation and other laws, to suit the needs of the country as they change from time to time. We must look beyond the present obstacles and view the whole subject from a statesman's standpoint. Under an enlightened policy of public regulation, but not repression, the railroads will be placed and kept in a strong position to meet increased traffic demands, as well as to live healthfully in times of depression.[65]

There could be little doubt that Rea still saw the principle of public regulation as a real protection of railroad interests.

Another result of increased government intervention was the growing popular view of railroads as quasi-public utilities. With rate regulatory powers and the power to order immediate compliance given to the Interstate Commerce Commission, even the general public and the shippers abandoned their beliefs that a crude *laissez faire* competition should characterize railroad affairs. Although rail management had held this view for years, the general acceptance of the principle of "limited competition" must be counted as a gain for the railroads. After some half-hearted I.C.C. inquiries into rail monopoly in the east, the question of railroad monopolization attracted less interest than before the passage of the Hepburn Act. Although the Commission, from time to time, and the Transportation Act of 1920 referred to the "maintenance of competition," there was little suggestion that this meant a return to the old ways of the eighties and nineties.

In disposing of their holdings of stock in eastern railroads, the Pennsylvania and the Central had created the illusion that their dominion over the east was broken. Shippers once again seemed to have four separate trunk lines to choose from, with the distinct possibility that others could be constructed if there was need. However, it was this very possibility of a fifth system, which loomed always as a threat to the Pennsylvania and the Central, as well as to the Baltimore and Ohio and the Erie, that was to offer encouragement to later mergers. The residue of community interest was much stronger than generally realized. By virtue of their size, their banker connections, and their earlier prominence, the Pennsylvania and the New York Central still dominated eastern railroads. The years of subjugation by the Pennsylvania had left the Baltimore and Ohio badly weakened, and the depressed financial condition of the Erie left it a poor threat to the Central.

TABLE 5

FINANCIAL CONTROL OF AMERICAN RAILROAD
NETWORK, 1915[a]

Financial Group	Mileage	Percent
Union Pacific — Southern Pacific	34,543	13.7
Morgan Interests	29,407	11.7
Hill Interests	28,053	11.1
Vanderbilts	23,675	9.4
Pennsylvania Interests	13,834	5.5
Sante Fe System	11,546	4.6
Chicago Minneapolis & St. Paul	10,442	4.1
Rock Island	8,330	3.3
Missouri Pacific	7,292	2.9
New Haven	7,105	2.8
Total	174,229	69.1

[a] E. R. Johnson and T.W. Van Metre, *Principles of Railroad Transportation* (New York: Appleton and Company, 1917), pp. 90-91.

The integration of railroad properties through banker control had not been halted by the growth of government regulation. Among railroads in New York State, Morgan money maintained almost complete control, and, through his association with the New Haven, Morgan also was able to dominate the New England roads as well.[66] The degree to which banker or financial groups controlled American railroads was revealed in a 1915 study which indicated that ten financial groups held firm influence over sixty-nine percent of American railroad trackage. As the above table shows, the Morgan-Vanderbilt-Pennsylvania interests had direct influence over at least 25 to 30 percent of the rail network. Intercorporate stock ownership and a variety of financial alliances probably extended this three cornered financial power to about 50 percent of the net.[67]

Despite occasional threats of prosecution for limiting competition, railroads continued to buy each others security issues. In 1906, 46 percent of American railroads' total capital stock issue of $9,000,000,000 was held by railroads themselves. About 15 percent of the bonded debt similarly was internally owned.[68] According to Ripley, this intercorporate relationship remained substantially unchanged for a number of years.[69] However, after 1910, railroads again began to acquire additional securities in other roads. In most cases, Ripley pointed out, this represented the convenient drawing of alliances rather than the primitive suppression of competition; however, the distinction between these two motives was really rather unimportant.

Another construction of community of interest, the partitioning of the anthracite and bituminous coal business by the Central and the Pennsylvania, had never been completely accomplished. The end of community interest, however, did not mark the plan's abandonment. The Hepburn Act, in the so-called "commodities clause," had struck a heavy blow at the carrier domination of the coal companies. The act specified:

> . . . it shall be unlawful for any railroad company to transport from any state, territory, or the District of Columbia to any state or territory, the District of Columbia or any foreign country any article or commodity, other than timber and the manufactured goods thereof, manufactured, mined or produced by it, or under its authority, or which it may own in whole or part, or in which it may have any interest, direct or indirect, except such commodities as may be necessary and

intended for its use in the conduct of its business as a common carrier.[70]

Nevertheless, the New York Central, through its Morgan connections retained a deep interest in the anthracite traffic. Not until 1920, with the Reading Case, was the commodities clause upheld in the courts; however, the railroads and their coal subsidiaries had by then devised a variety of techniques for getting around this provision.[71] In 1909, the courts, by a unique construction of the Hepburn Act, held that majority ownership of stock in a coal company by a railroad did not constitute legal ownership of the coal properties. Other devices were also found. Railroads sold their coal before it left the mine thus avoiding the commodities clause. Roads separated their coal and rail functions into two corporate entities (in some cases three), but the stockholders, of course, remained the same. Meanwhile, some railroads constructed holding companies to own both rail and coal properties. At any rate, coal prices remained fixed by mutual agreement and the railroads continued proportional sharing in traffic. The coal roads were to become the focus of New York Central and Pennsylvania attention during the merger movement of the 1920's, when they were again a major inspiration of empire-building activity.

Finances and Operations to World War I

Community of interest had focused the attention of railroad management, as well as the public and government, on the aggregation of corporate power. The acquisition of rail properties by the Central, the Pennsylvania and other eastern roads had usually been for its own sake and without much thought to the creation of improved traffic routes. A survey of management correspondence during the period gives the distinct impression that the officers and directors, and certainly the bankers, of the larger eastern railroads had very little understanding of traffic flow and transportation demand along the roads they sought to control.[72] President Cassatt of the Pennsylvania made no mention to his board of directors of the operational benefits accruing to his railroad as a result of its purchase of the Baltimore and Ohio and the Chesapeake and Ohio stock.[73] Similarly, the New York Central justified its purchase of Lake Shore, Michigan Central and Big Four stock simply as "improvement of financial organization."[74] The Central's affiliation with coal roads was largely a function of banker control although these acquisitions doubtless afforded some operational advantages to the road. The Boston and Albany lease is perhaps the only significant acquisition which gave direct operational advantage to the Central.[75]

Neither the railroad companies nor the regulatory agencies showed much concern in obtaining useful operating statistics. After 1906, the I.C.C. and the New York Public Service Commission improved their collection and the reporting accuracy of railroad income statements, and, to the discomfort of some carriers, required expanded accounting for the basis of evaluating rates. Nevertheless, the data collected was relatively useless for estimating traffic flow and demand over specific routes and lines. Among eastern railroads and regulatory agencies alike there appeared to be no technical understanding of the problem of excess capacity in the eastern rail network. Roads which had difficulties paying their fixed charges were considered weak roads, and those with relatively low charges were considered good, although the fixed charges themselves gave no insight to a roads' real earning power. Generally, when a road or the industry fell upon hard times, business cycle conditions were cited as the cause. On the other hand, when the economy was prosperous and rail earnings, even on marginally productive roads, were high, business conditions for the railroads were viewed as "normal," rather than abnormally good. With this outlook toward railroad earnings, the physical network's relationship to structural changes in flows and demand was never really understood. Not until World War I, when the railroads collapsed under the extraordinary traffic, did the necessity for greater knowledge of this interrelationship become apparent.

In large part, the growing national prosperity after 1900 served to diminish railroad interest in operational problems as such. Between 1900 and 1910 real Gross National Product for the United States grew by 35 percent.[76] As the following table shows, American railroad earnings nearly doubled during the same period, with freight and passenger gross revenues increasing by more than 90 percent. Traffic increasingly was taken for granted; however, in the relatively bad depressions of 1907-1908 and 1911-1912, railroad traffic declined enough to cause respectively about a 14 percent and a 6 percent reduction.[77]

TABLE 6

MISCELLANEOUS RAILROAD STATISTICS FOR THE UNITED STATES, SELECTED YEARS, 1880-1910 [a]

(000 omitted)

Year	Mileage [b]	Cap. Stock	Fund. Debt.	Gross Earn.	Net Earn.	Dividends [c]	Interest [d]
1880	93,236	$2,708,673	$2,530,874	$613,733	$255,557	$77,115	$107,866
1885	128,320	3,817,697	2,350,894	765,310	266,488	77,672	119,681
1890	166,654	4,590,171	5,053,319	1,078,835	341,666	83,575	217,922
1895	181,065	5,181,373	5,648,569	1,092,035	323,196	81,685	239,698
1900	194,262	5,804,306	5,758,592	1,501,695	483,247	119,288	214,199
1905	217,341	6,554,557	7,250,701	2,082,482	691,880	188,175	294,803
1910	242,107	8,113,657	10,303,474	2,750,667	928,037	293,836	370,092

[a] *Financial Review, 1903* (New York: William B. Dana Company, 1903), p. 67, and *Financial Review, 1912* (New York: William B. Dana Company, 1912), pp. 86 and 88.

[b] Variations in reported mileage between this table and Table 1 reflect different calculations for fiscal and calendar year. This table is based on Fiscal Year.

[c] Interest on Bonds only for 1880-1900 and on all funded debt after 1900.

[d] Dividends paid out of current income only.

Eastern trunk carriers proved to be more vulnerable to cyclical downturns which usually meant important losses of such export items as grain, coal and manufactured goods. In 1908, the Pennsylvania, New York Central, Baltimore and Ohio, and Erie respectively reported declines in net earnings of 19, 17, 17, and 10 percent; but, after each downturn, business and rail earnings rebounded well, and the hard times were quickly forgotten.[78] Although eastern railroads lagged behind the industry's national growth performance, the pre-World War years were nevertheless very good.

The rise in railroad earnings were viewed almost exclusively as a source for immediate profit-taking, with relatively little to be poured back into the railroads for improvement and betterment of equipment. Under the prevailing budgeting methods of the railroads, at least up to the passage of the Transportation Act of 1920, sinking funds, refunding programs, and depreciation allowances were rarely used to provide for capital improvement contingencies. This preoccupation with profit-taking was evidenced in that 66 percent of American railroad corporations in 1910 paid dividends of nearly $400,000,000, or about an 8 percent return for those stocks paying any dividends. About three-quarters of this total was paid from current income and the other quarter was appropriated from surplus.[79] Meanwhile, railroads reported using only $57,000,000 of current income for capital improvements.[80]

Between 1900 and 1910, the capitalization of all American railroads increased from $11,500,000,000 to $18,500,000,000. This 60 percent increase mostly was accounted for in the doubling of bonded debt during the period.[81] The growth in capitalization to a large degree reflected attempts to tighten the internal financial structure of rail systems. Collateral trust bonds were a favored instrument in such consolidations, with these instruments secured by the capital stock of the merged or purchased roads. Many roads reported as "improvements in road and equipment" the purchase of outstanding securities in roads already under their control or in roads they were attempting to control. Depressingly little of the new investment found its way into the physical improvement of the roads.

The ending of community of interest did not appreciably slow the rate of increasing capitalization. In fact, the capitalization of eastern railroads increased faster in the four years after the Central and Pennsylvania withdrew from their community arrangements than it did in the previous six years. The Pennsylvania, by the admission of its official historians, spent only "modestly" for physical improvements between 1906 and World War I.[82] Only $69,000,000 of its increased capitalization was allocated for additions and betterments of the mainline and its branches. At the same time, more than $200,000,000 was spent to secure control over railroad corporate properties already within the Pennsylvania sphere.[83] Just prior to World War I, under President Samuel Rea, the Pennsylvania embarked upon an ambitious terminal improvement program in Baltimore, Chicago, and New York. However, of the $210,000,000 added to the book value of the road by 1925, at least one-third resulted from the acquisition of corporate property or the integration of other lines into the system.[84]

The New York Central had followed a similar course in expanding its capital structure. In 1909, $10,000,000 in 4 percent bonds were issued to secure more control over the Big Four. In 1910, another $5,000,000 bond issue was authorized by the directors for securing $5,000,000 of first preferred stock in the same company. In December, 1911, in an unsuccessful attempt to gain control of the New York Ontario and Western, the New York Central offered $30,000,000 for the New Haven's majority holdings in that road; however, the action was not approved by the New York Public Service Commission.[85]

The Central was especially burdened by debt. Between 1902 and 1913, the total capitalization of the Central had increased from $309,000,000 to $649,000,000 — more than half of this being additions in debt. The New York Central System had been put together through the extensive use of leases and collateral trust bonds, with only one-fifth of the system's trackage owned outright by the parent company.[86] As a result, management was obliged to provide for considerable fixed charges before appropriations for dividends could be made. Nevertheless, during this period, dividends remained relatively high and were regularly paid, at the frequent cost of neglecting road and equipment. Not until 1914, with the reorganization of its capital structure, was the heavy indebtedness reduced, but, by this time the physical plant was badly run down, and a series of spectacular wrecks directed public attention to the dilapidated road bed and rolling stock of the company.[87] Under the reorganization, many of the Central controlled properties were formally consolidated under the new company. Although, in doing this, the Central was able to lower its annual fixed charges, capitalization, mostly reflecting the expansion in capital stock issue in the new company, grew from $650,000,000 to $880,000,000.

Few of the other roads in New York State followed as ambitious capitalization policies as the New York Central. The Erie, the only other trunk line operating in the state, was in a very bad condition. With short term notes in excess of $5,000,000 due in 1908, the road was saved from the courts only by the intervention of Morgan and Harriman.[88] But the Erie was too weakened to rebound. It paid no dividends on common stock between 1904 and 1920 and ceased paying on preferred after 1907.[89] William Ripley observed in presenting his 1921 consolidation plan to the I.C.C.: "The Erie stood almost alone, dependent largely upon through business. Its location seems almost to avoid the great cities and the interior ports."[90] As a result of this operational vulnerability and its burdensome over-capitalization, the Erie could not pursue expansionist capital policies, and of necessity, had to curtail its physical improvement programs.

The expansion in railroad capitalization soon attracted regulatory attention. In 1908, the I.C.C. produced a special report on the capital structure of American railroads, but the Federal commission was quite powerless to do much more. From the beginning of its operations in 1907, the New York State Public Service Commission had shown concern over the increase in capitalization of roads under its jurisdiction. With authority to control new securities of longer than one year issue, the Public Service Commission developed some general rules for permitting such issues. Of special importance was its ruling that new issues would only be approved if they were for the acquisition of property, for construction or extension of facilities, for improvement or maintenance of service, or for approved refunding of debt obligations.[92]

In 1908, the Commission authorized the Erie to issue bonds in anticipation of several year's interest on the understanding that an equal amount of improvements would be put back in the road. Again in 1912, the Erie was allowed to capitalize by $12,000,000 after it had shown improvements of an equal amount.[93] In the same year the Public Service Commission disallowed a Lehigh Valley petition to issue bonds to reimburse its treasury for property replacement, asserting that replacement was not a capital cost but should be funded from current income.[94] Although these actions were refreshing, the Commission was limited in its effectiveness in cases where one road issued securities to acquire another. Here the Commission was restricted in estimating the real valuation of the original issues. To what degree the collateral trust bonds usually issued against the older securities really reflected old "watering" remained bitter conjecture between the Commission and the rail operators up to the passage of the Transportation Act of 1920, when the I.C.C. was finally given authority over all new security issues. Meanwhile the zealousness of the New York State Commission in hampering new security issues was checked from time to time by the courts and the New York Legislature, since both tended to side with the railroads.[95]

While neither the state commissions nor the I.C.C. had proved especially effective in restricting the railroads' capitalization policies, rate regulation was another matter. After 1910, the railroad industry became increasingly embittered by the Interstate Commerce Commission's reluctance to meet rate hike demands. The Commission's recalcitrance on this matter led the industry to charge that the deterioration of rail property was really caused by the I.C.C.'s actions on rates. As noted earlier, the Commission denied a general rate increase to eastern railroads in February 1911, an increase which to the trunk lines alone might have meant as much as $27,000,000 in increased annual revenue.[96] The request was based upon an alleged need to cover wage increases granted the year before. Inopportunely, the denial came at a time of serious business recession in the country and when rail revenues were sharply reduced.

The editorial writer for the *Financial Review,* a currently popular financial publication which specialized in analyzing the railroad securities market, attacked the federal agency, observing:

> In February, after eight months of delay, the commission finally acted. The outcome was not only a complete disappointment, but it was stupefying and bewildering . . . Some railroads had contemplated the possibility that the carriers

would not get the full amount of the increase asked for,
and some there were who imagined that possibly one set
of roads or the other might have to forego the right of
marketing higher rate; but no one was prepared for veto,
such as the Commission handed down, of all rate increases
whatsoever.... The Commission sought to make it appear
that the railroads everywhere were, and had been, enjoying
unwanted prosperity, and that they could take care of
wage advances without rate increases and without in any
way impairing their assumed prosperity.

   With the stability of railroad income in jeopardy, it
was no time for extension and development work in the
railroad world.... Accordingly, hundreds of millions that
might have gone into reproductive railroad work, if conditions had been wholly favorably, were withheld.[97]

Such attacks on the I.C.C. by the railroads are to a considerable extent misleading since they tend to suggest the development of a strong anti-railroad bias on the Commission that
did not in fact exist. To be sure, the I.C.C. was "a man
between." On the one hand, it was almost constantly badgered
by railroads seeking higher rates; on the other, it was sub-
jected to pressures from consumers and shippers to hold rates
down. While such a middle position lends itself easily to the
conclusion that the I.C.C. acted pragmatically and Solomon-
like to split the difference fairly between the contending parties,
this somewhat standard historical analysis of Progressive Era
government regulation is not entirely justified. Perhaps the
I.C.C. was sometimes reluctant to meet railroad rate demands,
but the fact remains that in the very year that the *Financial
Review* editorialist attacked the Commission for denying a
general rate advance, the rail industry nevertheless paid the
greatest dividends in its history. The alleged "hard times"
imposed by the Commission's rate policy is very difficult to
document over the period between passage of the Hepburn
Act and World War I. Nevertheless, it must be admitted that
strong disagreements over rates and ratemaking did exist between railroads, shippers, and the I.C.C.

   The situation called for a clearer policy on the whole question
of rate setting and fair return on investment, and, in 1913,
a progressive-minded Congress passed the Valuation Act.[98]
The act prescribed that the Interstate Commerce Commission
ascertain the "true value" of railroad property. Once such a

valuation had been made, it would provide the basis for approving "reasonable rates" which would allow a fair return on real investment. While Section 20 of the Act of 1887 required annual reports that showed "cost and value of the carrier's property and equipment," the Commission believed that this capital figure would in almost all cases show enormous "watering."

Using variously as its measures to determine fair valuation, concepts such as "original cost to date, cost of reproduction, and cost of reproduction less depreciation," the Commission put together a staff of accountants and began work.[99] By 1920, $18,925,000 had been spent complying with the Valuation Act's specifications, and about 1200 of the nation's 1895 railroad properties had been valued.[100] The industry generally opposed the valuation work of the Commission, believing it to understate the true value of the roads. Their oppositon grew in the twenties after the passage of the Transportation Act of 1920 which specified that a 6 percent return on I.C.C. valuation of rail property constituted a "fair return."[101] However, industry oppositon was really only an academic matter. Few roads after 1920 were ever to earn more than 6 percent on either the existing capitalization or the I.C.C.'s valuation. Meanwhile, the courts threw out the original valuation work of the Commission in 1929, holding that the Commission's valuation had not been adequately based on "reproductive value *to date.*"

Summary

From the beginning of the century up to World War I, the accent in railroad affairs had been upon financial activity. In the east, this activity had been directed toward the corporate domination by the New York Central and the Pennsylvania over the remaining eastern railroads, in an effort to control industry competition produced by excess capacity. Attempts to build a community of interest and to bring about a large degree of intercorporate harmony had absorbed staggering amounts of railroad capital. Needed physical improvements in rolling stock and plant had suffered. While rail revenues doubled between 1900 and 1912, the number of locomotives in operation grew only 55 percent and the number of box cars 50 percent.[103] These improvements were especially inadequate considering the

important technological changes in rail equipment which had
taken place during this time and that the old equipment was
in very poor condition. This neglect was to hasten the breakdown in railroad operations during the enormous traffic demand
stimulated by World War I, and it was a major cause for
eventual government operation of the railroads.

The period from 1900 to 1916, while marked by the increase
of regulative poweres at both the state and national level, cannot be called a victory for public regulation. The "Progressive
Era" did not effectively restrain or redirect railroad corporate
policy in any really significant way. Regulation clearly brought
some discomfort, but it did not bring railroad corporate activities under a strict public control which ran counter to what
the industry saw as its own "best interest." The imposition of
non-competitive rate making had had both industry and public
approval at the outset, although railroads came to be less
enthusiastic about the setting of rates by the I.C.C. The growing
domination of the eastern railroads by the Pennsylvania and the
New York Central through a banker-developed financial hegemony had not been halted by the public authorities. Nor had
the I.C.C. and the state commissions been able to stop the
excessive capitalization during this period. To a much larger
degree than is generally appreciated, railroads had been able
to have their own way.

While the railroads had succeeded in ending the competitive
clashes of the nineteenth century, the fundamental problem of
excess capacity remained. Freight tonnage, total revenues, and
net earnings of American railroads had more than doubled between 1900 and the outbreak of war in Europe, but in the
recession of 1913-1914, the vulnerability of the network to even
modest declines in traffic was demonstrated. During this business
downturn, a 7 percent reduction in traffic had lowered railroad
net operating income by about 16 percent.[104]   And between
1913 and 1915, more than 15,000 miles of railroad trackage
went into receivership. As the European War began, railroads
with a total capitalization of $1,400,000,000, about one-tenth of
the total railroad investment, were in the courts or operated
by court trustees.[105]   However, bad as it was, things could
have been much worse. Although the average receipts per ton
mile in the United States in 1914 were actually below these of
1900, most industry leaders would have admitted that without

the solid industry front on rate setting and the decision by the Interstate Commerce Commission to approve a 5 percent rate hike in 1913, earnings would have fallen much more.[106] It was understood by rail leaders that enough underutilization probably existed so that reversion to earlier competitive rating practices would have been more disastrous than the rate wars of the 1870's and 1880's.

III

RAILROADS DURING WARTIME AND UNDER THE TRANSPORTATION ACT OF 1920, 1917-1929

The experience of New York railroads between 1917 and 1929 must be seen as only a part of national developments. For the nation, the war pointed up serious operational weaknesses in the rail net which had gone unnoticed or neglected for many years, and the railroad crisis at the peak of defense mobilization necessitated the federal operation of the roads. At this point, federal railroad policy shifted from mere interstate rate regulatory activity to attempts at national transportation planning. With the passage of the Transportation Act of 1920, the government moved, in theory at least, toward a comprehensive examination of the structure and operations of the American railroad network, and, initially, the act seemed to evidence a federal commitment to rigorously controlling rail operations. But, the result of this policy change was to draw the railroads closer together in intercorporate cooperation, and, among eastern carriers in particular, it encouraged the continuation, now with federal approval, of objects initiated under the community of interest proposals of two decades earlier.

Government Control During the First World War

At twelve noon on December 28, 1917, at the height of American war mobilization, President Wilson authorized the federal government to take over operation of American railroads.[1] For three years before the government takeover, the

European War had been creating traffic demands far greater than the railroads could handle. In justifying the government's move, the Interstate Commerce Commission cited the most obvious deficiency of the railroads as the breakdown of inter-system traffic control. "Permissible cooperation between carriers was not used successfully ... as indicated in the breakdown of car interchange rules during periods of heavy traffic."[2] The result was that heavy traffic flows of defense materials and European export items to eastern seaports, combined with in-adequate car accounting by the eastern railroads caused great shortages of rolling stock at points of traffic origination and gluts at eastern terminals.

At first, President Wilson's advisors had thought it prudent to allow the railroad industry to solve such problems by corpor-ate cooperation. However, the Railroad War Board, which had been formed in the spring of 1917 as a virtually powerless private management consortium, proved ineffective in com-pelling the roads to return the empty rolling stock to traffic origination points.[3] Even the special Interstate Commerce Com-mission powers granted under the Esch Act of 1917 to handle car allocations were insufficient.[4] At New York City and in the New Jersey yards, the empty car bottleneck was so great as to hamper the unloading of new arrivals.[5] However, as the newly appointed Director General of Railroads soon found out, railroad problems were much deeper than the failure of car service interchange among the operators.

The geographic distribution of rail operations worked against the railroads under the unique traffic demands of World War I. Northeastern United States, with 15 percent of the nation's territory and 50 percent of the population, had about 30 per-cent of the rail trackage. In normal times, eastern roads ac-counted for about 55 and 50 percent respectively of freight ton-miles and passenger miles operated. Under the wartime traffic conditions, these roads were obliged to move about 70 percent of the freight and passenger traffic.[6] Director General Walker D. Hines pointed out that the northeastern railroads' rolling stock and physical plant broke down under these de-mands. In his judgment, the northeastern operators had starved their roads of capital and technological improvements over the past decade.[7] Simply, the railroads, long used to underutilization of their plant, were not prepared for the war generated boom.

During the general traffic increase from 1914 to government control in 1917, the railroads could argue that they had not reaped much benefit. The Pennsylvania reported gross revenues of $191,000,000 in 1913 and earnings of $42,000,000. At the height of traffic demand in 1917, gross revenues had climbed to $255,000,000, but net operating income was down to $29,282, 000.[8] Hines admitted that a variety of problems prohibited railroads from sharing in the gains from increased war traffic. Rising labor and material costs, new full crew and accident laws in certain states, the Adamson Act's reduction in work hours and raising of wages had all driven costs upward. Meanwhile, interstate rate increases failed to match this upward trend in operating costs, and state regulatory authorities successfully forced down rates on point to point traffic within state boundaries.[9]

Hines' justifications for government operation did not receive much support from eastern operators who cited other causes for railroad failures. A few years after the war, the Delaware and Hudson's official historians noted that the government's wartime transportation requirements had been laid down without the discussion or approval of the railroads. The necessity of handling "tagged," high-priority cars with great haste vitiated any existing cost-accounting procedures and all attempts at maintaining a high level of operating efficiency.[10] Moreover, the European War unfavorably affected the railroad money market. The dumping of large amounts of European owned securities on the American market rapidly depressed security prices after 1914. New railroad security issues for capital improvements had to offer higher yields, thus driving financing costs upward.[11]

In New York, twenty-seven railroad companies were operated by the United States Railroad Administration during the war. These roads operated 7,827.9 miles of first line trackage in the state. Twenty-eight steam railroads, controlling 449.3 miles of track retained private management.[12] However, these roads were so small and virtually dependent upon the larger companies for traffic that the Railroad Administration's control in New York was complete. The New York Central, Erie, Lackawanna, and New York Ontario and Western, all centering on

New York port facilities, were burdened under an enormous volume of business as the New York trunk lines gained much traffic that was rerouted from the Pennsylvania and the Baltimore and Ohio. This resulted from the Railroad Administration's diversion of traffic to what was deemed the "most efficient and expeditious routes."[13] The traffic diversion, however, was to chafe the Pennsylvania managers, who felt their competitive position was being undermined by the wartime operations.[14] President Smith of the New York Central, they frequently pointed out, directed the Eastern Region during the federal operation of the railroads.[15]

Although statistical information for the separate roads is not available, the immensity of war service demands on the eastern trunk lines is evident in the statistical information on Port of New York debarkation. In 1913, tonnage debarking New York amounted to 3.3 million tons. By 1916, this had grown to 6.5 million tons and reached a 7.9 million tons high in 1919.[16]

The effectiveness of federal railroad operation was to be a sensitive question for many years after the war. For many operators, the years of government control were to be used as a handy explanation for most of the financial and operational weaknesses of the roads during the next two decades. Years after government control ended, a Pennsylvania spokesman explained:

> ...the management felt that the company's competitive position had been seriously impaired by the war diversion of traffic from its rails to other routes without sufficient reason, and that the property had been returned to it in a physical condition inferior to that which existed at the beginning of Federal Control.[17]

Worst of all from the company's standpoint was the loss of operating efficiency during the war years. The Delaware and Hudson management echoed the Pennsylvania's charges noting that, "the railroad property was not adequately maintained while in the possession of the government, nor was it returned in as good repair nor as completely equipped as when it was taken."[18] To substantiate these charges, the Delaware and Hudson pointed out that car service interchange, an alleged reason for government control, was a greater problem after the war. The road had had 56 percent of its cars on hand during

1914-1917. At the end of federal operation, only a little more than 12 percent were on hand. [19]

To these and other criticisms later leveled at wartime government operation, the Director General offered that government control, in fact, had improved the position of the railroads. A great deal of equipment and control standardization had been introduced. The Director General pointed out that $110,000,000 in annual operating savings had thus been obtained. [20] Moreover, the administration had purchased $1,750,000,000 in new equipment and the carriers received more than $2,000,000,000 for foregone earnings during the two years of government operations. [21] Since all this amounted to a cost to the Federal government of $1,123,500,000, Director General Hines' contention that the railroads had received a substantial government subsidy was not without merit. [22]

Government investment in plant and equipment averaged $100,000,000 more per year than under immediate pre-war private control. [23] In the northeast, the tottering New Haven received $44,000,000 in refinancing aid which temporarily lifted it from the financial doldrums created by Morgan and Company's unfortunate pre-war reorganization. [24] In New York, government control had not produced a universally adverse effect. As examples, the Lackawanna's net earnings remained well above a seven percent return on investment, and the Delaware and Hudson experienced the greatest industrial expansion along its right-of way in more than a dozen years. [25]

In general, however, all roads reported enormous increases in operating costs during and after government control. This was, of course, not exclusively the result of government administration. The war and postwar period brought on a dizzying spiral of price inflation. While operating revenues for American railroads climbed from $3,000,000,000 to more than $6,000,000,000 between 1914 and 1920, net income fell from $500,000,000 to only $100,000,000. [26] As the general price index climbed nearly 100 percent between 1914 and 1920, railroads watched wage bill increases of more than 100 percent. The Delaware and Hudson reported that wages climbed 116 percent, the Pennsylvania, 111 percent, and the New York Central, 110 percent. [27]

The rise in labor costs were not solely the result of government operation. The hiring of larger workforces which raised the companies' wage bill were in most cases essential to handling the increased traffic. The upward wage push was a national trend despite the probable accuracy of the owners' charges that the Railroad Administration was often unduly responsive to railroad labor demands. Even if the roads had remained in private control, it remains doubtful that the rise in operating costs would have been much smaller. Nevertheless, the rather repetitious argument that government control had produced enormous inefficiencies was given wide circulation by the railroad operators during and immediately following the war.[28] The railroads' agitation on this question doubtless led to the inclusion in the Transportation Act of 1920 of a provision for low interest federal loans and grants to make up for deficiencies resulting from federal operation.

The railroads undertook a vigorous public relations program immediately following the war and while Congress deliberated on the Transportation Act. A considerable propaganda and lobbying effort was directed at the legislators, both to eliminate serious discussion of nationalization of the industry which had from time to time been discussed by a few progressives and to get the kind of bill the industry wanted. With regard to the general public, the railroads were equally active, proclaiming with great effect in frequent newspaper advertisements and broadsides distributed to rail passengers that private ownership of the railroads was not only consistent with American social institutions but economically desirable.[29] Typical of much of the resulting official and academic opinion as well as reflecting general public sentiment on government ownership, one observer noted the problem this way:

> As for Government operation, that suggestion should be resolutely laid to one side until we have developed a public civic consciousness that will stand the strain. Today we are illfitted to undertake such a responsibility.
> In fact there is no precedent anywhere.... There are two serious objections to it, an economic and a political one. From the economic point of view, we should unquestionably lose all the benefits that spring from private initiative, and we should realize all the deadening influence of bureaucracy. It is unreasonable to expect men of the calibre of our railroad executives to remain indefinitely as Government employees.... The political effects of Government ownership are too well realized to require extended com-

ment.... The multitude of ways in which a pestiferous
politics minded Congress could interfere in the affairs of a
great industry like our railroad system is appalling....[30]

Nevertheless, an important outgrowth of the era of federal
operation of railroads was the decisive increase of federal authority in transportation matters. Before the war, the individual
state transportation agencies had enjoyed considerable freedom
on rate setting and other matters. After 1917, Director Hines
noted:

> The exigencies and pressures during the period of hostil-
> ities were such that there was not satisfactory opportunity
> for the Railroad Administration even to look to the state
> commissions for advice. For example, in the general rate
> advance in May 1918, the Railroad Administration did not
> consult state commissions in advance at all, but upon
> issuing the order explained to them the necessities of the
> situation and the reason why consultation in advance was
> not feasible.[31]

The war had eroded the state regulatory powers in a number of
ways. Not only did the I.C.C. afterward become more assertive
on rates and service, but the passage of the Transportation Act
of 1920, with its requirements for an I.C.C.-created consolidation plan and its extension of Commission powers to include
abandonment and financial issues of railroads, made no mention
whatsoever about state regulative authority.

The Transportation Act of 1920

The conclusion of military operations in 1918 immediately
raised the question of what to do with the railroads. Three
solutions were possible: 1) immediate return of the railroads to
private control, 2) federal ownership, and 3) the extension of
federal control. As we have already noted, the last two possibilities were largely eliminated by the railroads' successful
propaganda campaign which condemned government wartime
operation of the railroads as wasteful and inefficient. Meanwhile,
the first solution without some guarantees of operational improvements was practically unthinkable since memories of the
rail collapse of 1917 were still vivid. Thus, having lost any
opportunity for nationalizing the railroads, the federal government now moved to assert its authority in the area of rail

reorganization, and in doing this it received considerable popular support, even among railroad operators, for blueprinting a national railroad plan of consolidation under private ownership.[32] Since the outset of federal control, a variety of plans for eliminating the economically weak roads by absorbing them into a few large supersystems had been discussed by the press, the I.C.C., and the owners.[33] The proposals had had wide public approval, since, without raising the ugly question of government ownership, shippers and travelers agreed that unified wartime rail operations had vastly improved service.

On July 15, 1919, the House Committee on Interstate and Foreign Commerce began three months of hearings on a bill to return the railroads to private ownership.[34] Almost from the beginning, it became apparent that some plan for the combination of American railroads into a limited number of more efficient systems would be provided for in any legislation. Superficially, at least, this appeared to be a drastic change of policy from that taken by federal authorities during the era of community of interest. Approval for this new view toward railroad combination no doubt stemmed from a growing public belief that railroads were virtually public utilities with rates and routes so rigidly determined that private ownership could not lead to economic exploitation. As we shall see, this view was not entirely accurate. The federally sponsored consolidation movement provided a spokescreen for railroad ownership's return to its pre-war tendencies toward the elimination of corporate competition and the development of monopoly power.

The result of the congressional hearings of 1919 was the Transportation Act, or Esch-Cummins Bill, of 1920. While returning the railroads to private ownership, the act provided that the Interstate Commerce Commission "prepare and adopt a plan for the consolidation of railway properties of the continental United States into a limited number of systems."[35] The mergers were to be accomplished under private initiative and the Interstate Commerce Commission was given no power to enforce or require the railroads' compliance, except to disallow mergers inconsistent with the general plan. The I.C.C. was to develop a consolidation plan which 1) generally preserved competition, 2) maintained existing lines of traffic, and 3) held to uniform rates.[36] Such restrictions to a general plan worked at cross purposes since railroads widely varied in earning capacity and traffic strength. Questions raised but not answered by the Transportation Act of 1920 were: How could the larger systems to be created by consolidation be enticed to absorb the weaker roads, thus "maintaining existing routes;" and how could uniform rates and competition be maintained among carriers with different economies?[37] There were bound to be bitter disagreements between the Commission and certain roads and among the roads themselves in developing any comprehensive plan which satisfied these three conditions. However, the I.C.C., armed only with the power to disallow consolidations contrary to its general plan, could do nothing to forcibly decide such arguments. By the provisions of the Transportation Act of 1920, the Interstate Commerce Commission was obliged to proceed from the assumption that the private economic interests of each carrier and the desired general benefits of consolidated rail systems could be accomplished simultaneously. The legislative failure to give the I.C.C. power to enforce mergers had resulted from considerable lobbying from railroad interest groups. However, it is doubtful, based upon its own pronouncements, that the Commission really wanted this power. Without it, as we shall see, a consolidation plan conforming to the Transportation Act of 1920 was impossible.

On January 31, 1921, Professor William Zebina Ripley of Harvard University submitted his recommendations for consolidation which the Commission had requested.* Ripley's study divided the United States into six territories and nineteen major rail systems. In the eastern region, or Trunk Line Territory, Ripley called for the creation of five trunk lines, with the New England territory treated separately as a unit. These were to be based upon the stems of 1) the New York Central, 2) the Pennsylvania, 3) the Baltimore and Ohio, 4) the Erie, and 5) a combined Nickel Plate-Lackawanna route. Ripley noted that the creation of five systems of similar economic power was difficult, stating:

---

* Ripley was a noted railroad authority. Author of a number of books on railroad economics (*Railway Problems* (1907), *Railroads — Rates and Regulation* (1912), and *Railroad — Finance and Organization* (1914) he had served as a director of the Rock Island Railroad and had worked for the United States Industrial Commission. Ripley's 196-page report was published by the Interstate Commerce Commission. See *Consolidation of Railway Properties of the United States into a Limited Number of Systems,* 63 Interstate Commerce Commission 455 (1921).

A self-sufficient system of trunk lines is complicated by the fact that the disparity in size and competing strength of the various properties as well as by the fact that a considerable number of the roads consist of disjointed links lying east and west of Niagara Falls or else divided at the head of Lake Erie. Furthermore, some of the strongest systems enjoy the superfluity of approaches to strategic points, acquired perhaps for 'nuisance value' at some time in the past, while other competing roads are denied access to these strategic points. The Allegheny Territory, with its north-south valleys and ridges, in any event leaves but a few available east-west passageways which are capable of utilization.[38]

Ripley's plan attempted to follow the charges given to the Interstate Commerce Commission in the Transportation Act of 1920. It had been created with an eye to the traffic flows and financial structure of the eastern roads. Although recognizing that some roads were inherently weak and their inclusion in the overall system created redundancy and excess capacity, Ripley attempted to "maintain existing lines of traffic." No abandonments were called for in the Ripley Report. The weaker roads, instead, were to be allocated to the stronger.[39] Some of the roads, particularly the Pennsylvania and the Central, were to lose important segments of line in building up the two weaker trunks — the Erie and the Nickel Plate-Lackawanna. The distribution of the interior roads was to be made so as to make each of the five systems as stable as possible.

According to the Transportation Act of 1920, competition was to be "preserved" in any consolidation plan; however, the meaning of this charge was not altogether clear. For one thing, it was understood by practically all observers that "competition" did not mean the return to *laissez faire* market conditions, with price or rate competitiveness. Competition in this sense had been destroyed by the growth of the rate regulation powers of the I.C.C. and by railroad cooperativeness. However, on the surface, the reduction of the many separately capitalized railroads in the East into but five giant systems appeared to be antithetical with the maintenance of competition and seemed to go far in attaining goals pursued by eastern rail leaders since community of interest days. Nevertheless, the reduction of the rail industry into a limited number of properties was consistent with a new concept of competition which the I.C.C. (as well

TABLE 7

ROUTE MILEAGE UNDER THE RIPLEY PLAN

	N.Y. to Chicago (miles)	N.Y. to St. Louis (miles)	Highest Elevation (feet)
Pennsylvania	908.9	1052.9	2192
DL & W – NP	919.0	1115.4	1115
New York Central	978.7	1157.6	920
Erie-Wabash	998.5	1174.3	1173
B & O	1013.8	1117.8	2374

Source: 63 Interstate Commerce Commission (1921), p. 486.

as Congress, it would appear) had been developing over a number of years. Competition, according to this interpretation was not many small firms struggling against one another in the market but a few large firms with relatively similar shares of market and financial power acting with restraint and under public regulation. By requiring "competition" then, the Transportation Act really intended to require the balancing of market and financial power among the railroads. In the east, this was to mean balance between a few large trunk systems rather than domination of a great number of railroads by two strong firms. To facilitate the maintenance of market and financial balance, the Transportation Act had also given the Interstate Commerce Commission new authority over the financial issues and reorganization of railroads.

Ripley had honestly attempted to follow the charge of "preserving competition," and the implementation of this concept in his proposed consolidation plan was to become the crucial issue in the ensuing twelve years of discussion over consolidation. The Ripley Plan, and practically all succeeding I.C.C. plans, attempted to rectify by artificial means the corporate power distribution which had evolved over fifty years. Evidence of Ripley's intention to create competitive balance is perhaps best seen in his disposition of access to the anthracite and bituminous coal fields. In this case, all of the trunks were to compete within the anthracite region, and the New York Central, Pennsylvania, and Baltimore and Ohio were given access to the bituminous region. Such a plan posed a substantial threat to the existing power of the Pennsylvania and the aspirations of the New York Central. On this Ripley noted:

> The dynamic aspect of consolidation must also be kept in mind. The purpose being to promote a more evenly balanced competition, especially by means of equalization of opportunity in originating traffic as well as its interchange and delivery. It is conceivable that congestion may be in a measure relieved by this plan.
>
> The growth of business in future years must accrue largely to the existing stems. Sound public policy demands that this growth should be distributed as to avoid blockade and embargoes on the strong roads, while the weak ones are coincidentally drifting toward starvation.[40]

Although the passing of the community of interest plan in 1906 had signaled the end of formal intercorporate agreement between the Pennsylvania and the Central, the old alliance was sufficient to produce, at first, a unified opposition to the Ripley Plan.[41] Both roads had maintained, even with the passage of community of interest, strong financial and working agreements with most of the other eastern roads which they were now expected to give up. Moreover, they were also expected to absorb a number of weak roads in which they had no interest. No traffic increases were apparent while three new trunk line competitors were to be given considerable strength.

The extent of control exercised by the Central and Pennsylvania, not altogether clear to even the I.C.C. at the time, was discovered a few years later in a congressional investigation of monopoly activities among the eastern railroads. This investigation revealed that all but four of twenty-one major eastern roads were connected in one way or another with the Pennsylvania and its bankers, Kuhn Loeb and Company, or with the New York Central and Morgan interests.* Four roads, including the Pennsylvania, were serviced by Kuhn Loeb and seven dealt with J. P. Morgan and Company or Morgan's National City Bank of New York. Moreover, Kuhn Loeb and the Morgan houses worked closely together in the marketing of new security issuances and in corraling proxies.

The Ripley Plan received almost universal condemnation from

---

* For an elaboration of the investigations's findings, see Appendix II.

railroad management. The opposition in the east seems to have
stemmed from the practically common banker control or financial connection of the eastern trunk lines. Morgan interests
were strong if not dominant in four of the five proposed eastern
trunks.[42] What advantages this plan of reorganization offered
to a group which already held effective control over the trunk
territory and could initiate its own consolidations must have
seemed obscure indeed. President Smith of the New York
Central, after contacting his bankers, George Baker and Thomas
Lamont, opposed the five system plan of Ripley and argued that
any consolidation should be based upon the existing major trunk
systems.[43] His justification was a blatant defense of corporate
power as the basis for railroad consolidation, as he argued:
"The control of passageways must be in the hands that can
make the best use of them."[44] In opposing government-planned
consolidation, he argued that the railroads themselves are the
best judges of what was good for rail transportation:

> Briefly, allow the railroads to be joined together as they
> may best render service to the country. Give them fair com-
> pensation and place upon them a yardstick of duty and
> exact it under as little interference of regulation and
> initiative as possible.[45]

Many of the smaller roads showed equally little enthusiasm,
for some, such as the Delaware and Hudson, the Lackawanna,
and the Lehigh Valley, were healthier than the trunk lines to
which they were allotted. President Loomis of the Lehigh
Valley saw the proposed consolidation as "materially lessening
competition."[46] Speaking for many of the smaller roads which
were to be grafted upon the Erie or the Nickel Plate-
Lackawanna stems, he said:

> If consolidations are to be made, it would seem unfair to
> put a strong road like the Lehigh Valley in with a road
> like the Erie; and if such action should be taken, the
> Lehigh Valley stockholders should be very largely
> compensated.[47]

President L. F. Loree of the Delaware and Hudson produced
the bitterest complaint in noting that his road "would look with
apprehension upon consolidation academically achieved and
arbitrarily imposed."[48]

Despite such condemnation, the Ripley Plan's publication set the railroad operators to work. The swapping of roads and the creation of systems on paper appears to have dominated owner interest through 1921.[49] The railroads were badly split with regard to offering a concrete alternative to the Ripley proposals; however, it became increasingly evident that the larger roads were adamantly opposed to the creation of a "fifth system" eastern trunk. It would appear that much of this opposition came directly from the Morgan banking interests since this would have created a new line in which its financial connections would not have been as well developed as with the other four trunks. While it is doubtful that a Nickel Plate-Lackawanna trunk would have posed much of an operational threat to the other systems, it would have challenged the exisiting power structure among eastern roads, and this was a very important consideration to the Morgan group.[50]

The Interstate Commerce Commission adopted a tentative plan for railroad consolidation on August 31, 1921, which varied little with the original Ripley Plan, except that the Lehigh Valley did succeed in blocking its wedding to the Erie and replaced the Lackawanna as the eastern stem of the Nickel Plate systems. From March 1922 to January 1924, the I.C.C. held hearings on the proposed mergers.[51] Since the New York Central and the Pennsylvania had the most to lose under such a proposal, the two roads bitterly fought any attempt by the Commission to divest them of what they viewed as deserved power. Ripley had argued for partial dismemberment of these two systems to improve the competitive position of the other trunk carriers. However, as New York Central and Pennsylvania counsels pointed out, this clearly opposed the intent of the Transportation Act of 1920, which pledged "to maintain existing routes and channels of traffic."[52] The two roads eventually won their case and the dismemberment idea was permanently dropped. Without its acceptance, the fate of the hearings was decided, for no consolidation based on a "fifth system" was now practicable. Indeed, the decision not to dismember made any general consolidation plan practically impossible.

It should be emphasized that rail opposition to the I.C.C. general consolidation plan did not reflect a deep philosophical difference between railroads and that agency. The railroads had early recognized the possibilities for consolidation as a solution to instability in the industry. Their activities in the

twenties, although they were often wasteful and unwise squandering of capital badly needed for operating improvements, still
reflected a commitment to the old consolidation plans of J. P.
Morgan. Their difference with the I.C.C. lay on a practical
level — namely what kind of consolidation and on whose terms.

The Merger Movement of the 1920's

The first Interstate Commerce Commission hearings ended in
failure in January 1924. The bitterness and unconciliatory tone
of the hearings thoroughly discouraged the Interstate Commerce
Commissioners, and the result was the withdrawal of I.C.C.
initiative in developing a consolidation plan.[53] The unfavorable
reaction to the ambitious consolidation plan of 1921 had provoked the Commission to report:

> In our opinion... the experience we have gained... has
> led us to doubt the wisdom of the provisions of the law
> which now require us to adopt a complete plan for the
> consolidation of the railway properties of the continental
> United States into a limited number of systems, to which
> plan all future consolidations must conform. The differences
> of opinion which have developed both within and without
> the Commission, in regard to the form which such a com-
> plete plan of consolidation should take are so numerous
> and so difficult to reconcile... that a majority of the
> Commission have been impelled to the belief that results
> as good... are likely to be accomplished... in a more
> normal way.[54]

The "more normal way" was to allow private mergers to
develop with private initiative and to approve them or dis-
approve them on their individual merits. Congressional action
on the Commission's recommendation was not forthcoming;
but, between 1924 and 1929, the I.C.C. abrogated what consolidation planning functions it had been given. The railroads,
principally the most powerful, succeeded to the I.C.C. position
as the architects of consolidation.

After the failure of the first hearings, the eastern roads
commenced their own private discussion on mergers which lasted
through 1924 and 1925.[56] These meetings, or "Four Party
Conferences," brought together executives of the New York
Central, the Pennsylvania, the Baltimore and Ohio, and the
Erie, which was only recently acquired by O. P. and M. J.

Van Sweringen, wealthy Cleveland real estate promoters.[57]
The chief intent of the meetings was to create a consolidation
plan for Commission approval which was based upon the
four existing trunk stems.

The Transportation Act of 1920 had provided new techniques
for the acquisition of property. Most roads doubted that consolidation in advance of any general plan would be approved
by the I.C.C. However, under the act, properties could be
acquired by outright lease or stock purchasing. Leasing required
Commission approval. Stock purchases of less than 50 percent of the outstanding stock could be made without I.C.C.
permission. In most cases, much less than 50 percent was
sufficient to gain working control, and the major systems resorted to this device after 1924 to complete their own consolidation plans.

While the Commission had been hearing testimony on its
consolidation proposal in 1923, the Van Sweringens had inaugurated the "private" merger movement by putting together a
trunk line territory of their own which did not coincide with any
Commission plan. Starting with borrowed Morgan money in
1916, the Van Sweringens purchased control of the Nickel
Plate from the New York Central.[58] The "Van's" dependence
upon Morgan in these undertakings was not discovered, however,
until much later during special Senate hearings in the mid
1930's. After acquiring the Lake Erie and Western, the Toledo
and St. Louis, and the New York, Chicago, and St. Louis,
again with Morgan aid, they purchased control of the Erie in
1923.[59] The early acquisitions had been approved by the I.C.C.
since they conformed to the Tentative Plan of the Commission
of 1921; however, the Van Sweringen's attempt to create a
third "supersystem" was torpedoed in 1926 by the I.C.C.
when the brothers' petition for corporate merger of their holdings was rejected.[60] While the Commission's decision was
mostly based on the financial boondoggling evident in the reorganization of the roads, it also noted that in combining the
Nickel Plate with the Erie, the Van Sweringens had violated
the 1921 plan and destroyed the basis for a "fifth system."[61]
However, the brothers still had control of the Erie, even if they
could not merge, and a few years later devised a scheme for
reorganization which bypassed the Commission's protest.

In 1924, the Pennsylvania demonstrated the possibilities for empire creation through partial stock control. After an I.C.C. reprimand for attempting to lease the Norfolk and Western, the Pennsylvania purchased enough stock to gain control of the road then through the management of the line attempted to purchase control of the Virginian, another southern coal road.

The New York Central took no special interest in acquiring properties in this manner with the exception of the Lehigh Valley.[63] The Central management long had been interested in obtaining improved access to the Pennsylvania anthracite region which the Lehigh Valley seemed to provide. Both the Ripley Plan and the Tentative Commission Plan of 1921 had denied the Central the sought after coal connection, and the road moved to remedy this oversight. It was on this issue that the thirty-year rapprochement between the Central and the Pennsylvania began to crumble. The Pennsylvania managers perceived New York Central control of the Lehigh Valley as an important step toward eventual competition with its own New York to Pittsburgh traffic.[64] In particular, the Pennsylvania opposed any property acquisition which changed the relative balance of power between the two systems.

The Pennsylvania split with the New York Central, while by no means complete, was serious. The Pennsylvania had the most to lose in any I.C.C. plan. The Ripley Plan would have reduced the Pennsylvania's connections into the anthracite coal region with the effect that coal traffic over its lines would have been cut by more than half.[65] Moreover, such a redistribution of anthracite roads would have vastly increased the Central's share since the Central and its ally the Erie would have gained most of the Pennsylvania's losses.[66]

The inflexible opposition by the Pennsylvania to changes in relative power in the bituminous and anthracite coal regions in fact ended the Four Party Conference in 1925. The Pennsylvania's apprehensions had sound basis, for, after the Pennsylvania withdrew from the talks, the other trunks submitted a proposed four trunk consolidation plan which would have realized the Pennsylvania's worst fears. In the 1925 proposal, agreed to by the Central, the Baltimore and Ohio, and the Van Sweringens, the Central would have gotten the Lehigh Valley, the Ontario and Western and a strong foothold in the anthracite region. The Baltimore and Ohio would have received the Reading and thus have both anthracite and bituminous connections.

The Van Sweringens would have received the Lackawanna to strengthen their coal properties. The Pennsylvania would have gotten only the Norfolk and Western over which, by 1925, it had already gained control.[67] Although the plan was doomed to fail without Pennsylvania approval, the I.C.C. still opposed it because of its "noncompetitive" four trunk basis of organization.[68]

For the next three years after the failure of the Four Party Conference, the Pennsylvania's continued efforts to keep the *status quo* in the east dominated private merger activity in the trunk territory. While the New York Central, the Baltimore and Ohio and the Van Sweringens attempted to make good the apportioning of eastern roads as agreed upon in 1925, the Pennsylvania acted to blunt these policies. In particular, the Pennsylvania gave support to two proposed "Fifth Systems" which would have destroyed the Four Party Plan and, perhaps, so divide property in the east as to maintain the Pennsylvania's present dominance in the trunk territory. First, it gave secret support to the plans of L. F. Loree, president of the Delaware and Hudson and a former Pennsylvania vice president, who proposed to build a fifth system based on the properties of the Delaware and Hudson, the Lackawanna, the Lehigh Valley, the Wabash, and the Western Maryland.[69] The Pennsylvania pledged to buy $50,000,000 of Wabash stock in support of Loree's plan. For this the Pennsylvania was given the options of receiving Delaware and Hudson stock, the new system's stock, or the Delaware and Hudson's holdings in the Lehigh Valley, in which Loree had obtained a 44 percent stock interest, all depending upon I.C.C. approval of Loree's "fifth system." At any rate, the Central's attempt to obtain the Lehigh Valley would be halted by such an action. The Loree Plan, however, failed when the I.C.C. disallowed Delaware and Hudson control of the Buffalo Rochester and Pittsburgh, a crucial part of the system.[70] Loree, failing in a proxie fight with the Morgan forces in an attempt to gain control of the Lehigh Valley, then sold his shares in the Lehigh Valley and the Wabash to the Pennsylvania.

A second effort to establish a "fifth system" was offered by Frank Taplin, head of a West Virginia mining syndicate and operator of the Pittsburgh and West Virginia Railroad. Taplin's plan was essentially a reconstruction of George Gould's earlier proposals to build a line from tidewater through the bituminous region to the Great Lakes. Again the Pennsylvania gave support —this time to block access to bituminous coal to any of the other trunks.

In an effort to stop Taplin's plan which called for the merging of the Pittsburgh and West Virginia, the Western Maryland and the Wheeling and Lake Erie, the Central, the Baltimore and Ohio and the Van Sweringens purchased control of the Wheeling and Lake Erie in 1927. Invoking the Clayton Act's Section 7, the Interstate Commerce Commission quickly broke up this compact the following year after finding that the Wheeling and Lake Erie competed with the Central and Baltimore and Ohio. However, Taplin's proposal was never to develop much beyond the planning stage. Like Loree with the Lehigh Valley stock, Taplin eventually sold his holdings in the Pittsburgh and West Virginia to the Pennsylvania's new holding company, Pennroad, for $37,000,000. Taplin's preference for the Pennsylvania when he discarded his "fifth system" plans certainly had been assisted by an earlier loan of $2,000,000 advanced to him by Pennroad.[71]

Thus, by using the threat of a fifth system, the Pennsylvania had been able to block the expansion activities of the other trunks into her coal areas, and, in the case of the two "fifth systems," the Pennsylvania had actually emerged holding the crucial rail properties. The Pennsylvania ownership of the Pittsburgh and West Virginia "did not seriously affect competition" but ownership of Lehigh Valley and Wabash stock led to I.C.C. action under the Clayton Act.[72] This move by the Commission in 1930, like the previous action against the New York Central, the Baltimore and Ohio, and the Van Sweringen holdings of Wheeling and Lake Erie and Western Maryland stock, was based on its policy of keeping the *status quo* in the east until Congressional action relieved it from the general consolidation mandate. However, the Pennsylvania successfully fought the Commission's action, arguing that Pennroad, not the Pennsylvania Railroad, was the owner of the Lehigh Valley and Wabash stock. This interesting legal construction satisfied the courts that there had been no violation of the Clayton Act.

During the closing years of the decade, the eastern trunks turned to the holding company as an increasingly popular device for facilitating consolidation, a technique aptly described by critics as "marriage without benefit of ceremony."[73] By

organizing a parent corporation to own the assets of the properties under their control, the rail owners were able to form,
at least on paper, consolidations of acquisitions made after
1924 without I.C.C. approval. From July 1928 to the end of
1929, these holding companies and the eastern trunkline railroad companies spent more than $300,000,000 in the purchase
of railroad stocks.[74] The Van Sweringens, through their Allegheny Corporation, brought control of a vast, 30,000-mile
network under one corporate structure despite the fact that the
system was a complete repudiation of the Interstate Commerce
Commission's consolidation plan. The Pennsylvania, through
its holding company, Pennroad, acquired the New Haven and
the Boston and Maine, obtaining a foothold in New England.[75]
The New England venture, from an operating standpoint, was
unwise, and Pennroad's activities in this case seemed to be
characterized by nothing more than a power display.[76]

The merger movement of the 1920's is best explained in
terms of the power balance among eastern railroads. First,
the Pennsylvania and the Central were opposed to any five
system plan which would have curtailed their existing influence,
although, as we have seen the Pennsylvania would accept a
weak fifth system not formed from its own lines. Second, both
of these roads wished to retain their respective dominance over
the weaker Erie and Baltimore and Ohio stems. Third, the Central and the Pennsylvania were involved in a struggle for power,
with the anthracite region as the battlefield. The jealousy between the Central and the Pennsylvania was deep and real and
it could not be healed, as such problems usually had been in
the past, through banker hegemony. The split between the two
eastern rivals was not permanent but many years were to pass
before the two could work together cooperatively again. The
New York Central's occasional alliances with the Baltimore and
Ohio and the Van Sweringens were understood by the Pennsylvania as nothing short of treason and they reacted accordingly.
Meanwhile, the I.C.C., unable to fulfill its charge to consolidate
the roads in systems which would maintain competition and
handicapped by its inability to control holding companies,
could only fight delaying actions, selectively allowing or disallowing mergers which did not upset the existing balance of
corporate power.

The scramble among the eastern trunk lines was clearly the

result of the complete failure of the general consolidation plan. The prosperous business conditions of the late twenties, without much effort on the part of the railroads, had driven upward the earnings of all carriers. Talk about "weak roads" had practically ceased, and the old problem of excess capacity seemed to have disappeared. The rising stock market seemed to indicate the permanent arrival of prosperity and to justify any merger or corporate expansion. The various railroad managements explained their actions as consistent and "in furtherance of the consolidation policy of the Transportation Act;" but, not all the managers were so optimistic about the railroads' consolidation policies. President Willard of the Baltimore and Ohio, who more than once had frightened colleagues with "disloyal" talk, wrote to Commissioner Eastman of the I.C.C.:

> The failure of the Commission to prepare a plan for the general guidance of the railroads had been responsible for bringing about what might be termed "a return of Harrimanism" and that the situation had now gotten into a condition where... it was wholly out of the control of the Commission.[77]

The I.C.C.'s response was to propose in 1929, a "final" consolidation plan.[78] Still refusing to accept the fact that no fifth system was practical after the buying spree of the past five years, the commissioners produced a plan which basically validated these acquisitions. The plan still shut the New York Central out of the anthracite field and was practically identical to the 1921 arrangements for the Central, except that it was assigned the Virginian rather than the Western Maryland. A-side from obtaining a few additional coal roads in Pennsylvania, the Pennsylvania system was unchanged. Meanwhile, the Baltimore and Ohio received access to New York State, having been given the Buffalo Rochester and Pittsburgh. Most important, the Van Sweringen purchases were validated in a fourth system built on the Chesapeake and Ohio, Erie, and the Nickel Plate. This system had parts of three separate systems of the 1921 Plan. Its existence made the "fifth system," still a goal of the Commission, a virtual monstrosity. Called the Wabash-Seaboard, it combined the Wabash Lehigh Valley, Wheeling and Lake Erie, Seaboard Air Line, and miscellaneous pieces of trackage rights into an imposing but basically weak system.[79]

From 1929 to 1932, the new I.C.C. Plan was the technical foundation for all railroad merger activity, but it was still unacceptable to the railroads. As a later congressional report noted:

> After 1929, the focus of railroad consolidation activities shifted away from the stock market. For the next three years, the four party conferences, which were revived in 1930, held the center of the stage.... The stock purchases, holding company activities, and fifth system promotional ventures did not, however, come to an abrupt halt.... "Harrimanism" did not die a sudden death, it tapered off.[80]

The New York Central gave up its Lehigh Valley holdings and in its only expansion venture after 1929, acquired access to the anthracite region by gaining control of the Lackawanna.[81] The Baltimore and Ohio exhausted itself obtaining the Buffalo Rochester and Pittsburgh, and the Pennsylvania continued to buy New England railroad stocks.[82] As the depression worsened, it became obvious that the I.C.C. Final Plan would never be completed. In 1931, four party talks began again, and, in October, 1931, the four parties again submitted a proposal for consolidation based on four eastern trunks.[83]

The I.C.C. made some modifications but finally accepted in general principle the four-trunk plan. [84] The four trunks met again and announced on September 23, 1932, that "the executives of the four systems have agreed and composed all differences between themselves and arising from the I.C.C. Four System Consolidation Plan of July 1932."[85] Fittingly, even this announcement was not quite accurate since, unknown to the public or the I.C.C., the four powers had still made some horse trades of properties which the managers thought an improvement to the Commission's arrangements and to be "inconsequential."[86] Senator Burton Wheeler's study of this era of consolidation some years later concluded:

> Looking back on the Commission's 1932 plan, it is apparent that the Commission's action was not so much a declaration of a plan of its own as the ratification with some changes of a private agreement among the four most powerful eastern systems. Nor was this private agreement in any sense a "plan;" it was merely the outcome of the

trading and bargaining which has been discussed in this
report....

Furthermore, the Commission's plan was in large part a
ratification of acquisitions which had been carried out
either in open disregard of the Commission or by devices
intended to shelter the transactions from the Commission's
jurisdiction. The Pennsylvania Railroad had increased its
Norfolk and Western holdings despite the Commission's
suggestion in its 1921 plan that the Norfolk and Western
be a separate system. The Van Sweringens had assembled
their roads from the outset with little regard for the 1921
plan.

The whole process was characterized by financial short-
sightedness and sharp practice. The Wabash and the Delaware and Hudson scrapped basic accounting principles and
resorted to concealment of their buying activities. The Van
Sweringens, disguised as one corporation or another, developed a multiple business personality to avoid the effect
of Commission decisions which did not please them and to
obtain money from the public. Through the Pennsylvania
Company and the Pennroad Corporation, the Pennsylvania
Railroad management played fast and lose with the Commission and enticed investors into an absurd proposition.
But all this was officially forgiven.... The speculative era
ran its course, and the railroads were left with staggering
losses, the investors with defaulted bonds and worthless
stocks. The net result of the "scramble" was the dis-
crediting of railroad managements, complaints against the
Commission, exacerbation of hard times, and the nulli-
fication of the consolidation program which had furnished
the excuse.[87]

An Assessment of the Merger Movement of the Twenties

The "final" plan was never to be put into effect, for the
worsening business depression soon dashed the optimism of the
proponents of consolidation. In fact, the Van Sweringens had
already lost control of their vast Allegheny Corporation properties a year before the last four-party conference, and their
great holding companies were pledged for bankers loans.[88] In
1931, the brothers had purchased Missouri Pacific stock, amounting to about one-third of their Allegheny Corporation assets.
Meanwhile, in a catastrophic real estate venture, they pledged
their Allegheny holdings, worth about $15,000,000, as collateral

for a bank loan. As the value of Missouri Pacific stock fell in 1931 and 1932, the Van Sweringens were obliged to make up the difference between their real estate pledges and depreciating Allegheny values.[89] Unknown to the public or the Interstate Commerce Commission, the brothers secured a $40,000,000 loan from J. P. Morgan and Company, using their remaining rail securities as collateral.[90] It had really only been with Morgan Company approval that they had appeared at the 1932 four-party meetings. Necessarily, their actions in opposing the Commission's five-system plan must be understood as reflecting the position of the Morgan banking interests.

The domination of the Van Sweringens by Morgan interests was a well kept secret. As late as March 1934, an article in *Business Week* could focus upon the empire building activities of the brothers Van Sweringen, praising their speculative abilities, without mentioning their dependence upon Morgan money.[91] Indeed, the external appearance of the "Vans" railroad properties gave no indication of its shaky capital organization.

While the depression finally destroyed the merger plans set up under the Transportation Act of 1920, the original intent of the act had long before been forgotten or set aside. The provisions of the act had been conceived broadly to deal with all American railroads and specifically with the "eastern problem." However, the framers and initiators of the act and the eastern rail executives and banking groups had acted from entirely different motives. In general, both had accepted the principle of a limited number of rail systems in the east, to be built around four or five major trunks. Both had more or less accepted the notion that only "limited competition" should be encouraged among the carriers, although clearly the rail operators showed a greater desire to limit competition. However, the federal authorities, at least at the outset, had pressed for mergers based on lessons learned during the years of government operation. The original Ripley plan and various I.C.C. proposals until 1924 were mostly concerned with creating "natural traffic systems." Ripley had worked very hard to construct railroad systems with reasonably similar capital structures and return to investment. The physical welding together of properties showed some genius in ordering the roads to supply maximum transportation service. This included the grafting of weak lines to the stronger trunks.

The railroads' views toward mergers were not shaped by the wartime experience as much as by the community of interest ideas of two decades earlier. Railroad management never seemed to grasp the intent of any merger plans which first considered operational aspects, rather than financial, as critical to reorganization. As they had shown indifference to operational and traffic demands in the first decade of the century, they appeared no better informed under the government sanctioned mergers of the twenties. The Wheeler Report summed it up:

> At no point did the executives approach the (railroad) problem as a piece of public planning, or endeavor to measure needs of communities or shippers for particular routes or combinations. Their thought processes were those of the Vanderbilts, Cassatt, Gould, and Morgan thirty years earlier. An empire was to be divided; negotiating skill and financial resources were the instruments of survey.[92]

The more or less independent Pennsylvania and the New York Central with its Morgan banking connections, really dominated merger activity. As noted before, without both these roads' agreement, any consolidation plan in the east was impossible. As clashes between these two systems had earlier drawn them together in community of interest arrangements, in which their duopoly control of the eastern railroads served as a kind of business peace-keeping device, their corporate jealousy was a basis for their actions in the twenties. Any merger plan, to the satisfaction of the Pennsylvania and the Central, must not have unfavorably changed their relative strength as trunk carriers. Suspicion of changes in strength accordingly destroyed merger plans, as when the Pennsylvania refused to endorse the 1925 four party plan. In particular, the Pennsylvania wanted to maintain its across-Pennsylvania monopoly and the Central wished to keep expanding its coal connections. However, the creation of four or five relatively strong trunk systems would have meant stripping property from these two giants and frustrating their ambitions. Since they opposed such action, no plan of consolidation based primarily upon the operational merits of mergers was ever possible.

The Interstate Commerce Commission had always shown special concern for the railroads' private merger ambitions and never strictly interpreted its role in planning consolidations. The I.C.C. had made modifications in the original Ripley Plan in 1921 to meet Pennsylvania and New York Central objections; and the Commission, in the growing national prosperity after 1924, began to show less concern in wedding the "weaker" roads to the "stronger ones," as the general rise in rail earnings gave practically all roads a misleading sense of well-being. This reflected a drastic departure from the intent of the Transportation Act of 1920, which had sought to eliminate the problem of excess capacity through mergers. The final I.C.C. acceptance of the carriers' own carving up of the railroad network amounted to a complete rejection of the Transportation Act.

The Transportation Act had been represented as a basis for the development of a public-directed national transportation policy. The apparent intent of the act was to eliminate financial preoccupation with the creation of powerful rail empires and to shift concern to property and service improvement. Regrettably, the act failed to instruct the I.C.C. to enforce mergers which it drew up. Without this authority, all power in constructing rail combinations fell to the private operators. Meanwhile, the vastly improved business conditions of the twenties, which saw rail earnings rise by 40 percent between 1920 and 1928, tended to produce a forgetfulness over past problems. The potential "object lesson" of collapse and government takeover in 1917 was lost as railroads returned to their earlier business habits. The result was that in New York and other eastern states, the future economic well-being of many railroads was considerably weakened. It was soon apparent in the depression years of the thirties that American railroads had reaped few benefits from the Transportation Act of 1920.

The Interstate Commerce Commission, the Railroads, and
Transportation Planning up to the 1930's —
An Historiographic Note

Writing in 1922 in his study, *Railroads and Government,* Frank Haigh Dixon said of the passage of the Hepburn Act:

> It was in 1906 that the railroads fought their fight to a finish against federal regulation.... Backed by President Roosevelt and an aroused public sentiment, Congress revolutionized the Act to Regulate Commerce.... It was at this

time that the administrative authority of the Commission was clearly established . . .⁹³[93]

Dixon then proceeded to assert the importance of the regulative powers invested in the Commission in managing the railroads for the "public interest." Dixon's view has largely been the traditional position on the I.C.C. and the expansion of its powers after passage of the Hepburn Act. Later, and of more consequence, this view was embodied in I. L. Sharfman's monumental and authoritative study of the Interstate Commerce Commission.[94] On the Commission's regulative authority, Sharfman noted:

> In seeming contradiction of the tenets of individualism under which the system of free enterprise is reared, the commission exercises far-reaching control over privately owned and privately operated common carriers. The broad scope of this control is evidenced both by the extensive group of carriers subject to the Commission's jurisdiction and by the sweep of power which it asserts over them . . . . The entire cycle of their (railroads) organization, financing, charges and practices is embraced within the ambit of the Commission's authority . . . . While there is continuing lip worship of the doctrine that interference with management is both undesireable and invalid, the freedom of the carriers is so circumscribed in all significant directions that true managerial independence as distinct from freedom in the affairs of internal organization and administration, is largely a matter of the past in the railroad industry. Moreover, not only does each individual carrier find practically all of its major policies and practices effectively conditioned by the legal environment resulting from the vast grants of authority conferred upon the Commission in the public interest, but from many angles the carriers as a whole, despite multiple corporate ownership and control, are conceived as a national transportation system and are made to serve general transportation needs, without regard to individual interests.[95]

In brief, Sharfman's thesis was that: 1) out of the abuses of monopoly and excessive building during the closing decades of the nineteenth century, there developed a need for "independent control" over railroads to protect the public; 2) the I.C.C. was created as this independent agency, to function in the public interest; and 3) the gradual accretion of power to the Commission after 1887 enabled it to develop as a competent independent regulator.

To Sharfman, the I.C.C. was not simply a negative regulator, interfering with private decision-making. Rather, it was a creator of policy guidelines and the initiator of needed national transportation planning. It seemed to be the spirit of the new "progressivism" of a managed capitalism wherein the market was improved by government guidance. Sharfman saw the railroad system of the country "under the fostering guardianship and control of the Commission." [96] Through four highly detailed and documented volumes, the writer labored to justify this thesis. In light of the then (1931) obvious failure of the Commission to develop a national plan of railroad consolidation and to deal with the self-interest of the carriers, Sharfman's work was a remarkable document. It is even more remarkable when it is noted that his interpretation remained the standard study of the Interstate Commerce Commission and a model for studies of government regulative agencies for the next two or three decades.

At the time of his study, the I.C.C. was clearly not as Sharfman represented it. Despite the unclear origins of agitation for railroad regulation, the railroads themselves were not universally opposed to regulation.[97] Given their problems of competition and excess capacity, regulation of some kind was vitally important. Private regulation through pools and spheres of influence had failed, not so much from public opposition as from the competitive self-seeking of the railroads themselves. Sharfman's contention that the creation of the Interstate Commerce Commission was in the "Public Interest" obscured the point that to many railroad leaders it was *also* in the private corporate interest.

Sharfman contended that the I.C.C. was especially interested in restoring competitive rates and operations among railroads. This clearly the railroads did not want. Moreover, "administered competition" was an impossible logical contradiction and the Commission never succeeded in developing such a concept in practice. From the beginning, the railroads effectively blocked any efforts to sharpen competition. To be sure, the Commission did enlarge its regulative powers, especially after 1906, to deal with the worst abuses of corporate power, but I.C.C. actions were not especially inimical with the philosophy of such business leaders as Morgan, Cassatt and others.

In contrast to Sharfman's high praise for the Interstate Commerce Commission as acting in the "public interest," it should have been apparent that the Commission's understanding of this obligation tended in large part to accept economic principles advanced by the carriers themselves. For example, on the question of abandonments and the "public interest," Sharfman held that the Commission, in reaching any decision, always balanced the interests of the carriers and the affected public. Even he suggests, however, that the economic burdens of the carrier were of primary concern.[98]

While the effect upon the community was doubtless considered it appears that "public interest" considerations in abandonments rarely led to denials of the carrier's petition. In the period between 1921-1930, the Commission received 540 separate abandonment petitions. All but forty of these were granted, although 151 of those granted were contested.[99] In oth words, the actions of the Commission did not seem to clash sharply with those of the railroads in applying public interest measurements. In these cases, the I.C.C. placed much stock in the railroad's own statistical studies as a basis for proving certain operations uneconomic. Since this evidence was usually provided by the carrier without investigation by the Commission or without off-setting evidence from other sources, the carrier's testimony was always quite persuasive.

When Commission policy and corporate policy did clash, as in the planning of consolidations, evidence suggests that the railroads were adept at gaining their way. As noted earlier, the I.C.C. was virtually powerless to enforce its merger plans under the Transportation Act of 1920; however, in the east, the large roads developed techniques such as holding companies, to implement their own plans.

The mandate for regulation given to the Interstate Commerce Commission by successive acts of Congress, of course, could be no stronger than congressional desires to subject railroads to rigorous financial and operational regulation. The Transportation Act of 1920, in particular, indicated that the rail industry still had an immense fund of good will in the Congress and that it had little heart for establishing too restrictive regulatory policies. In support of this interpretation, it should be noted that consolidation, which the Transportation Act authorized, was a solution to railroad economic problems which the industry had long advocated. Moreover, in requiring that the rail proper-

ties be reduced to a limited number of systems, Congress had
carefully given the I.C.C. no authority to enforce the consolidations. Thus, by default, the railroads retained the real
authority in initiating mergers. The Transportation Act had
also gone far in eliminating troublesome state regulative authority
over rates, abandonments and financial issues. In these matters,
the railroads had always found stricter and less sympathetic
regulation at the hands of state commissions which zealously
sought to protect local shippers and regional interests.

Another feature of the act which could scarcely be termed
detrimental to the railroads was Section 15a which provided:

> ...in the exercise of its power to prescribe just and
> reasonable rates the Commission shall initiate, modify, es-
> tablish or adjust such rates so that the carriers as a whole
> (or as a whole in each of such rate groups or territories
> as the Commission may from time to time designate)
> will... earn an aggregate annual net railway operating
> income equal... to a fair return upon the aggregate value
> of the railway property....[100]

Such a rule of rate making came about as near providing
a guaranteed return to rail investment as could be expected.
Under Section 15a, the Commission, with authorization provided by the Valuation Act of 1913, was to calculate the true
value of rail property and could authorize returns on investment
of up to 6 percent for the industry.[101]   One half of earnings
in excess of the industry limit of 6 percent was to be held
in a fund which could be tapped by the individual carrier when
its earnings were below the "fair return." The other half of
earnings over 6 percent was to be paid to a general con-
tingency fund, administered by the I.C.C., which could be used
as a source of loans for needy carriers.* The 6 percent guide
for "fair return" became for the railroads both the minimum
and the maximum expected return on investment; but, most
important it was a figure almost never attained in the past by
the industry. For example, between 1893 and 1913, returns
on the industry's book value never exceeded 5 percent. As a
consequence, it soon became industry policy to demand this
return and to base rate requests and abuse of the I.C.C. on the

---

* The Emergency Act of 1933 repealed the recapture clause.

industry's earning position relative to this goal. From 1921 to
1926, the industry return, with help from I.C.C. rate boosts,
increased from 2.96 percent to 5.15 percent.[102] Moreover,
the calculation of these returns was based on the carriers own
book values of property rather than the I.C.C.'s valuation.
The plan for the 6 percent fair return was uneconomic. There
was little stimulus for firms earning near the fair return to improve their economic efficiency, since all earnings in excess
would be held in a general fund. Moreover, to arrive at an
aggregate industry return of 6 percent, it would be essential
to raise rates so that uneconomic properties would not hold
down the industry average. Strictly speaking, the provision for
fair industry return violated good economic principles by taxing
increasing returns firms and subsidizing decreasing returns (inefficient) firms.

Other benefits accruing to the railroads under the Transportation Act of 1920 included exemption from a number of
Clayton Act restrictions and the permission to pool under I.C.C.
approval.[103] Under the latter privilege, the industry gradually
developed its own informal regional rate bureaus, accomplishing
what had been denied in the original 1887 Act.

Sharfman's understanding, then, of the I.C.C. as a vigorous
protector of the "public interest" in an evolving pattern of a
national commitment to transportation planning appears to be
greatly overworked. In the sense that regulation and planning
took place independent of the railroads' own economic interests
and as a neutral function, his thesis is poorly supported by
empirical evidence. Instead, the Commission, by its own actions
and in performance of congressional mandate, had, through the
1930's, subordinated itself to the policies of the railroads. As
the following survey of the 1930's, 1940's and 1950's will show,
the ineffectuality of the I.C.C. as an independent originator
of national transportation planning continued.

The importance of an accurate interpretation of the Interstate
Commerce Commission's role in recent railroad development
should be obvious. If, as Sharfman alleges, it was an adequate
independent regulatory agency, then the gathering railroad crisis
after the 1930's may be explained as a function of exogenous
economic and technological forces. In this case, there would
be much merit to the argument that the railroad decline was
not the result of the railroads' own corporate policies, since

these policies would have been modified or offset by the I.C.C.s own national transportation planning.* However, if the I.C.C. was really inconsequential in the development of corporate policies or tended only to validate the private market decisions of the railroads, then the Commission has not followed an independent path, and it has, indeed, failed to develop national railroad planning. As a result, the corporate behavior of the railroads becomes more important in understanding their economic problems. It is along this latter path that this study follows.

---

* A recent study (Marver Bernstein, *Regulating Business by Independent Commission* (Princeton: Princeton University Press, 1955)) which has gained general acceptance among transportation economists, offers a partial variation on the Sharfman thesis. Bernstein accepts much of Sharfman's conclusions with regard to why railroad regulation developed and the position that the Interstate Commerce Commission was an "independent" agency. However, he argues the Interstate Commerce Commission developed "quasi-judicial" regulative procedures and never acted as a "planner," at least in the sense that it attempted to develop and impose a plan for resource allocation for the railroads. The narrow role adopted by the I.C.C. has thus created a "policy of drift" with regard to national transportation planning.

While the Bernstein thesis suggests that railroad regulation was therefore inadequate due to the narrow judicial function accepted by the I.C.C., it fails to note that this inadequacy really shifted the development of a national policy to the industry itself. This interpretation is more sophisticated than Sharfman's but it does not seriously modify the interpretation offered in this study. In effect it merely adds justification to this writer's contention that public regulation of railroads, as it has developed in the United States, did not serve as a serious restraint to private action. Moreover, as the rail industry became more effectively integrated in the development of corporate policy, even the purely judicial functions of the I.C.C. became captive of the industry it supposedly sought to regulate.

While a number of recent railroad studies have more or less correctly placed the blame of the current railroad problem upon the I.C.C.'s failure to develop a national transportation plan, they have not taken a next logical step — examine the industry policy which grew up in the absence of governmental planning.

IV

THE DEPRESSION AND NEW DEVELOPMENTS IN NATIONAL TRANSPORTATION POLICY, 1929-1940

The depression decade of the 1930's was an important watershed in American railroad history, for it inaugurated a new era for the railroads — persistent economic decline, only briefly abated by the boom years of World War II. During the twenties, the operational problems which had been pointed up by World War I and which had led to the federal mandate for a general plan of railroad consolidation were forgotten in the improved business conditions. As traffic expanded, the urgency for dealing with excess capacity and the chronically weak roads correspondingly decreased. The merger movement had abandoned the creation of a planned national railroad system and followed the simple rule of self-interest in acquiring properties, in which the yardstick for consolidation became both immediate financial gain and preserving non-competitive market conditions. The operational deficiencies of the American railroad network, often hidden by the fact that even the weaker roads shared in the prosperity of the twenties, were unresolved when the boom came to an end after 1929.

The magnitude of the depression far exceeded the wildest nightmares of railroad operators. More than a decade of comparative economic calm and rising income had passed since the last serious crisis. Time had to a large extent insulated management from recalling the special difficulties that depression brought to railroads. All of the old operating problems which had been deferred, or forgotten, or purposely neglected now came back to haunt the industry, and they reappeared with a vengeance. From the railroads' point of view, the elimination of competition was more essential than ever, and selective abandonments and cessation of service were finally accepted as solutions to excess capacity and unprofitable operations. Increasingly, the railroads looked to the Interstate Commerce Commission and to Congress for the solution to operating problems. And, at least in the case of a number of important requests, they were not disappointed. Threatened with the economic collapse of the railroads, public policy, while technically still committed to bringing about a general railroad consolidation, offered aid and support to the industry's attempts to solve its operational problems.

The Economic Collapse and the Eastern Railroads

The onset of the depression after the stock market collapse in 1929 was not sudden but gradual. However, for the railroads, always early affected by changes in business activity, revenues were down 15 percent in 1930 over the year before. By 1932, they were about half that of 1929.[1] Nevertheless, as late as 1932, there was still some residual optimism among railroad management. The new president of the New York Central, Frederic E. Williamson, foresaw future improvement, concluding that "the bottom has been reached."[2] At the time Williamson voiced this optimism, "the New York Central dividend was down to one dollar quarterly (lowest since 1899). The stock had tumbled more than 200 points from its 1929 level; the earnings before fixed charges had dropped 70 percent in the same period."[3] Despite Williamson's hopefulness, worse was yet to come. Within a few months, in New York, the level of revenue traffic had fallen so low that perhaps 70 percent of the state's trackage earned revenues less than the fixed charges apportioned per mile of track.[4] Railroad management began talking less hopefully about the future.[5] Operating revenues for New York railroads continued to fall from 1930 to 1940. In fact, by 1940, more than half of the large roads operating in the state reported operating revenues below those earned in 1920. Most important, net income fell even more radically.

A brief survey of the income statements of New York railroads reveals the seriousness of operating problems. For railroads operating in the state, revenues fell 40 percent in the three years after 1929, to slightly over $1,100,000,000 in 1932.[6] In the face of declining revenues, management attempted ruthless cost-cutting. In the winter of 1931-1932, wage cuts averaging between 10 to 15 percent were effected on virtually all roads operating in the state. Railroads also eliminated about 150,000 jobs and shifted many workers to part-time status. Although not all of this job loss affected New York State rail employees, probably 40,000 New York rail workers lost their jobs and at least an equivalent number did not draw full pay by 1932. Perhaps the most vigorous employment reductions were enacted by the Pennsylvania as it reduced its work-force from 186,319 in 1928 to 109,071 by 1935. In making these reductions and by slashing wages, the Pennsylvania was able to reduce its wage bill by about 47 percent. [8]

Such cutting of costs lowered operating expenses to about $850,000,000 for New York railroads by 1934 — about 35 percent below 1929.[9] However, the cost cutting was not sufficient to prevent net income from falling to a $26,444,172 deficit.[10] By 1935, only the Pennsylvania still paid dividends; however, its payment of $13,000,000 to stockholders was only a 2 percent return on stock of $620,000,000.[11] The token dividend, in fact, was paid from the road's dwindling earned surplus. By 1935, the New York Central's surplus was down to $195,000,000, less than half its peak holdings of seven years before. Virtually all roads had to tap their reserves, for no company operating in New York State was paying its fixed charges and taxes out of current operating income by 1935.[12]

The Erie was in the poorest condition among the trunks.[13] By 1932, operating income was down to $73,000,000. Out of this, the road was obligated to pay $15,000,000 in fixed charges. With few reserves and little credit left after the collapse of the Van Sweringen empire, the Erie found its fixed charges an unbearable burden. After running through a Reconstruction Finance Corporation loan of $20,000,000 in 1935, the Erie had to apply for an additional $6,000,000 in 1937.[14]

There was a brief respite from the general business decline in 1936. Carloadings increased during the latter half of the year and into mid 1937; and there was vague talk among rail

leaders that the worst of the depression had passed. But, beginning in the second half of 1937 and continuing through 1938,
the national economy fell off into what appeared to be a deeper
depression than that of the early thirties. Eastern railroads
were especially hard hit by the secondary depression, and the
Pennsylvania and the New York Central reported operating
revenue losses of from 20 to 25 percent in 1938. [15]

By 1938, no large road operating in the state, with the exception of the Pennsylvania, earned its interest charges. The
New York Central earned only 59 percent, the Erie 25 percent, and the New Haven, 16 percent of fixed charges.[16]
Management's response was even more vigorous cost-cutting than
that seen in 1933-1934. The Central reduced its work-force by
30 percent in 1938, and employment on the Pennsylvania fell
a similar proportion. By 1938, the Pennsylvania employed only
95,000 full time and part-time workers, a drastic reduction from
its 1920 high of 280,000.[17] The Pennsylvania also announced
the discontinuance of its company pension plan.[18]

At the end of 1938, the Association of American Railroads,
itself born out of the adversity of the depression, reported that
American railroads were earning only one-half of one percent
on investment. Nearly one-third of the nation's mileage, 77,560
miles, was in bankruptcy or receivership.[19] The Association
noted that since the beginning of "a new phase of depression"
in 1937, the bottom had fallen from under American railroads.
In the first three months of 1938, railroads "piled up a deficit
of more than $100,000,000."[20]

The depression had unleashed enormous criticism of American
business. From Labor, from the New Deal government of
Franklin Roosevelt, and from the remnants of the old Progressive movement, business was battered by an unending stream
of attacks and charges, practically all of which assumed that
the economic crisis was business's fault. Railroads, as they had
always been in times of depression, were considered to be
special transgressors, and in the press and occasionally in
Congress they received special abuse. In defense of the railroads
the A.A.R. cited such authorities as the I.C.C. and congressional
documents to show that the decline was 1) not the result of
inefficient operation, 2) not the result of "abnormal" over-
capitalization, 3) not the result of excessive dividend payments
and 4) not the result of excessive management salaries. From

the Association's standpoint, the economic decline was a function of the regulatory agency's inability to give the roads needed help. Specifically, it had failed to raise rates.[21] The Association also called for increased cost-cutting—particularly wage slashes and tax reductions as short-term solutions to the problem of declining income.[22] Taxes were also noted as a serious problem, for taxes had climbed, the A.A.R. noted, from about 6 percent of rail expenditures in 1929 to more than 10 percent by 1938.

By 1938, over 3500 miles of Class I trackage operated in the north-eastern states had gone into bankruptcy. In 1935, the New Haven, still weakened by Morgan's reorganization and its own immodest expansion programs of three decades before, had gone to the courts. Late in 1937, the New York Ontario and Western and the New York Susquehanna and Western, their coal earnings eroded by the depression of coal prices and traffic, fell into bankruptcy.[23] As noted before, the Erie had been especially hard-pressed since the early thirties, and, turned down by the R.F.C. for an emergency loan in 1937, it failed to meet its debt obligations and went into receivership on January 18, 1938.[24] Despite aroused efforts by citizens of northern New York and Vermont, the Rutland defaulted on its interest payments the same year.

In northern New York, where the railroad was still considered to be a sort of economic umbilical cord which tied the region to the rest of the country, the Rutland's troubles stimulated a number of novel efforts by local citizens to head off bankruptcy. Communities forgave taxes. Labor cheerfully accepted wage cuts. Private donations were made to pay fuel, water and maintenance bills. In Burlington, a parade was staged to drum up railroad business.[25] However, little help was given the Rutland by its leading stockholder, the New York Central, and default on interest eventually led it to the courts. The secondary depression of 1937-1938 had cut earnings to the point where no New York railroad could cover interest, taxes and other fixed charges from current earnings. The way of the Erie, the Rutland and the New Haven seemed to point out the direction for all New York railroads when the European War and American defense mobilization began to stimulate recovery in late 1939.

A New Corporate Approach to National Railroad Problems

The operating and capital condition of the eastern rail network as noted earlier, put a halt to merger and consolidation activity on the part of the railroads. In July, 1932, the Dow-Jones rail average stood at 13.23, down from 144.72 in December, 1929.[26] By 1935, the great eastern railroad holding company operations, the Allegheny Corporation, Pennroad, and New York Central Securities Company, had come unraveled or had been forced to curtail their market operations to the point that their effectiveness in putting together consolidations was at an end. The former Van Sweringen properties were soon tied up in the courts in a maze of suits and counter-suits by stockholders, the government and subordinate companies. As a sign of the times, J. P. Morgan, Jr. and a number of officers of Guaranty Trust were indicted in Federal court, charged with stock manipulation in Guaranty Trust's financial aid to the Van Sweringen brothers.* The battle for control of the remnants of the Van Sweringen empire continued on in the courts until 1943, when Robert R. Young, former president of the Chesapeake and Ohio and later president of the New York Central, and Allan P. Kirby gained control of the Allegheny Corporation.[27]

The other holding companies came to less spectacular ends, but it was evident that the expansive era of the holding company was over. They had attracted federal attention in 1931 when the Interstate and Foreign Commerce Committee of the House of Representative held hearings on the "regulation of stock ownership in railroads."[28] Two years later, under the provisions of the Emergency Transportation Act, and at the direct request of President Roosevelt, the railroad holding companies were placed under I.C.C. control.[29] Looking back on the era somewhat defensively the official Pennsylvania historians remarked:

> The application of hindsight, conditioned by the psychology of the depression, resulted in the subsequent criticism of these purchases, which were made by Pennroad during

---

* Morgan and the others were eventually acquitted but Guaranty Trust was held liable for $1,000,000 in damages in suits initiated by Allegheny Stockholders.

the prosperous period of 1929 and early 1930. But in all fairness it must be remembered that at that time it was the almost universal opinion of statesmen, bankers, financiers and responsible business leaders that prosperity had become a prevalent state and would continue to grow and expand, and that, while there might be minor ups and downs in the business cycle, the old-style depression was a thing of the past, and the general trend over the year would be for the better.[30]

While the speculative attraction of mergers withered with the depression of the securities market and the general diminishing of business confidence, the operational advantages of consolidation from the point of view of the large roads evaporated as well. There were no exceptions to the general operational decline in the east. Through the mid and late thirties, there were no strong roads east of Chicago, only some were less weak than others.

More important than the ending of consolidation and speculative activities, the depression also signaled an important change in railroad corporate policy. In particular, it marked a shift in the source of initiation and implementation of policy. As has been noted, up to and after the passage of the Transportation Act of 1920, the policies of eastern railroads with regard to such problems as excess capacity and competition rarely originated as the independent creation of railroad managers. Instead, the board rooms of major eastern financial institutions were of greater importance in setting out broad policy plans. The day to day running of the roads, of course, was left to the companies' own experts.

In the early 1930's, J. P. Morgan and Company, First National Bank (New York), Bankers Trust and Guaranty Trust, all bearing the mark of Morgan influence, together dominated the board of directors of the New York Central, New York New Haven and Hartford, Delaware and Hudson, Lehigh Valley and Erie.[31] Other formal and family financial connections drew in the Pennsylvania and the Baltimore and Ohio to the Morgan orbit. Kuhn Loeb and Company had directors on the Pennsylvania, the New Haven, the Lehigh Valley, the Delaware and Hudson and the Boston and Maine among the eastern roads.[32] Since these roads in turn, through intercorporate holdings, were connected with other carriers, the Morgan-

Kuhn Loeb financial influence was calculated by the National Resources Committee to extend to over 98 percent of all American railroad assets. A 1931 congressional inquiry revealed that five large banks and nine brokerage houses — all affiliated with Morgan and Kuhn Loeb interest owned $415,000,000 in rail securities, or slightly more than 5 percent of the outstanding voting strength.[33] This was a considerable concentration of power since real control in any one company could be obtained with much less than majority stock ownership.

Harry Laidler, President of the National Bureau of Economic Research, looking at the resulting pattern of interlocking directorates, found "that the directors of all Class I railroads were directors of 132 larger banks and trust companies."[34] Professor William Ripley, however, indicated that this still obscured the fact that among the many banking houses, there was considerable mutual understanding as "bankers and brokers allocate to one another sponsorships for this, that, and the other corporation."[35] In perhaps the most succinct explanation of how the banking houses worked, Ripley commented in a New York Times letter:

> Under such an arrangement, House "A" passes the hat about the district receiving proxies for enough "street" stock from the concerns to give working control.... Thus, and through the prestige of the great banking houses, coupled with the larger corporate holding by insurance companies, trusts, foundations and the like, virtual concentration of control in this industry is substantially perpetuated. Of all railroad financing during 1930, 10 banking houses headed issues amounting to $850,000,000, more than 90 percent of the total. Kuhn Loeb led with 30.3 percent of the total. J. P. Morgan ranked second with 28.29 percent.... Chase Securities (a Morgan affiliate) had charge of 6.78 percent. [36]

The actual impact of banker control is difficult to document directly. The thousands of pages of company records and correspondence subpoened by the Wheeler sub-committee in its 1936-1940 studies of "Railroad Combinations in the Eastern United States," like the 1931 House inquiry into holding companies, revealed little in the way of direct financial-corporate relations. Virtually all evidence of financial control of railroad corporate policy during the twenties and early thirties aside from statistics on interlocking directorships amounts to nothing more

than the fact that actual railroad policy was invariably beneficial to the financial houses and that financial houses had
"their men" on the railroad boards. As noted earlier, the banking houses had successfully opposed the I.C.C. sponsored merger
plans which might have increased competition in the east or
which might have placed limitations on the earning power of
the more powerful roads by merging them with less prosperous
lines. Meanwhile, in the late twenties, coasting on a speculative
stock market wave, banking houses had enjoyed a thriving
business in railroad securities.

Beginning with the depression, however, the banker orienta-
tion of railroad policy began to ebb as two important modifications in railroad corporate policy took place. First, with the
formation of the Association of American Railroads in 1934,
intercorporate agreement became more formal and showed an
even greater degree of industry concensus than had been created
under banker influence. Second, the direction of policy began
to show greater concern for management and operational considerations while the role of the promoter or owner ebbed in
the deepening economic plight of the railroads.

The relative decline of "banker influence" roughly paralleled
the railroads' abandonment of external sources for capital expansion. As the depression worsened, the need or ability to
obtain new capital funds through private money markets diminished as railroads found government loans or internal financing
to be the only available capital sources. Later, the industry
came to finance its capital developments increasingly from internal sources, and external capital markets virtually ceased
as a source. Internal financing, of course, made the railroads
less dependent upon the old banking establishments, and, at
the same time, gave rail management greater authority over the
roads' capital organization.

Meanwhile, the creation of an industry-wide, policy-making
body had received increased government encouragement since
the beginning of the depression. In response to the railroads'
problems, President Hoover had established a National Transportation Committee in October, 1932. The committee, composed of former President Coolidge, former Governor Alfred
Smith, and bankers Alexander Legge, and Clark Howell, was
charged with the investigation of "all phases of the railroad
problem and to recommend a solution which will insure an
opportunity for the railroads of this country to be put on a

business basis."[37] Along with their suggestions to cease inefficient rail service and to improve financial management, the committee recommended that the railroads should act cooperatively to "reduce competitive expense."[38]

During the 1932 campaign, Presidential Candidate Roosevelt similarly advocated coordination among railroads to eliminate competition. Although he urged that railroad holding companies be placed under public regulation, this threat to the industry was softened by his opposition to any policy of "enforcing competition among railroads." Roosevelt's plan for industrial cooperation was soon unveiled in the National Industrial Recovery Act of 1933 which encouraged, under certain conditions, the creation of industrial associations to eliminate "costly competition." Passed by Congress on the same day as the National Industrial Recovery Act, the Emergency Transportation Act specifically asked for the elimination of waste and duplication in the railroad industry.[40] The act also provided for a Federal Transportation Coordinator who was charged with studying possible savings in transportation through the development of intra-industry cooperation. To aid the coordinator, the railroads were ordered to establish three regional coordinating committees, in the east, the west and the south. General William Atterbury, President of the Pennsylvania, saw this legislation as a special benefit for the railroads, and the Pennsylvania railroad staff prepared a number of reports for the coordinator pointing out possible savings through the elimination of duplicating services. In general, these studies emphasized the possibility of labor savings that might be accomplished by coordination and service reduction; however, the Emergency Act restricted labor displacement, maintaining that workers' jobs must be protected in any economy moves.[41]

Perhaps, one of the more extreme proposals offered for private coordination was made in May 1934, by A. J. County, Vice President in charge of finance of the Pennsylvania Railroad.[42] County called for the creation of a "united Eastern Railroad System." This would be a single integrated rail system under a board of directors composed of all the presidents of the eastern railroads. Strictly speaking, it was not a resuscitation of the consolidation movement, but more nearly resembled a giant railroad pool. Individual roads were to retain their corporate and financial identity but the new corporation would govern day to day operating matters and direct the allocation of capital improvements.

The County Plan probably requested too much in the way of creating an eastern railroad monopoly. Although eastern rail leaders debated its merits for a few months, there was little official endorsement. Meanwhile, President Roosevelt "unofficially" urged the creation of a single national railroad organization which could make policy for the industry.[43] When the formation of the Association of American Railroads was announced in September of 1934, federal sanction was quickly offered by Joseph Eastman, former Interstate Commerce Commissioner and new Federal Coordinator. Eastman noted:

> The announcement that the railroad executives of the country have agreed upon one national railroad authority to deal effectively with all matters of national interest to the railroads of the United States is gratifying. I believe that it is a step in the right direction which offers promise of substantial benefit to the railroads and also to the country. For a long time the need for a better central organization of the industry which could act authoritatively, somewhat in the capacity of a general staff, has been evident.[44]

On the surface, the government's position represented a significant shift in the philosophy of public regulation. It was difficult to interpret Eastman's or the President's remarks as anything except an official government concession to the cessation of competition. Although this concession may be rationalized as an out-growth of the unique conditions and the peculiar economic philosophy of the "New Deal," the Association of American Railroads did not treat it as a temporary change of official mind. It was, after all, what the railroads, especially the eastern roads and their banking houses, had sought since Morgan had engineered the "Corsair Compact" and, later, community of interest.

The Covenant of the Association of American Railroads openly proclaimed the organization's intent to create a solid, industry-wide policy on railroad matters. It specified:

> ...the Railroad Companies of the United States do hereby establish an authoritative national organization which shall be adequately qualified and empowered in every lawful way to accomplish said ends whose covenent of policy and

action are required. For the purpose of facilitating the realization of this constructive objective, the members do hereby declare that these announced policies shall be authoritative and will be supported.[45]

With membership open to all Class I railroads of greater than 100 miles in length, the administrative power of the Association was vested in a Board of Directors comprised of a President, five directors from the eastern territory, six from the western territory and three from the southern territory. The Association recognized and integrated into its own machinery such existing railroad agencies as the Eastern President's Conference, the Western Association of Railroad Executives, and the Southeastern President's Conference.[46]

Five administrative departments were created in the covenant. The Law Department was "to deal with questions of legislation, governmental action and policies, and matters of a legal nature, which in the opinion of the Board of Directors or of the Executive Committee, will affect the members of the Association." Other departments included: Operations and Maintenance, Traffic, Finance, and Planning and Research. Although the definition of the duties of the administrative departments was not explicit, most of the administrative action of the Association were to replace similar activities previously undertaken by individual companies.[48]

The Association's power was centered in the Board of Directors, with special authority given to the President in the "general supervision over the affairs of the Association."[49] The covenant also called for arbitration on "all controversies between members of the Association," with the Board of Directors deciding by a three-quarters vote on all arbitration submitted to it.[50]

Although the original plan of organization made no specific mention of rate maintenance and pricing agreements, such a direction for concerted action was certainly implicit in the Association's principles. In fact, the Association received "official" assurances that such action to restrict competitive practices would not prompt I.C.C. intervention.[51] While later antitrust action against the Association held that its policies of rate maintenance and the operating of pools violated the Sherman Act, the Roosevelt Administration apparently saw no such threat in 1934.

Another less easily evaluated function of the Association, and not specifically outlined in the covenant, was that of "political education." Three years before the creation of the Association, its predecessor, the Association of Railway Executives, had directed 26 Class I railroads to organize regional railroad associations in each state.[52] Primarily, these groups were to act as levers upon local congressmen.[53] The dimensions of this lobbying activity were partially uncovered by the Wheeler Committee Report in 1940, which revealed that $182,000,000 had been spent by national, state and regional railroad associations between 1930 and 1936. The report could only speculate that a large portion of these expenditures had been made for "political education."[54]

The Association of American Railroads quickly estimated the useful possibilities for such lobbying efforts, and moved to establish its own educational program for legislators, although it sought to do this surreptitiously. In April 1935, the Transportation Association of America was formed as a national "political educational" group specifically interested in obtaining legislative exemption for the railroads from Federal anti-trust laws. The Wheeler Committee investigation of lobbying in the rail industry reported in 1940 that the A.A.R. was instrumental from the beginning in the activities of the Transportation Association, although it made "every effort to conceal its role."[55] A detailed analysis of the dimensions of the Association's commitment to political action remains for another study. The shift to political action by the railroads, however, should not be seen as an entirely new trend in corporate policy. Railroads, as well as shippers and merchant groups, since the earliest beginnings of the industry, had used political leverage to advance special legislative interests in both state legislatures and the Congress. Nevertheless, the political education activities carried out directly and indirectly by the Association of American Railroads represented the first unified national effort on the part of the rail industry. As such, it marked a new departure for railroad corporate policy.

Although the Roosevelt Administration had taken the position that the A.A.R. was a legitimate intercorporate policy-making body, critics charged that it was thoroughly dominated by the banking and ownership interests of Kuhn Loeb and Morgan organizations. As a front for the banking interests, it was alleged, the individual roads could conspire collectively in opposition to the public's interest. During the dreary depression years such criticism was stifled by the deteriorating economic position of the railroads and the attitude of the administration that, under the Emergency Act and other legislation, there was adequate public protection. However, in 1944, in similar suits, the state of Georgia and the United States Department of Justice initiated anti-trust action under the Sherman Act against the A.A.R. and certain railroads and individuals. The Georgia suit charged that the Pennsylvania Railroad and other roads conspired "to establish and to maintain freight rates which are unjust, unfair and harmful to the States and the people of Georgia."[56] At issue was the use of "informal" regional rate bureaus in maintaining regional rate differentials.[57]

The federal suit named 140 individuals and corporations as defendants to the charge that they had attempted to artificially maintain rates in the western territory. Among the defendants were the Association of American Railroads, the Western Association of Railway Executives, J. P. Morgan and Company, Kuhn Loeb and Company and forty-seven western railroads.

Both suits charged that rates were set to favor the eastern "official" territory. The federal action specifically named the A.A.R. as the operator of rate bureaus which functioned to maintain eastern rate preference. The federal suit further alleged that ownership and financial interests demanded non-competitive and high rates to protect the value of railroad securities. To support these charges, the brief pointed out that a steering committee of nine railroad directors which had drawn up the Association's covenant in 1933-1934 were all affiliated with Morgan and Kuhn Loeb financial interests. Evidence was marshaled to show that the banking interests maintained strong formal and informal ties with the Association and the regional rate bureaus.

To the charge that the Association of American Railroads maintained regional rate bureaus to eliminate intra-industry competition, the Association was clearly guilty. That this action violated the Sherman Act is practically indisputable. However, the rate bureaus had received tacit I.C.C. approval and surely seemed consistent with the economic philosophy advanced by the National Industrial Recovery Act and the Emergency Trans-

portation Act. The question was finally resolved in 1948, with
the passage of the Reed-Bulwinkle Act which gave the railroads
authority to operate rate agencies if they received advance I.C.C.
approval. The passage of this act over President Truman's veto
came only after a vigorous lobbying campaign by the railroads.
Despite the hue and cry of "Railroad Monopoly" created by the
passage of the act, Reed-Bulwinkle only validated the intent of
the Emergency Transportation Act of 1933.

The charge that the Association of American Railroads was
dominated by eastern financial interests and, hence, that Association policy was "banker policy," despite the mountains of
circumstantial evidence set forth in the government's case,
missed the point and was much too simplistic. The depression
and the appearance of competing transport modes in the 1930's
had created previously unknown operating problems for the
railroads at the same time that speculative financial interest
in railroad securities ebbed. While certain financial houses
specializing in mergers and reorganizations doubtless saw profit
in these areas and, therefore, continued to influence the consolidation movement, the concern of most ownership interests
was simply to keep the railroads operating at income levels
which would pay out fixed charges and permit at least modest
dividend payments. Banker and ownership perspectives and the
outlook of the management, which was directly concerned
with questions of profit and loss, did not differ as greatly
as they might have in the earlier years of railroad building or
during the consolidation efforts of the twenties. The Association
of American Railroads, perhaps "banker dominated" as charged,
still was preoccupied with questions relating to the day to day
operation of the railroads. To suggest that it acted simply as
a modern-day institutional tycoon misunderstands the degree
to which the depression changed the corporate psychology of the
American railroad industry.

A further example of the increased concern for railroads'
operational problems is reflected in the installation of new presidents by the Pennsylvania and the New York Central. In 1931,
the Central directors chose Frederic Williamson. Noting that
Williamson had virtually no professional or family contacts
with the "interests" but had made his way up through the
management ranks, *Fortune Magazine* observed:

It may be assured that in laying this responsibility on Williamson's shoulders at this time, the Directors and bankers have given him tacit assurance of their cooperation; and that at the same time, they look forward to a president capable of managing their affairs with a strong and fearless hand.[58]

In 1935, the Pennsylvania similarly sought leadership with managerial experience as they elevated Martin Clement from Vice President in Charge of Operations to the Presidency.[59]

Government and Railroad Cooperation

The official recognition and encouragement of formal industry cooperation by the Roosevelt Administration was undoubtedly a significant gain for the railroads, but much more was needed and expected from the federal government to permit the companies to weather the depression. An informal program of economic relief drawn up by the railroads through the A.A.R. offered at least three separate proposals: 1) the provision of needed capital aid to meet maintenance and replacement demands which could no longer be financed out of private security sales or current income, 2) the obtaining of legislative insulation from the competitive threat of the fast-growing trucking industry, and 3) the commitment of the Interstate Commerce Commission, as well as the Congress, to an openly sympathetic policy on rate setting, trackage abandonment and service discontinuance, financial operations, and merger requirements.

The issue of federal economic aid to the railroads, given the depressed state of business conditions and the special plight of the railroads, was the least controversial issue in the emerging railroad program. Direct economic subsidy dated from the very beginning of railroad building in America, and no large American industry ever had the special access to the public treasury that the railroads had enjoyed. Federal Coordinator Eastman calculated that, up to the beginning of the depression, federal aid of all types to railroads had been equivalent to about $1.5 billion.[60] Between 1932 and 1938, additional direct aid of almost $1 billion was provided. The Reconstruction Finance Corporation, a Hoover program enlarged by the Roosevelt Administration, became the chief distributor of capital funds. Of the R.F.C. and its operations, Joseph Schumpeter observed:

Primarily intended as support to banks and cognate institutions, and as an agency to carry part of the burden of loans that were noneligible in the sense of the reserve bank legislation, its scope naturally included the only type of big business that was seriously threatened, railroads.[61]

Virtually unable to borrow in private money markets, the railroads obtained authorization for $625,000,000 of R.F.C. loans between 1932 and 1937.[62] Roads operating in New York State accounted for $173,000,000 of these loans.

An often overlooked but, to eastern railroads, almost equally significant source of federal aid was granted under the Federal Emergency Administration of the National Industrial Recovery Act. Of an original appropriation of $3,300,000,000 in emergency funds, $119,607,800 was allocated for railroad loans "to aid in the financing of such railroad maintenance and equipment as may be approved by the I.C.C. as desirable for the improvement of transport facilities."[63] Unlike the Reconstruction Finance Corporation moneys which required rather stringent repayment schedules and set modestly restrictive collateral requirements, Federal Emergency Administration loans were easier to obtain. Maintenance loans could run for ten years, and equipment loans ran from between fifteen and twenty years. Nominally the interest rate was 4 percent, but no interest was charged for the first year and the average rate was between 3.6 and 3.75 percent. Amortization could be in annual or semi-annual installments.[64]

Eastern railroads especially took advantage of the F.E.A. moneys. Eight eastern roads, of the thirty-two American railroads receiving Emergency Administration aid, absorbed $120,000,000 of the $201,000,000 in loans granted by 1937.[65] This aid facilitated most of the major equipment and maintenance outlays in the east during the mid 1930's. With a $70,000,000 loan, the Pennsylvania electrified its Washington Division and purchased new electric engines. The New Haven was able to add a streamlined passenger train. The Lackawanna, Baltimore and Ohio, Erie, and Lehigh Valley bought new cars and locomotives, and the New York Central and the Ontario and Western made major maintenance outlays to improve track and roadbed.

In all, the response by the Roosevelt Administration to the

railroads' economic plight was most helpful. The railroads had been encouraged to work cooperatively to increase efficiency and had received very considerable financial aid. The industry responded approvingly, although it usually maintained a public pose that the aid received should have been greater. Under the growing leadership of the Association of American Railroads, the industry continued to press for further sympathetic government action.

In the eastern states, the general depression of rail freight traffic in the thirties had been aggravated by the continued shift of transport demand from railroads to trucks. Although accurate figures on this shift are not available, the I.C.C. reported that railroads' national share of inter-city freight fell from 74 percent to 61 percent while truck traffic grew from 4 percent to 10 percent between 1930 and 1940.[66] This could be translated into a decline for the railroads from 390 billion freight-ton-miles to 375 billion and a rise for trucks from 20 to 65 billion freight-ton-miles. Moreover, this was obviously only the beginning of the trucking threat. With advanced motor vehicle technology and better highway building programs, trucks would certainly increase their traffic share.

The railroads' reaction to this thriving competition was to turn to the federal regulative authorities and to Congress for relief in the form of expanded regulation over trucking. Quite conditioned by their own experience with non-competitive rate-making, the industry now sought to expand this approach to other transport modes, thus eliminating all price competition. With their present domination over freight movement, the railroads saw in rate equality between the two transportation modes a way to maintain their positon in the new "inter-modal" competition.[67] Although such a position seemed consistent both with railroad policy and with New Deal thinking, having gained support in the administration from Transportation Coordinator Eastman and others, this line of regulatory policy soon proved unsound.[68] Nevertheless, the Motor Carrier Act was passed in mid 1935, placing interstate trucking under I.C.C. control and accepting the principle that rail and motor rate-making should be more or less the same on similar commodities. The railroads were to find, however, that this idea of rate parity really amounted to a subsidy for many trucking operations and a restriction upon their own inherent transportation advantages in others. However, many years were to pass before the railroads admitted their error.

Another thrust of corporate policy was to enlist the direct support of the I.C.C. in those areas over which it presently had existing authority. Indeed, the railroad industry's decision to use the I.C.C. as a supporter of its own economic policy goals is perhaps the most significant long-range effect of the new corporate approach emerging from the depression. To a considerable extent, in appealing for regulative aid, the railroads sought to blunt the more "radical" solutions to their economic problems that were from time to time proposed. Clearly, the Interstate Commerce Commission was viewed as a buffer between the natural aspirations of rail management and the growing public criticism.

The railroads' economic problems, particularly the problems of the eastern railroads, had again raised the question of government ownership or operation. For nearly a decade and a half after the passage of the Transportation Act of 1920, public ownership of the railroads had been largely an academic question — discussed in college economics classrooms and occasionally challenged at business club luncheons. For most rail managers and government officials, it seemed that the Transportation Act had closed the door to this method of solving the railroads' problems. However, the protracted business depression and the political climate of the "New Deal" gave credence to ideas which had earlier been considered only as "radical reforms."

On April 15, 1936, Senator Burton K. Wheeler, after a Senate speech which reviewed the troubled financial and operating conditions of the eastern railroads, introduced a bill proposing the creation of a public owned corporation which would acquire all railroads engaged in interstate commerce.[69] Since Wheeler served as chairman of the powerful Senate Committee on Interstate Commerce, his bill appeared to be more than a passing threat. The gravity of the railroads' economic plight evoked a number of sympathetic reactions to the bill. Joseph Eastman, Transportation Coordinator under the Emergency Act, expressed his approval for the general outlines of the Wheeler plan.[70] The railroads, individually and through the recently formed A.A.R. reacted predictably. Although government intervention was sought, it was not desired along these lines. Rather, the railroads contended that their operating positions could be improved with public financial aid. Shippers who still believed that competitive rate making might someday be restored also opposed the Wheeler plan. Quickly, a National Committee for Prevention of Government Ownership of Railroads was organized by the National Industrial Traffic League, an organization closely related to the A.A.R..[71]

Controversy raged over the Wheeler Bill through 1936 and 1937; however, the bill never had much chance of passage. Public ownership, it soon turned out, was not an instrument in the New Deal economic tool box. As noted earlier, a more popular technique of market reform had been the use of industrial agreement and self-regulation, or if that failed, limited regulation through public agencies. Even Joseph Eastman admitted that the Wheeler Bill had little chance of passage, although he noted:

> There is no agressive sentiment opposed to public ownership and operation. The financial world is less hostile to the idea than in the past, because some institutional bondholders think it might improve their situation, and because of doubt as to whether the railroads will be a source of large profits in the future. Fundamental objections to the operation of an industry by the government tend to disappear in direct ratio with profits. The man on the street appears to be indifferent rather than hostile.[72]

However, there was little support in the Roosevelt Administration or in the I.C.C. for such radical action as government ownership or operation. "On the whole," Eastman added, "there is now little effective support in public agencies for public ownership and operation."[73]

John J. Pelley, President of the A.A.R., urged that discussion of public ownership be set aside in favor of an "enlightened government policy." To Pelley, and presumably to most of the rail leaders, enlightenment did not mean a return to *laissez faire.* Specifically, it meant the loosening of I.C.C. rate setting power, tax reductions, the ending of subsidies to competing carriers and the rescinding of the general consolidation specifications of the 1920 act.[74] Pelley and the Association, however, were prepared to accept "non-competitive regulation" and industry-initiated consolidation and rate setting with "enlightened" I.C.C. approval. The argument was to become a familiar one. Under the A.A.R.'s proposal, regulation was to be on the industry's terms, and, as later events showed, this industry position was substantially implemented by legislative and I.C.C. action.

The spectre of government ownership of the railroads never entirely disappeared. During the thirties it was raised again and again in countless popular publications. As late as 1939, the Investment Bankers Association, obviously fearing the seizure of rail assets, asserted that the coming European war could serve as a pretext for government nationalization of the railroads.[75] Secretary Morgenthau, no favorite of the business community, however, assured Americans that government would only "assist not control" the railroads in wartime.[76] Early in 1940, as war demands placed increased traffic pressures on the railroads, the I.C.C. announced that there appeared to be no need for government operation and that the railroads were much stronger than they had been in 1917.[77]

The possible uses of the I.C.C. were not simply limited to evading the public ownership question. An I.C.C. committed to the principle of keeping the railroads going could render extraordinary operating benefits to the railroads. No longer was the industry hesitant to employ public regulation for its own benefit. The agitation by the railroads for truck regulation was one example but there were many others. One such case was the railroads' attempt to get special relief from the heavy fixed charges of their financial structure. In March of 1937, U.S. Congressman William Chandler proposed the creation of a reorganization court which would aid railroads facing bankruptcy by reorganizing their debt structure so as to lower fixed income charges.[78] With considerable encouragement from the Association of American Railroads, the I.C.C. proposed a similar plan which would allow the railroads to forego certain fixed charges temporarily, without being thrown into the courts.[79] Among the eastern railroads these proposals were especially attractive. As Daniel Willard, President of the Baltimore and Ohio, testified before a Senate Committee hearing on the Chandler Bill, more than half of the eastern rail trackage was presently in the bankruptcy courts or was immediately threatened.[80] In late July the Chandler Bill was signed into law with President Roosevelt's praise, and, under its provisions, railroads were able to reduce voluntarily their fixed debt payments if three-quarters of their creditors would agree.[81]

The increased war earnings of the railroads soon made the Chandler Bill and similar proposals unnecessary, as roads allocated much of their war income to the reduction of fixed charges. However, this act and other legislation had created precedence for preferential federal treatment of the railroads' financial and operational problems. During the war years this meant the adoption of new tax "write off" policies which allowed the railroads to charge off unamortized debt payments as operating expenses.[82]

In many respects, railroads at the time counted as their greatest legislative gain the passage of the Transportation Act of 1940. The act seemed in every respect to be a railroad victory. It revoked the general plan for railroad consolidations, released land grant railroads from the burden of carrying government property at reduced rates, and included water carrier commerce under I.C.C. regulation. However, from the point of view of the A.A.R. the greatest gain was the announced commitment of the federal government to a "national transportation policy" in which Congress was

> . . . to provide for fair and impartial regulation of all modes of transportation subject to the provision of this Act, so administered as to recognize and preserve the inherent advantages of each, to promote . . . and foster economical condition in transportation and among the several carriers, to encourage the establishment and maintenance of reasonable charges for transportation services, without unjust discrimination, undue preferences or advantages or unfair or destructive competitive practices . . .[83]

Under the Transportation Act, the railroads had finally obtained legislative sanction of their long-held position that "competition was destructive." Moreover, non-competitive rate making was to be applied to all transportation modes.[84] The legislative victory for the railroads was the result of a number of factors. For one thing, the railroads' depressed financial condition, compared to the robust health of other transport types, served to point up the need for "fair and impartial regulation" of all carriers. Meanwhile, the impending war clouds also pointed up the probable military and defense gains from a healthy rail industry and from coordination of all carriers.

Like earlier enactments which had been passed to protect the regulated industry as well as the consumer, the Transportation

Act of 1940 was a paradox. Just as the Transportation Act of 1920 had tried to maintain competition while it reduced the rail industry to a few monopolistic firms, the 1940 act attempted to preserve "inherent advantages" among the different transportation modes while eliminating "undue preferences or advantages" and "destructive competitive practices." As a basis for developing a national transportation policy, this was asking too much. For the railroads, the act's great promise was never to be attained.

The End of Planned Consolidation as National Transportation Policy

As we have noted, the Transportation Act of 1940 finally freed the I.C.C. from developing a general plan for railroad consolidation. Technically, this had been the basis of public policy toward the railroads since 1920. However, at least by the time of the failure of the 1925 talks, it was evident that no general plan was possible, and the commission itself began to assume a more passive role toward the question.

The I.C.C.'s failure as a creator of national transportation policy, at least its failure to obtain a general consolidation, brought forth a number of proposals for reforming the Commission. In 1926, Walter M. W. Splawn, a former Texas Railroad Commissioner, advocated dividing the Commission into regional administrative offices, each region charged with developing its own policies with regard to rates, mergers, and general regulation. In 1929, the National Industrial Traffic League, as well as the President's Transportation Committee in 1932, argued for greater policy creating power for the Commission. Alfred E. Smith suggested in 1933 that the I.C.C. be replaced by a more powerful cabinet post of Secretary of Transportation.[85] However, for all the threatening talk, the I.C.C. never moved toward asserting itself as the initiator of national transportation policy. When authorized additional regulative power, it was slow to act. For example, when the Emergency Transportation Act of 1933 awarded the Commission investigative and regulative authority over the actions of non-carrier holding companies, the I.C.C. let the new authority lapse.

On the other hand, the I.C.C. stood ready to provide what operating aid it could give to the railroads during the thirties.

The Commission still maintained its commitment to the principle of preserving a fair return on railroad investment, although the traffic decline, of course, made this impossible. Under I.C.C. pressure, the recapture provisions of the 1913 Valuation Act were repealed by the Emergency Act of 1933. Meanwhile, the I.C.C., as we shall see in the next section, was quite agreeable to the abandonment policies pursued by the railroads. Usually these abandonments were permitted solely on the basis of financial evidence collected by the petitioning railroad. The Commission never undertook an overall study of the dislocative economic effects of abandonment just as it had ceased to study the economic effects of consolidations it approved.[86]

The passage of the Emergency Transportation Act of 1933 was the last federal legislative attempt to solve the railroad problem through planned consolidation. Under that act a Federal Coordinator of Transportation had been created to promote financial and operational reorganizations. As an inducement to stimulate approved private mergers, the specification that security issues of the reorganized company could not exceed the aggregate value of merged properties was eliminated from the Transportation Act of 1920.[87]

The tenure of Joseph Eastman as Federal Coordinator was not especially eventful. Before his office disappeared for lack of Congressional renewal in June of 1936, he could claim no accomplished mergers. The coordinator, however, did produce a number of useful studies on railroad operations and spent considerable energies on at least one new consolidation proposal — the Prince Plan. The work of Boston banker Frederick Prince, this plan had gained considerable support among eastern financial groups by late 1932, when it was evident that the "Final I.C.C. Plan" would fail. Eastman was known to be sympathetic to some of its proposals, and as a result, President Roosevelt had both the Prince Plan and Joseph Eastman in mind when he proposed the Emergency Act of 1933.[88]

The Prince Plan called for the most drastic reorganization of any of the merger plans — reducing American railroads to but seven systems, with only two lines operating in the east. The plan's proponents argued that savings of about $750,000,000 annually could be obtained. Attractive to the banking community was the condition that the federal authorities guarantee "fair return" to the seven super-systems.[89] The division of railroads in the east, under the Prince Plan, called for the building of two trunks — one built around the Pennsylvania and the Baltimore and Ohio and the other around the Van Sweringen and New York Central properties. The plan called for the ruthless trimming of excess capacity through abandonment and integration of terminal and route facilities.

The Association of American Railroads opposed the plan. Doubtless much of its opposition stemmed from Section 7b of the Emergency Transportation Act which virtually prohibited the reduction of employment resulting from mergers. Although the Prince Plan never became an "official" merger plan, the Coordinator's studies of the plan and his attempts to produce voluntary consolidation along its lines, met with a mixed response from the eastern railroads.[90] The Pennsylvania, financially the strongest of the eastern railroads, offered to acquire the Baltimore and Ohio which had been assigned to it under the plan.[91] The Pennsylvania had long shown an interest in the Baltimore and Ohio, and the apparently legalized wedding of the two under the Prince Plan provided the motive for such an offer. However, the Pennsylvania made no moves to acquire the road's stock, as the reluctance of President Williard of the Baltimore and Ohio and the worsening business conditions put an end to merger discussion.

Meanwhile, the New York Central disclaimed any interest in further acquisitions.[92] Although the Prince Plan combined the Central and Van Sweringen properties, both systems had very nearly common banker control and gains to the owners from a merger were not altogether evident. Like the Pennsylvania, the Central also lacked capital resources to accomplish any merger.

The Prince Plan soon was abandoned; and during the remainder of the thirties only one merger was accomplished. In 1937, the I.C.C. approved the acquisition of the Nickel Plate and the Erie by the Chesapeake and Ohio. This merger conformed with property allocations under the 1932 Four Party Plan, but it really only validated the existing financial control of the Erie and Nickel Plate by the Chesapeake and Ohio. It is noteworthy, however, that before the Chesapeake and Ohio could take possession of the Erie, the Erie went into receivership.[93]

The ineffectiveness of the Federal Coordinator in bringing about consolidation was probably increased by the railroads' irritation over the appointment of Eastman to this office. To many rail officials, Eastman represented an economic philosophy which was alien to their own and alien generally to the actions of the I.C.C. As a *Fortune Magazine* writer stated it, "Mr Eastman is the most socialistic commissioner appointed to the I.C.C."[94] Eastman was once charged by John J. Cornwell, general counsel of the Baltimore and Ohio, with having "depreciated the market value of public utility and railroad securities by several billions of dollars by simply publicly expressing his valuation ideas."[95] Eastman, as might be expected, had few laudatory comments for rail management either. He characterized their economic philosophy as "intensely individualistic and suspicious of collective action."[96]

Eastman, of course, was no socialist. As an Interstate Commerce Commissioner he had opposed the railroads' constant pressuring for "fair return." Eastman held that "public interest" meant the maximizing of public service, not the assurance of maximum earnings. As Coordinator, Eastman changed his views somewhat. He backed off from his earlier position that consolidation meant the creation of monopolies and conceded that real economic gains to the public might be obtained through merger. By 1934, his views were much like those of F.D.R. on railroad regulation, that is to say, "Big Business" could be effectively regulated by an interventionist "Big Government." Eastman still harbored predilections for government ownership of the railroads, but he became less vocal on these matters as the years went by. However, he was no more effective in impressing his views favoring consolidation upon the railroads than he had been as a dissenting commissioner in usually opposing rate increases and service reductions. With important opposition provided by the Association of American Railroads, Congress neglected to renew the office of Federal Coordinator when it expired in June of 1936.

In 1938, "official" policy moved to admit what had long been known, namely that general consolidation was impossible. President Roosevelt appointed two "semi-official" committees to recommend alternatives to the existing consolidation policy under the Transportation Act of 1920.[97] The Committee of Three, made up of Eastman and I.C.C. members Mahaffie and

Splawn, urged the elimination of the general consolidation plan of the Transportation Act of 1920, the appropriation of federal aid to carriers seeking to merge along lines approved by the I.C.C., the elimination of "destructive competition" between and among the varying types of carriers, and the expansion of Commission power as well as the creation of a Federal Transportation Authority to oversee all these matters. The Committee of Six, composed of three industry representatives and three members from the railroad brotherhoods, similarly called for the expansion of regulation of all types of transportation by the I.C.C. and the creation of a Transportation Board to supervise national affairs. It is noteworthy that both reports called for the expansion of Interstate Commerce Commission power while also requesting repeal of the general consolidation mandate of the 1920 act. Both reports urged the creation of what amounted to a "National Transportation Policy."[98]

Acting on the evidence provided by the committees and other experts, as well as President Roosevelt's personal recommendations, Congress, as we have noted, dealt with the problem of consolidation in a new Transportation Act, passed in May 1940. Under this legislation, proposals to "purchase lease, merge, consolidate or otherwise acquire control of rail properties" would be examined and approved or denied individually by the I.C.C. A new set of criteria was sketched for the Commission to use in reaching any decision:

> In passing upon any proposed transactions under the province of this paragraph (Sec. 2 Par. 5), the Commission shall give weight to the following considerations among others: (1) the effect of the proposed transaction upon adequate transportation service to the public; (2) the effect upon the public interest of the inclusion, or the failure to include, other railroads in the territory involved in proposed transaction; (3) the total fixed charges resulting from the proposed transaction; and (4) the interest of the carrier's employees affected.[99]

As noted earlier, the 1940 Act called for expanded I.C.C. authority and urged the creation of a national transportation policy, but it also eliminated what the railroads had considered the most onerous aspect of national planning — a general consolidation plan. In effect, the act went a long way in assuring that initiative for any national transportation planning would

continue to reside with the individual roads. The best comment
the A.A.R. could offer with regard to the general consolidation
plan was that it had been only "...an irridescent dream...
fine as an ideal... but absolutely impractical in its application."[100] This was surely a considerable understatement of the
industry's opposition to the general plan, for while a national
consolidation plan might have been only a dream, it had seemed
to have a nightmarish potential for taking control of the railroad network from the railroads themselves. The Transportation
Act of 1940 promised to remove that threat.

The Railroads Turn to Abandonment

The physical network of American railroads changed little
during the 1920's. Between 1921 and 1930, the net decline in
mainline trackage amounted to less than 4500 miles, and the
total I.C.C. approved abandonments of all types of trackage
amounted to about 8000 miles. Geographically, New England,
the southern states, and the southwest accounted for most of
the outright abandonments during this period. In the trunk
line territory, there were comparatively few discontinuances, and,
in the case of New York State, much of the abandoned trackage was accounted for by the closing down of old mining and
milling operations in remote areas.[101] Abandonments in the
eastern states, except in the case of the abandonments of un-
successful interurban and suburban electric railroads, did not
represent important functional changes in rail transportation or
new directions for management policy. Although there was
increased discussion within the industry on what to do with
operations which were clearly excess capacity, Frank H. Dixon,
a well-known contemporary student of the railroads, asserted
that "abandonment mileage mostly reflected abandonment of
roads built for temporary use." [102]

Nevertheless, even modest reductions of trackage evoked some
official and public concern. Albert B. Cummins, author of the
1920 Transportation Act, argued before a meeting of the eastern
railroad presidents that "scrapping the 'lame duck' roads is a
blow to the country."[103] Cummins doubtless echoed some
official opinion in suggesting that some of the "lame ducks"
could and should be revitalized if railroad management so
desired. Meanwhile, the American Short Line Railroad Assoc-

iation urged federal action to keep rural property values from being "destroyed and the people ruined" by the abandonment of feeder lines.[104]   For many Americans the reported fact that annual abandonments exceeded new annual construction in the rail industry was incomprehensible.[105]   Without much effort to evaluate the causes for abandonment, much nostalgia was evoked about the impending end for the railroads, since they had apparently begun a slow but steady trek downhill. Periodically through the 1920's the *Railway Age* featured articles on abandoned lines, which contributed little to understanding the causes of abandonment and greatly overemphasized its actual importance at that time.

The Transportation Act of 1920 had placed the abandonment of trackage under I.C.C. control, stating:

> ... no carrier by railroad subject to this part shall abandon all or any portion of a line of railroad, or the operation thereof, unless and until there shall first have been obtained from the Commission a certificate that the present or future public convenience or necessity permit such abandonments.[106]

Previously, control of abandonments had been reserved for the states, where they were dealt with by regulatory commissions or by the courts.[107]   In general, the state commissions, acting in the interests of local shippers or affected communities within the state rather than in the interest of absentee railroad corporations, tended to decide against abandonments.[108]   But, whatever the bias of the state commissions, abandonments did not become an important issue until after their control had passed officially to the Interstate Commerce Commission. With the passage of the 1920 act, the I.C.C. was supreme in this area, and while state commissions were permitted to present evidence at hearings and initiate action to deny the abandonment, the I.C.C. could reverse the state's decisions. The supremacy of the I.C.C. was noted by Sharfman:

> Although abandonments are frequently restricted by railroad charters and are subject to the jurisdiction of many of the state commissions, the new provisions of the Transportation Act of 1920 make it mandatory on the carrier to secure prior approval of the I.C.C.; and where the continuance of the service is likely to burden interstate

commerce, the Commission may authorize the abandonment even in contravention of the jurisdiction and judgment
of the state authorities.[109]

The accession of I.C.C. authority over abandonments naturally
had the general approval of the railroads. Not only did it set
up national standards for measuring and determining the need
to abandon, but the I.C.C. was generally understood to be more
sympathetic on the whole question. However, abandonments
were not very frequent in the 1920's, and the potential clash
between state and federal authorities on this issue was deferred
to a later time. In New York, total abandonments of all kinds
during this period amounted to only about 200 miles, with net
loss in trackage totaling only 100 miles. Eastern railroads were
then preoccupied with the consolidation provisions of the Transportation Act which sought to eliminate the problems of excess
capacity through the merger of the weak roads with strong ones
rather than through their abandonment.

Following the general economic collapse after 1930 and the
failure of the consolidation movement, abandonment became an
increasingly common device for dealing with excess capacity.
Most eastern lines had considerable stretches of road that had
not paid their way for as long as fifteen years. The increased
pressures from declining revenues and rising costs over the
whole road very often dictated that unprofitable segments be
cut off. In the case of some roads that were weak over the
entire length of their operations, hope of being bailed out by
merger was replaced by a fear that only outright abandonment
of the system was the solution. The sudden increase of abandonments after 1930, therefore, was not the result simply of
depression-induced traffic declines. More frequently, it was the
forced resolution of old and lingering economic problems that
had been hidden from view by the flamboyant merger activity
of the twenties.

In many respects the case of New York railroads during the
1930's was unique. Although abandonments did increase in the
state, the proportion of mileage abandoned was well below the
national average. Between 1921 and 1946, 33,514 miles of
mainline were abandoned in the United States, or about 13.3
percent of 1921 trackage. In New York, only about 10 percent of the 1921 base was abandoned.[110]   With the exception

TABLE 8

ABANDONED MAINLINE MILEAGE IN NEW YORK STATE
AND THE UNITED STATES,
1930-1943[a]

Year	United States		New York State
1930	694		—
1931	795		37
1932	1,452		58
1933	1,896		4
1934	1,995		31
1935	1,843		31
1936	1,523		57
1937	1,140		29
1938	1,783		201
1939	1,897		51
1940	1,299		61
1941	1,509		1
1942	1,516		59
1943	1,096		12

[a] *Railway Age*, Vol. 116, January 1, 1944, pp. 112-114.

of two abandonments in 1938, one of sixty-two miles and one of fifty-seven miles, none affected long stretches of track.[111]

Nevertheless, New York railroads were not without serious operating problems. The Rutland, the Lehigh Valley, and the Lackawanna were especially hard pressed. By 1935, the Rutland reported a net income of only $86,000 to cover taxes and fixed charges of $650,000.[112]   Talk of abandonment of the entire line was rife in the north country press, and even the *Wall Street Journal* reported that all efforts had failed to resuscitate the road and that the end looked near.[113]   The observation proved correct as the road went into receivership, but the end did not come until 1962.

Typical of the decision to trim excess capacity, the New York Central sought I.C.C. approval to close a number of loss-producing spurs. In 1937, it abandoned its sixty-two mile-long Tupper Lake-Helena line, formerly the property of the old New York and Ottawa. Some indication of the problem of excess capacity as it was viewed by the railroads was given in the Central's calculation that the road serviced communities with an aggregate population of only 3100 people. Moreover, the road generated revenues of only $17,000 while paying taxes in Franklin County alone of $11,000. The I.C.C. was convinced that the $76,400 loss in 1935 was sufficient to permit abandonment.[114]

The following year the Central was allowed to close a thirty-three mile section between Canadaigua and Caledonia after showing that the 2200 people in the affected communities all had access to surfaced highways.[115] Similarly, the Lehigh Valley was permitted to abandon a twenty-one mile stretch of track between Canastota and Camden, when the road proved that all communities were serviced by "good roads."[116]

The closing of the New York and Pennsylvania in 1936 was the only complete abandonment of a fairly large railroad. With investment of somewhat more than $1,000,000, the fifty-seven mile road in Steuben and Allegany Counties in New York and Potter and McKenna Counties in Pennsylvania was a good example of a chronically weak line. It had earned profits only briefly after its construction in 1896. In 1917 it discontinued passenger service, and by 1935, it carried only 34,513 tons of freight, none of which originated on the route.[117]

With control of abandonments in the hands of the Interstate Commerce Commission, state regulatory authorities were powerless to oppose abandonment plans of the railroads. Even in areas where the Public Service Commission felt that it reserved power, as in the case of the abandonment of the Jamestown Westfield and Northwestern, an electric railroad operating wholly within the state, with little traffic originating or terminating in interstate movement, the Public Service Commission's decision was contested by the I.C.C.. In this case the Public Service Commission's denial of abandonment was set aside by the national agency which argued that even if the road was electric and operated wholly within the state, its service was not materially different than steam roads covered by Section 1 of the Transportation Act of 1920.[118] The effect of this decision was a clear assertion of federal authority in all types of route abandonment.

The attitude of the New York Public Service Commissioners was not unlike that of regulative authorities in other states.

Almost instinctively, abandonment was looked upon as undesire-able. Yet the inflexible opposition to abandonment was not simply a function of protecting regional interests. Chairman Milo Maltbie of the New York commission had frequently pointed out that no abandonment could be decided upon out-side of the context of the petitioning road's total operations. The Commission's position was perhaps best explained in its 1945 report:

> In the case of railroad abandonments under the authority of the Interstate Commerce Commission, *public convenience and necessity* does not, for the most part, appear to be the major consideration. In case after case, the federal com-mission has permitted the abandonment of track and facil-ities upon a showing by the railroads that a line, or a part of it, proposed to be abandoned is unprofitable. The New York Commission is opposed to this principle as the sole basis for discontinuance of rail service.[119]

The Commission held that segments of roads which were unprofitable might still be operated by reallocation of profits earned elsewhere. Since railroads were virtually a protected public monopoly, the commissioners maintained they could be expected to render service as required not just as it happened to be profitable. The argument rested on the assumption that social benefits from rail operations were not best measured by profit-loss accounting. With regard to how an evaluation of comparative benefits to communities and to railroads could best be calculated, the Public Service Commission argued for regional control over regional railroad matters:

> The position of this commission was stated fully in 1944 by Chairman Maltbie before a United States Senate Committee in connection with proposed legislation to change the power of the Interstate Commerce Commission in this respect.... He declared that lines which render purely in-trastate service should be left to state commissions having jurisdiction because such bodies are in a better position to determine the need for continuation of local and branch lines. He also took exception to the Interstate Commerce Commission practice of allowing discontinuance of a rail-road on a mere showing by the company that a local line is in whole or in part unprofitable, and he urged that the federal commission should make findings based upon its own investigation rather than on the claims made by railroads.[120]

While the Public Service Commission had lost control over abandonments, it retained authority over service curtailment until 1958, when state regulative control of any kind was practically abolished. In particular, the Commission had authority to authorize reductions in rail service or allied station operations. While the existence of the Commission's power in this area probably served to inhibit the railroads' requests for curtailment of service, it should be noted that the state commission did exhibit concern for rail operating problems. Between 1931 and 1945, the Commission received 484 petitions for the abandonment or reduction of station agency services. In general, the petitions reflected the decline of "less-than-carload" freight and the dwindling of traffic at the little stations which were located about every seven to ten miles along the mainline. Only fifty-six petitions were denied by the Commission while it approved the closing of 152 stations, the ending of freight agency service at 168 points, and the cessation of less-than-carload freight operations at 108 stations.[121] When, in the late forties and early fifties, the railroads attempted to bring about drastic reductions in scheduled freight and passenger service, the Public Service Commission became more recalcitrant. However, in the thirties, aside from its ineffectual opposition to abandonments the Public Service Commission posed no real threat to rail management.

An Evaluation of the Thirties

To understand the meaning of the thirties, it is necessary to go back briefly and reconsider the development of railroad policy since the beginning of the century. Initially, it will be recalled, the railroads had understood their problems as largely temporary. Excess capacity and its constant threat of competition, as well as excessive capitalization, were seen as eventually disappearing in an expected general increase in traffic demand. Until that time, however, rail corporate policy was understood to require a high degree of intercorporate agreement and cooperation, largely to forestall sudden competitive flurries. To some extent, the general consolidation provisions of the Transportation Act of 1920 had seemed to be a concession to railroad attitudes toward competition, but the general merger plan was doomed for a number of reasons. First of all, it never resolved to the railroads' satisfaction the "weak road-strong road" problem of a general railroad consolidation. Second, neither the Transportation Act nor the I.C.C. in the 1920's really conceded to the railroads their point about the need to eliminate competition within the industry. And third, the prosperity of the twenties simply reduced the urgency of the problem from the railroad point of view.

The thirties, however, brought a return of crisis to the industry. As demand for rail transportation fell, the degree of under-utilization or excess capacity grew and the old problem of excessive capitalization returned. However, these problems were now quite different than before. Through both intercorporate agreement and regulatory policy, a return of price competition within the industry was no longer possible and thus not a problem; but, with the rise of competition from trucks, busses and autos and easily apparent shifts in product demand, no one seriously held any longer that total transportation demand would rise to validate the physical and financial proportions of the rail network as it now existed.

The new situation the railroads argued, demanded a new policy. Emphasis within the industry shifted from attempts to create financial empires as a brake against competition to forging new instruments of intercorporate managerial agreement. Indeed, within a very few years the Association of American Railroads became the real locus of corporate policy-making power. With regard to government regulation the railroads at first urged and then demanded that the federal government act to protect the industry, and the companies were not to be disappointed. "Public Interest" criteria for government action shifted from any pretended concern for shippers and consumers to a policy of simply keeping the railroads going. Rather than using the depression as a pretext for coerced mergers or nationalization of the railroads, federal transportation policy became quite permissive and supportive of the industry. It should be noted that even in the depths of the depression, there was never substantial opinion on the Interstate Commerce Commission, or in the Roosevelt Administration, which would have supported a position on consolidation, or any other matter, which was seriously opposed by the industry. The government policy was, of course, not a very dramatic shift since the railroads had never been seriously challenged by federal regulation and legislation anyway; but, now, they sought and received a long list of government supports.

Railroads received substantial amounts of financial aid for operating improvements. They were encouraged to develop a solid "industry-wide" policy on rates and service and they were permitted to pool. Their trucking competitors were placed under stronger federal regulation; and, the old bugaboo, "competition," was gradually removed from the vocabulary of the I.C.C. in most of its dealings with the roads, although its complete elimination did not come until the sixties. Meanwhile, the old general consolidation plan was abandoned and the individual roads were encouraged to merge as they saw fit.

This was the "new policy," then, that was emerging by the end of the depression. It called for greater intra-industry cooperation and greater government support in developing this cooperation. It demanded that the federal government and the I.C.C. become part of the firms' own policymaking process. It was, of course, not a "new policy" at all; but a logical and rational extension of ideas developed by Morgan and others before the turn of the century and generally accepted by the industry ever since.

The thirties had taught a further lesson to the rail industry which it gradually absorbed and soon incorporated as a leading component of policy. This was the view that excess capacity within individual railroads as well as for the industry could in the future be dealt with only by abandonment or curtailment of service. The illusion of an eventually expanded demand for service which would economically justify all rail operations was finally rejected. However, the conditions for abandoning this excess capacity, the measurements to be accepted in determining what was essential and what wasn't, naturally remained, from the industry's perspective, their decision alone to make. Indeed, this issue was to become the dominant policy question in railroad affairs after the depression and the war.

V

NEW YORK RAILROADS AND
NATIONAL RAILROAD DECLINE
AFTER WORLD WAR II, 1941-1958

As the title of this chapter indicates, it was to become more difficult after World War II to separate an understanding of the operations of particular companies or of railroads in a particular region from national developments. This is not to say that corporate or regional distinctiveness ceased to exist or was irrelevant. Whatever the aggregate statistical picture of American railroads, there remained a wide variety of individual operating situations. For instance, throughout this period, operating problems among eastern railroads were much worse than those in other areas of the nation. However, two important developments shifted the railroads' problem to an almost exclusively national dimension. First, the industry itself became increasingly centralized in terms of policy origination through the expanded influence of the Association of American Railroads. Second, governmental response to the railroads' economic problems, through new legislation and regulation, came almost entirely from the federal level.

The Development of an "Industry Policy"
During and After World War II

The creation and development of the Association of American Railroads in the 1930's provided the industry for the first time with an effective instrument of national policy-making.

The expansion of the Association's role as spokesman for American railroads was largely to shift railroad action on such matters as financial policy, railroad regulation, and miscellaneous operating problems away from purely regional or individual corporate undertakings to an industry-wide level of policy making. For the purposes of this study of the New York railroad network, therefore, it is necessary to digress briefly to look at the development of A.A.R. policy during and after World War II. Such a survey provides a general framework for understanding particular developments among New York railroads.

The Second World War placed sudden and enormous burdens on American railroads. In early 1941, a public opinion survey reported that about 50 percent of Americans, many apparently recalling the breakdown of the railroads in World War I, favored government operation in the event of war.[1] However, the railroads responded fairly well to the increased war traffic. Between 1939 and 1944, the wartime peak, freight movement grew from 900,000,000 tons originated to 1.6 billion tons, and passenger traffic was twice that of 1918.[2] The burden placed upon the eastern roads, both the trunks and the coal carriers, was especially heavy, and railroads operating in New York State reported carrying about 1 billion tons of freight in 1943, or about two-thirds of that originated in the United States.

To a large extent the "two front" nature of the war placed less stress on the rail network. With war materials moving both east and west, the demand for cars and yard service was more evenly distributed, and the backlog of loaded and unloaded cars which had jammed rail yards around eastern ports during World War I was avoided. Under the direction of Joseph Eastman, appointed by President Roosevelt to head the newly-created Office of Defense Transportation, a high degree of operational coordination was achieved.[3] Eastman, who as an Interstate Commerce Commissioner and Emergency Coordinator of Transportation had been a frequent antagonist of rail management, now enjoyed considerable private cooperation in working with the Association of American Railroads. Quite unlike World War I, industry leaders remained laudatory of government wartime intervention. However, given the public's willingness to accept government operation at the beginning of the war and the fact that much doubt existed about the railroads' capacity to respond to war demands, the maintenance of private operations might have been viewed as a significant concession to the industry. The effect of the decision to keep the railroads under private control was not lost on the Association of American Railroads. The Association maintained close ties with the Office of Defense Transportation and received numerous commendations from President Roosevelt.[4] In a very significant way, the war provided the Association with the official sanction of which it was to make good use later. At the same time, the war effort's demands for coordination among the carriers added more evidence to the old case against maintaining intra-industry competition.

To be technically accurate, it should be noted that the railroads were briefly nationalized from December 27, 1943, to January 18, 1944, when labor trouble threatened to impede the shipment of war materials. However, the roads still remained under private management's control, and the brief intervention, in fact, drew praise from the A.A.R. and rail management.[5] Although the eventual wage settlement which was granted was subsequently attacked by the industry as being "inflationary" an almost *pro forma* reaction, the exercise of federal authority against labor unions, in forcing the workers back to their jobs, was undoubtedly refreshing to management.[6] The precedent of federal intervention to maintain rail operations in the face of labor troubles was to be recalled later when the industry began its systematic attack on what it termed "featherbedding."

The war period brought a welcome respite from the economic problems of the 1930's. Between 1939 and 1944, total operating revenues rose from slightly under $4,000,000,000 to $9,500,-000,000. While costs generally advanced during the war, particularly labor charges, which doubled, and taxes, which expanded by 500 percent, net railway operating revenues reached almost $1,500,000,000 by 1943,[7] However, looking at national aggregates only is misleading. As a rule, eastern railroads shared to a lesser degree in these gains. Operating revenues for roads running in New York lagged behind the national average, and the rate of growth of net operating income was about half that of the national performance.

Of special significance during the war years was the change in railroad financial policies. In the past, increases in net income resulting from improvements in business conditions often had been seen as a source for immediate profit-taking. This had been the case immediately preceding World War I when the railroads, especially eastern railroads, limited road and equipment improvements to meet their high fixed charges and still provide ample dividends. Again in the 1920's, mergers and speculation siphoned off large amounts of earned surplus without improving physical property. However, earnings accumulated during World War II were not so hungrily appropriated for dividends or speculative and financial maneuvers. Instead, the railroads sought to apply earnings to the reduction of fixed charges.

It is difficult to account for the origination of these new, mainly conservative financial policies. Quite probably they reflected the virtual disappearance of the speculative rail promoter and the rise of managerial specialists in the creation of railroad policy. The depression had created much anguish over the debt structure of American railroads. In the past, debt had been looked upon as more or less permanent, to be refunded rather than repaid. Morgan's earlier efforts at railroad reorganization had been aimed at eliminating the more obnoxious debts, but even the roads he reorganized remained heavily indebted. So long as traffic and revenues stayed reasonably high, the debt obligations were not bothersome; however, general business downturns usually pointed out that most roads simply had more debt than they could carry. In the depression years, as revenues fell below what had earlier been considered possible, the squeeze applied by the necessity of covering fixed charges eliminated, first, investment in road and equipment and, then, profits. By 1938, as noted earlier, twenty-eight Class I railroads failed to pay their fixed charges.[8] In July of 1938, thirty-nine Class I railroads, amounting to 75,000 miles of track and $5,000,000,000 in investment were in receivership.

By the late 1930's, the A.A.R., with the approval of the Interstate Commerce Commission, began to urge railroads to reduce their debts.[9] The Commission's concern had come about almost entirely as a result of the depression experience. Not until 1933, had the Commission required the railroads to establish sinking funds for debt retirement on new bond issues.[10] Like the management of the roads, the I.C.C. had earlier accepted the permanence of funded debt.

The increased earnings of the railroads during the war years afforded a unique opportunity to reduce indebtedness and, with pressure applied by the A.A.R. and some banking houses, the railroads began to apply substantial parts of their earnings to debt reduction. Most roads resisted temptations to dip into their suddenly acquired wealth, although eastern railroads seemed generally to pay out larger dividends. Of $3,400,000,000 in net income earned between 1941 and 1945 by all American rail-roads, only $1,000,000,000 was paid out to stockholders. At the same time, long-term debt was reduced by about $2,000,000,000, or 20 percent.[11] As a result, fixed charges fell from about $444,000,000 annually in 1940 to $364,000,000 in 1945.[12]

The refunding operations mostly drew acclaim — although a few debt holders objected. Railroad credit was thought to be improved, and, by reducing fixed charges, it was hoped that the industry could avoid any repetition of the bankruptcies of the 1930's even if post-war economic conditions reverted to depression. In the years immediately following the war, the railroads began to make larger dividend payments, and, by 1948, almost 70 percent of all railroads payed some dividends. Of these, the rate of return averaged 5.2 percent.[13] Again, aggregates are concealing. The record of eastern railroads remained disappointing. In 1952, with railroads operating in New York State accounting for almost 30 percent of all United States railroad investment, their dividend payments were only 8 percent of the national total.

The accumulation of surpluses, aside from reflecting the war generated rise in traffic, was aided by changes in government tax-credit and depreciation policy. The Association of American Railroads had begun to argue early in the war for depreciation credit against taxes. The railroads held that the accelerated use of the railroad plant and equipment was not adequately accounted for by the present taxes. John Pelley, President of the A.A.R., set out the case, stating:

> To a considerable extent...the apparent earnings of the railroads are due to the fact that war conditions compel them to postpone maintenance and repair work which can be put off until after the war.... The I.C.C. has recognized the fact and has authorized railroads to treat as current operating expense the maintenance work which normally would be done now...but which cannot be done because

> of difficulties in securing materials and labor, by setting
> up now reserve funds to do the work eventually....
>   However, possibilities along this line are slight in view
> of the present state of the Internal Revenue laws, which
> still regard these deferred expenses as if they were truly a
> current profit. Any funds set aside...would be subject to
> income taxes, amounting to not less than 40 percent and
> as much as 81 percent. [14]

Pelley hoped that "this situation will be corrected at the present session of Congress."[15] However, a bill which would have
given special tax-credit to the railroads for deferred investment
did not pass the House until 1945, then only to be defeated
in the Senate. Nevertheless, I.C.C. interpretations of existing
general legislation permitted the railroads to more than double
maintenance of equipment depreciation between 1944 and 1945,
raising this total to $1,186,644,437.[16] By comparison, with
only slightly smaller book value, railroads claimed only $193,-
000,000 in depreciation in 1934. Further changes and adjustments in the Internal Revenue laws provided a Federal tax
reduction of 75 percent in 1945 and produced a net tax credit
for railroads of $12,000,000 in 1946.[17] The liberalizing of tax
credits had been less than what the industry asked for, but,
along with the general increase in revenues during the war
years, railroads, especially eastern railroads, entered the post-
war period in perhaps the best financial condition they had
ever enjoyed.

The A.A.R.'s position on railroad finances remained basically
conservative after the end of the war in 1945, advocating the
tightening of the debt structure as the best protection against
possible deterioration in earnings. In particular, the tighter financial approach meant the continued reduction of fixed charges
through debt retirement and the financing of new capital investment out of retained earnings. With the bankruptcy ex-
periences of the thirties and the wartime accomplishments with
regard to debt reduction as evidence, the I.C.C. also endorsed
these conservative financial policies of the railroads. As a result, railroads practically ceased to look for new funds in
capital markets. Although nearly $2,000,000,000 in equipment
obligations were assumed by the railroads between 1945 and
1960, mostly to pay for "dieselization," these were obtained
at relatively low cost due to the companies' improved credit.[18]

Moreover, the issuance of these debt instruments was offset by the almost equivalent reduction in other long-term debt. The book value of American railroads grew about 30 percent between 1940 and 1960, but the corresponding increase of corporate surplus from about 10 percent of book value in 1940 to 35 percent in 1960 reflected the roads' increased reliance on internal financing.

Railroad policies toward public regulation as formulated and presented by the A.A.R. were mostly extensions of positions developed in the late thirties. The prospect of increased competition from vehicular transportation loomed large, and the railroads sought to gain a measure of protection through favorable governmental regulation. In the eastern states, where the most developed highway systems were in operation and where important short haul rail traffic was especially threatened, rail management was most vigorous in proposing new public transportation policies which would insulate the railroads from other transportation competition. President Clement of the Pennsylvania observed in 1945:

> ...they (the railroads) will be able to meet the effects of reconversion if an understanding public, through its legislative and regulative authorities, permits them to have a fair opportunity to do so.
>
> The country's vast system of airways, highways and waterways will be expanded at the government's expense, while all of the improvements for the railroads will be privately financed. The problems with which the railroads are faced as a result of the war should have intelligent consideration by state and national authorities whenever regulation restrains the opportunity for railroads to move forward.
>
> The railroads want no subsidy; they want equity. They are a heavily taxed industry competing with subsidized industries and all they ask is equality of opportunity.[19]

Clement's ideas were embraced and expanded in an important position paper issued by the Association of American Railroads in 1947. In this report, the Association pronounced what was to be the industry's basic policy toward public regulation for at least the next decade. Now, two years after the war, the worst fears about declining revenues and increased competition were being realized. Income for 1946 was 10 percent below that of 1944.[20] As a redirection of public policy which would supposedly halt the deterioration of rail earnings, the Association's position paper called for: 1) more rigorous rate regulation of competing transport modes, 2) the cessation of "subsidies" to these modes, 3) more liberal use of abandonments and privately initiated consolidations to effect reductions in uneconomic excess capacity, and 4) the guaranteeing of "fair" returns on railroad investment in the Interstate Commerce Commission's rate-setting policies.[21] The latter proposal also assumed that the roads would be able to administer their own rates through regional rate setting bureaus. In general, the proposals picked up where the Transportation Act of 1940 and the war had ended discussion seven years before.

Pointing out that the building of publicly owned highways placed heavy burdens on the private railroads, the A.A.R. offered its own justification for equity:

> Subsidies are essentially undemocratic.... It is said that the railroads were subsidized in the early days by grants of public land and the answer is that these were not gifts but contracts, under which the government obtained reduced rates for three quarters of a century, and under which the values of the lands have been repaid many times over.[22]

The Association then argued for the ending of subsidy to other forms of transportation and for the increase of regulative authority over these modes' rates and service. At the same time, it requested that public regulation of transportation should permit the railroads to develop their own "inter-modal" transportation operations. The paper argued:

> The studies indicate rather clearly that our transportation situation would be greatly improved if instead of having railroad, airline, motor carrier, and water carrier companies, we had, instead, transportation companies, authorized and able to furnish to any shipper that particular class of service which the exigiencies of his business demand. Such a privilege would not permit the continued operation of independently owned railroads, trucks, busses, airplanes and vessels. But the function of these general transportation companies, under public regulation, would provide a pattern for economic operation that would tend to restrict each

form to the field in which experience has shown that it really belongs.[23]

The proposal may have appeared novel at first glance, but it was little more than an attempt to expand the concept of a non-competitive, regulated railroad industry to a larger non-competitive but regulated transportation industry. From a point of view considering efficient resource use only, the idea had much appeal and has continued to receive support from many professional economists.[24] Despite the boldness of the proposal and the fact that no legislation was forthcoming that would have facilitated intermodal transportation companies, the idea failed mostly because the railroads continued to face declining earnings and tighter financial situations which, they felt, prohibited costly experimentation with new transportation ideas. Nevertheless, the idea persisted, and, in a special federal transportation study prepared in 1960, it received important endorsement.[25]

On the question of railroad earnings, the Association pointed out that the depressed condition of returns on investment, which averaged only 2.74 percent on invested capital in 1946, had tended to make rail securities unattractive and had handicapped the roads in obtaining capital needed for "dieselization," and the rebuilding of war-induced equipment deterioration.[26] While the argument may have been persuasive, it was not entirely accurate. Although rail securities continued to remain rather depressed, at least in comparison to the large number of industries which were expanding in the post-war boom, the railroads were able to obtain very large amounts of equipment loans at low cost. Since the A.A.R. still urged the railroads to reduce their capital stock and debt structure, concern for the relative position of rail securities in capital markets was certainly not based upon projections of a capital expansion program to be financed externally. In fact, the depressed condition of rail securities had been of much help in the railroads' own refunding programs.

The low rate of return on investment, whatever its effect on rail security prices and their impact in turn upon the railroads' capital position, was mostly a source of irritation because it was less than what the railroads had come to accept as "reasonable." Pointing out that the now suspended Valuation Act of 1913 had specified that 6 percent was a "fair" return

of investment, the A.A.R. paper noted that American railroads averaged more than that figure in only one year since
1920 (6.3 percent in 1942). [27] The Association stated unequivi-
cally that the "industry desires a *guaranteed* return of 6 percent." [28] Clearly, the Association meant that it was the function
of the I.C.C. or the legislative authorities to adjust rates, permit economies, and regulate competition so that railroad earnings
would be assured.

At the same time, public policy toward consolidation was to
continue along the lines laid down in the Transportation Act
of 1940, with the railroads initiating mergers and the I.C.C.
validating them. According to the Association:

> The Transportation Act of 1940 calls for no consolidation
> plan nor any administrative agency to organize such a
> plan. The I.C.C. will act on each proposal submitted by
> the interested companies. The railroad industry favors the
> voluntary rather than compulsory consolidation.[29]

The report continued that, with the I.C.C.'s indulgence, "we
may confidently expect that, as financial and commercial conditions permit, the consolidation process will continue."[30]

While setting out these policy aims, it was also evident to
the A.A.R. that it had begun to encounter serious criticism
of its position as an industry coordinator. The urgency for dealing with the railroads, or any industry, in the manner which
had been acceptable in the days of the early New Deal seemed
less apparent in the general business upswing of the forties.
Accordingly, the Association sought to make permanent what
critics claimed was only a provisional monopoly power.

As pointed out in the last chapter, both the Federal government and the state of Georgia had initiated anti-trust actions against the industry. At issue was the concept of in-
dustry-operated rate bureaus, a procedure which had its roots
in Morgan's "community of interest" and which had developed
during the depression and war with I.C.C. approval. The rate
bureaus permitted single price settings in various traffic origination areas.[31] That such industry price setting be continued
was crucial to the railroads, for the destruction of this concept
could mean a return to a crude price competition. Accordingly,
the position paper cited the "undeniable urgency" for exempting
railroads from the general anti-trust laws. Meanwhile, in pur-

suit of ameliorative legislation which would have granted the railroads permission to operate rate bureaus, the A.A.R. carried on a spectacular lobbying program in Congress.

The overall effect of the 1947 position paper left little doubt as to the industry's attitude toward public regulation. In brief, it rested on the assumption that the Federal government in its legislative and regulative actions must be committed to a policy of keeping the railroads going — and going on terms acceptable to the industry. The response to the Association's statement of policy must be calculated as considerably less than what the industry desired. However, the government position cannot be counted as hostile. As discussed in Chapter IV, the lobbying activities of the A.A.R. and allied pressure groups were effective in gaining passage of the Reed-Bulwinkle Act. The act permitted common carriers of the same class (i.e. railroads) to make agreement on rates subject to I.C.C. approval.[32] In effect, this meant that the I.C.C. could suspend application of anti-trust laws as it saw fit. The act, therefore, placed more discretionary power in the hands of the I.C.C., while granting to the railroads the privilege of exemption from anti-trust action. The passage of the act must be counted as a great legislative gain, especially since the railroads were able to mount enough Congressional support to eventually override a Presidential vote. President Truman, of course, had never been considered a railroad ally, having served on the old Wheeler Committee in the Senate, which had opposed much pro-railroad legislation in the late 1930's.

With regard to their requests for rate adjustments to assure "reasonable" returns, the railroads had some success. After granting two general freight rate hikes, the I.C.C. approved an increase in passenger fares in the east in 1949 which raised fares to the highest levels in their history. By 1957, rate increases of more than 100 percent of their pre-war levels had been granted by the Commission.[33] To the railroads, however, the actions were tardy and inadequate, lagging well behind what the industry considered acceptable.

On the question of abandonments, the I.C.C. remained favorbly disposed to railroad requests. On abandonment petitions received after World War II, the I.C.C. acted affirmatively on 85 percent of the requests of "public convenience and necessity."[34] Commission attitudes toward consolidation proposals were, until the late fifties, less clear. Although it permitted a number of important mergers, it continued, to the irritation of rail industry, to interject criteria concerning the maintenance of inter-railroad competition.[35]

In making an overall evaluation of railroad corporate policy during the war and immediate post-war period, it is apparent that the railroads had obtained important gains from Federal legislative and regulative actions. The gains, however, were soon obscured by increased economic difficulties within the industry.

Changes in Demand for Railroad Transportation in the East

Martin Clement, President of the Pennsylvania Railroad, had observed at the close of World War II:

> Now that the war is over and the great job of handling troops and supplies is nearly done, the railroads can look back with satisfaction on having furnished every service they were called upon by their country to perform. . . . The railroads are a national necessity at all times. The greater the emergency, the greater the necessity. . . . As the railroads planned to meet the requirements of war, so they are planning for the opportunities of peace, and given a fair and equitable chance they will furnish the public the best in freight and passenger service.[36]

This hopefulness was quickly dashed. The return of peace meant, for the railroads, the return of the economic problems of the thirties, but with one important difference. Whereas the 1930's were illustrative of a general business depression with all industries suffering from stagnating demand, the post-war period was one of unprecedented economic growth in which the railroads shared very little. In the twelve years following the war, the American gross national product rose from $229 billion to $442.5 billion.[37] During this time, the real growth rate for the economy exceeded 3 percent and the industrial production index climbed 50 percent.[38]

For the railroads, the same years produced a steady operational decline. Between 1945 and 1957, freight traffic fell 12 percent. Total operating revenues climbed only 13 percent, well behind the consumer price index rise of 25 percent.[39] Overall, the demand for rail transportation was far below the increase in post-war demand for other goods and services.

Although it is practically impossible to measure the discrete effects of all of the factors affecting rail demand during this period, they may be generalized as three interrelated post-war developments: changes in rail transport demand due to the rise of competing transportation modes; changes in demand resulting from changes in consumer demand for products; and changes in rail transport demand due to shifts in the spatial distribution and intensity of economic activity.

The rise of auto, bus and truck traffic was felt by the railroads before World War I, with competition becoming stronger during the 1920's and the depression. Busses, passenger cars, and taxis operated in the United States grew from about 450,000 in 1910 to over 8,000,000 by 1920 and 23,000,000 by 1930. Trucks increased from under 10,000 in 1910 to 3,500,000 by 1930.[40] The ownership of motor vehicles in New York State proceeded at about the same rate as for the nation. With about 682,000 motor vehicles registered in 1920, New York had over 2.3 million in 1930 and 4.8 million in 1955.

The undesirable effect of this increase in motor vehicle ownership might have been even greater upon the railroads during the 1920's and 1930's if highway construction had paced their acquisition. As late as 1930, there were only 92,000 miles of heavy-duty surfaced highways in the United States. More than two-thirds of all rural mileage was not paved at all.[41] Although New York's record was somewhat better than most states, in 1930, more than 40 percent of the state's highways were still "unimproved".[42] In particular, the state lacked a well-developed inter-city highway system, and although Federal public works monies were available during the thirties, New York averaged less than 350 miles of state highway construction or rebuilding each year between 1933 and 1941.[43] Of this, only a small proportion represented the building of multi-lane or high-speed inter-city routes. While local governmental units improved about 12,000 miles of highways between 1935 and 1941, this chiefly affected short distance motor vehicle movement.[44] Nevertheless, the result of even such modest building programs was that during the 1930's motor vehicles began to compete quite favorably with railroads on short-haul transportation.

The first casualties to the motor vehicle were the numerous

suburban and interurban electric railroads. Most had been built in the decade and a half before World War I, and although they were a brilliant technological advance in high speed passenger transportation, the private motor car, especially as mass production lowered its price to within the range of most American's pocketbooks, was simply more attractive to most Americans.[45] It should be pointed out though that the "electrics" were in most cases handicapped by extremely heavy fixed charges, very often the result of financial mismanagement that surpassed even the excesses of steam railroad building.[46] New York steam railroads were only slightly involved in electric railroad operations with the Central and the Erie briefly operating interurbans.[47] Nevertheless, the financial collapse of most interurbans in the late 1920's and their disappearance in the depression was an ominous sign of things to come for railroads offering passenger or commuting service.[48]

As the following tables illustrate, the relative shift of passenger and freight movement to motor vehicles during the twenties and thirties in the United States was quite pronounced. Although the steam railroads suffered no absolute declines in freight traffic, the dwindling numbers of rail passengers paralleled the earlier experience of the interurban electric roads. Available data on the shift of commercial passengers, however, does not present the true dimensions the impact motor vehicular transportation had upon rail passenger traffic. In 1900, railroads moved 80 percent or more of all people moving between cities; however, by 1950, railroads and all other commercial transportation systems accounted for only 20 percent of all intercity passenger miles traveled. The comparative decline in commercial passenger movement was, of course, the result of expanded private motor car ownership and operation. By 1957, the Interstate Commerce Commission calculated that private automobile usage had grown to account for 88 percent of all inter-city passengers.[49]

The railroad losses in short haul freight shipment were apparent from the very beginnings of truck competition. All railroads felt these losses but they were especially burdensome to the small lateral lines. Continued competition and the general traffic decline in the thirties led a number of New York railroads to inaugurate affiliated truck operations to carry short distance, less-than-carload freight. By 1945, the Pennsylvania

TABLE 9

DISTRIBUTION OF INTERCITY FREIGHT MOVEMENT
IN PERCENT OF TON-MILES BY TYPE OF CARRIER,
1916-1960 [a]

Year	RRs	Motor	Water	Pipe	Total Ton-Miles (in Bill.)
1916	77	—	18	4	476
1930	74	4	16	5	524
1940	61	10	19	10	615
1945	67	6	14	12	1020
1950	56	16	15	12	1040
1955	49	17	17	16	1215
1960	43	22	17	17	1280

[a] United States, Interstate Commerce Commission, *Seventy-eighth Annual Report, 1964*, pp. 128-129.

TABLE 10

DISTRIBUTION OF INTER-CITY COMMERCIAL PASSENGER
TRAFFIC, 1916-1961[a] (IN BILLIONS OF PASSENGER MILES
AND PERCENT OF TOTAL)

	RRs		Inland Water		Bus		Air		Total No.
Year	No.	%	No.	%	No.	%	No.	%	Billion Pass.
1916	42	98	.5	2	—	—	—	—	43
1930	29	75.6	3	7.1	7	18.1	.07	.2	39
1940	25	67.1	1	3.6	10	26.5	1.0	2.8	37
1945	94	74.3	2	1.6	27	21.4	3.0	2.7	126
1950	33	46.3	1	1.7	26	37.7	10.0	14.3	70
1955	29	36.5	2	2.2	25	32.4	23.0	28.9	79
1957	26	31.9	3	2.4	25	30.6	29.0	35.1	82

[a] United States, Interstate Commerce Commission, *The Activities of the Inter-State Commerce Commission, 1937-1962*, pp. 128-129.

system reported operating about 9000 miles of scheduled truck service for less-than-carload lots and the New York Central operated slightly more than half this mileage with trucks.[50] However, the railroads' attempts to combat truck competition with their own truck services were not really successful. In the first place, many of the smaller roads, which were most seriously threatened by trucks, could not finance their own truck operations. And, while the larger lines' shifts to trucks may have provided a competitive weapon against the truckers, it did not solve any of the excess capacity problems of their rail operations. At any rate, the railroads' use of trucks did not halt the shift of more commodities and more business to truckers.

One important commodity which was lost by eastern railroads to truck transportation was milk. In 1920, New York railroads collected more than $14,000,000 from milk shipment.[51] While for the New York Central, milk movement accounted for only about 1.5 percent of its total earnings, the New York Ontario and Western and the Rutland derived more than 11 percent of their total revenue from this commodity and seven other small roads depended upon milk shipment to produce between 11 and 25 percent of their income.[52] By 1950, milk revenues for New York railroads had fallen to less than $7,000,000. During the next decade milk revenues practically ceased and the smaller New York railroads lost an important revenue source that could not be replaced.

The war years briefly inhibited the growth of motor vehicle transportation. Shortages of gasoline, tires, and vehicles and curtailment of road construction and maintenance temporarily arrested the railroads' competitive decline. However, by 1950, faced with a highway system which was calculated to be "50 percent structurally deficient," the State of New York launched a massive road building program aimed at constructing and rebuilding 15,000 miles of roads during the next fifteen years.[54] The 1950 plan called for the eventual spending of $3,000,000,000 with $976,000,000 allocated to the first state building of a "state thruway." The report made no calculation of the effects that such a road building program might have on the railroads, and its tone clearly indicated a new public commitment to road building. The State's Department of Public Works officially reported:

State Highways are everybody's highways. It is apparent
that the value of the benefits derived by all the residents of
the state from an adequate State Highway System will
greatly exceed the cost.... The state cannot afford again
to neglect its highways and the fact that the rehabilitation
is so definitely justified, both from the standpoint of economic need and financial return, merely emphasizes the
necessity of taking positive action now.[55]

Such enormous subsidies to competing transportation modes
were pictured as unfair by the railroads. As railroad earnings
sagged, the industry increasingly laid the blame upon the government subsidized road building programs. Before a Senate
Investigating Committee in 1957, President Alfred Perlman of
the New York Central testified that the Central's passenger
earnings had fallen 23 percent the year before, when the New
York State Thruway opened.[56] To Perlman, this loss in passenger revenue was almost exclusively a function of high speed
motor vehicle traffic encouraged by the state's highway building.

Another important element in the post-war changes of demand for rail transportation were the changes in the composi-
tion of industrial and consumer demand. In general, the rising
level of national income and the steady growth of population
meant increased demand for most products. As noted above,
however, railroads shared modestly or not at all in the expansion of demand. Moreover, certain products carried by
rail showed either relative or absolute declines in demand, and
in the case of one such product, coal, most eastern railroads
suffered serious revenue losses as a result.

The declining demand for anthracite and bituminous coal
posed special problems for the eastern railroads. Coal had long
been the most important freight revenue source for many New
York railroads. The search for profits in the transportation and
marketing of coal had been an important stimulant to much
of the railroad building in the eastern states in the 1870's and
1880's, and control of anthracite coal and the creation of
stability in the anthracite industry and among its carriers had
been a primary consideration in Morgan's building of community
of interest among the eastern railroads. For such roads as the
Pennsylvania, the Central, the Lackawanna, the Erie, the Delaware and Hudson and the Lehigh Valley, anthracite and bit-

uminous coal movement up to the late 1940's more or less
consistently accounted for about a quarter or more of all
freight revenues earned.

The phenomenal increase in the consumption of energy fuels
after World War I represented an important economic revolution in the United States. This expanded fuel consumption came
almost exclusively from the use of relatively new fuels — pe-
troleum, gas and electricity. Coal consumption after 1920 ex-
hibited a steadily dwindling demand. Most of the eastern railroads were tightly fastened to the fortunes of the coal industry,
and as coal demand fell, rail freight revenues similarly declined.

In New York, the Erie, the Lackawanna, the Delaware and
Hudson, the Lehigh Valley and a few smaller roads had more
or less consistently carried the 30 to 35 percent of Pennsylvania
anthracite production which made its way to New York markets. These same roads along with the Pennsylvania and the
Reading carried about 80 percent of all anthracite mined. As
anthracite production fell to about a quarter of its all time
high by the late 1950's and showed no sign of rebounding,
these roads had to count as lost one of their most important
freight revenue sources.[57]

The case of bituminous coal is roughly similar. Shares in the
bituminous market among the major ten or twelve carriers had
remained fairly constant since World War I. Although the decline in demand for bituminous was less acute than in the case
of anthracite, the relative losses suffered by the eastern coal
carriers between 1948 and 1956 were significant. The dollar loss
in revenues, however, would have been greater if the I.C.C.
had not approved several coal rate increases during this period.

More subtle in its effects upon the demand for rail transportation in the east than the rise of vehicular competition and
changes in product demand were the locational shifts in economic activity that began during World War II and continued
into the post-war years. These changes in the distribution of
economic activity can be classifed in two ways — as broad
national movements and as realignments within economic regions. Together they accounted for an important part of the
diminution of rail demand.

Viewing the pattern of national change, the most striking
feature is the comparative economic decline of the industrial

northeastern and mid-western states and the acceleration of economic activity in the western and southwestern states. By 1950, a Resources for the Future study reported, per capita income in the western states exceeded that of the east, with California's industrial output per worker reaching $5,573 in value while New York averaged only $3,324.[58] Population movement westward made California the nation's most populous state by 1962, while New York's growth remained somewhat lower than the national average during the post-war years.[59]

The meaning of this broad redistribution of population and economic activity in the United States has only recently attracted the attention of researchers. Its implications, therefore, are not yet entirely clear. But, for the purposes of this study, there are some obvious effects to be noted. The comparative decline of economic activity in the east meant that the eastern railroads would likely have a smaller share in American railroad transportation even if no other factors were considered. From available evidence, it would appear that this is exactly what has happened. Income and earnings of the western roads have remained relatively higher than that of eastern carriers, and a number of economic studies of recent railroad operating problems have suggested that the "railroad problem" has mostly been an "eastern railroad problem."[60]

Economic shifts within the eastern states complemented the effects of national locational changes in reducing, or at least modifying, the demand for rail transportation. Steady depopulation of rural areas, the economic stagnation and decline of small cities, and the phenomenal expansion of large metropolitan areas were the chief characteristics of regional economic change in the east. In New York, the decline of population and economic activity in rural areas, which had been proceeding slowly since the beginning of the century, meant special hardship for the smaller railroads and for the branch lines of the large systems. Meanwhile, the increased growth of urban centers created few offsetting benefits for the railroad network. Many of the new plants built in the growing metropolitan areas sought space and lower taxes outside the municipal limits of the urban areas. Removed from the old industrial complex with its usually adjacent rail terminal connections and sidings, the new plant buildings meant the redevelopment of railroad facilities if rail service was to be utilized. Many of the new plants, especially those using small quantities of raw materials and producing products for regional consumption, saw no need for locating near rail connections nor paying for the construction of such connections. Instead, they were to rely upon truck service. In the New York Metropolitan area, more than 60 percent of the new plants built between 1945 and 1957 had no rail sidings whatsoever.[61] As railroads continued to operate mainline and terminal facilities which were in almost all cases more than a half century old, they increasingly lost contact with the new patterns of industrial location. Although the location of rail lines had once determined the adjacent location of businesses, new economic forces were diminishing the locational importance of railroads.

The Economic Condition of Eastern Railroads Up to 1958

In evaluating the operating conditions of American railroads after World War II, it is apparent from the statistical evidence that the decline of demand for rail service was only a part of the economic problem. Rising operating costs put a powerful squeeze on railroad net earnings and this in turn contributed to the initiation of austere capital investment and improvement programs.

With regard to the dwindling demand for rail service, the comparatively greater problem in the east is evident in the case of New York. Between the wartime high in 1944 and 1954, the decline of freight revenues of railroads operating in New York, despite two general rate increases, was nearly four times greater than the national reduction in freight earnings. The decline in passenger traffic during the same period was about equal to the national loss which totaled about 50 percent; but, this hides the fact that much of the passenger mileage operated by New York railroads was high cost commuter service.[62]

The following table of miscellaneous operating statistics for railroads operating in New York illustrates the growing problem of railroad profits. By the 1960's, railroad net income had fallen lower than during the worst of the depression years.

On the other side of the balance sheet, railroad operating costs persistently advanced. In this case, the problem of the

TABLE 11

OPERATING STATISTICS OF RAILROADS OPERATING IN NEW YORK STATE, SELECTED YEARS, 1932-1962

Item	1932	1942	1952	1954	1956	1958	1960	1962
Miles Mainline	8,205	7,686	7,465	7,373	6,822	6,726	6,489	6,280
RR Operating Revenues (000,000 omitted)	$1,126	$2,456	$3,209	$2,760	$3,167	$2,697	$2,676	$2,561
RR Operating Expenses (000,000 omitted)	$ 848	$1,611	$2,610	$2,285	$2,251	$2,255	$2,238	$2,114
Tax Accruals (000,000 omitted)	$ 94	$ 341	$ 267	$ 196	$ 256	$ 227	$ 239	$ 209
Net Income (000,000 omitted)	-$ 27 (Def.)	$ 283	$ 131	$ 75	$ 157	$ 20	-$ 31 (Def.)	-$ 27 (Def.)
Dividends (000,000 omitted)	$ 11	$ 45	$ 38	$ 35	$ 78	$ 27	$ 24	$ 14
Tons of Freight (000,000 omitted)	387	840	723	610	738	555	571	551
Passengers Carried (000,000 omitted)	309	390	294	282	275	243	205	201

Source: Calculated from New York State, Public Service Commission, *Annual Reports*, Selected years, 1933-1963.

eastern roads was not much different from the experience of the rest of the industry.

The general price pressures of the immediate post-war period forced practically all railroad costs upward, but at a rate far exceeding national price inflation.[63] While national price averages increased about one-half between 1945 and 1958, railroad construction and maintenance costs, according to the I.C.C., practically doubled[64] Similar price advances affected the railroads in their purchase of new equipment. However, the greatest of the cost pressures felt by the railroads was labor costs. Between 1945 and 1952, total railroad wage and salary bills grew from $1.8 billion to $5 billion. Meanwhile, labor's share of railroad operating expenditures rose from 40 to 48 percent.[65] From management's point of view this was a very dangerous development and very quickly a broad campaign was put together to attack the labor-cost problem. During the 1950's, the railroads, both individually and through the A.A.R., battled in the press and through legislative lobbies against the Railroad Brotherhoods in general and against the "archaic" full crew laws in particular. Meanwhile, with as little fanfare as possible, the industry reduced railroad employment. Between 1952 and 1958, the total wage bill showed no important change; however, the number of rail employees were reduced by about one-third, to 840,000.[66]

Another perplexing cost problem was taxes. Between 1940 and 1955, federally mandated taxes on earnings, as well as for unemployment insurance and for retirement contributions, rose more than 2000 percent. The tax hikes had largely been initiated with the war as justification. While income taxes were reduced with the coming of peace, they did not fall to pre-war levels. Although American industrial leaders persistently complained about their tax burdens in public statements, very few could maintain that taxes prohibited profit-making during the post-war boom. However, railroad operators convincingly argued that their taxes were demonstrably harmful, especially since some of their tax payments were indirectly to subsidize their trucking competition. Especially despised was the 3 percent excise tax on all I.C.C. regulated freight shipments. Introduced as an attempt to reduce wartime consumer goods movement, this "emergency" tax showed every sign of becoming permanent. By 1956, it was returning to the United States

Treasury over half a billion dollars each year. While the railroads did not directly pay the tax themselves, the A.A.R.
pointed out that it spurred truck competition by inducing
firms to hire their own fleets of trucks to escape the tax.
State and local taxes similarly increased in the post-war years.
As the following table shows, they nearly doubled between 1940
and 1960, amounting for New York railroads to a much greater
burden than federal taxation. As a rule, railroads were taxed
according to the miles of track (of all kinds) that they operated.
For many little communities in the state, the railroad was the
only industry which would return a sizeable income from property taxes, and they were often looked upon as a "natural
resource," to be mined and exploited as need be to pay for
schools, roads and other municipal charges. However, many
towns were to find out that the resource was quickly exhausted
as the companies pulled up duplicating and multiple tracks or
closed operations altogether over low income lines to evade
the tax charges. Nevertheless, local and state tax bills in New
York State grew to an average of over $6,300 per mile of
mainline by 1960, a level of state taxation only surpassed by
New Jersey in the United States.[67]

Through the 1950's, the railroads responded to the cost

TABLE 12

TAXES ON NEW YORK RAILROADS BY NEW YORK STATE
AND THE FEDERAL GOVERNMENT,
SELECTED YEARS, 1912-1960 [a]

Year	Taxes Levied Within New York State (in millions)	Federal Tax on all U.S. Railroads (in millions)	Average Federal Tax Mile of Track for all U.S. Railroads	Average New York Tax Mile of Track for N.Y. Railroads
1912	$ 9.8	$ 4.6	$ 18	$1210
1920	17.8	37.3	148	2271
1930	28.0	59.4	239	3522
1940	24.1	182.0	836	3276
1950	34.6	868.0	4120	4801
1960	39.9	600.6	2883	6379

[a] Calculated from United States, Interstate Commerce Commission, *Yearbook*
(selected years).

pressures generated by rising wages and taxes with an increasingly loud public relations program carried on by the Association of American Railroads. By the late fifties, as we shall see later, this campaign was probably a contributing factor in the reduction of New York taxes, the elimination of the federal excise tax, and favorable court decisions with regard to industry charges of labor featherbedding. Nevertheless, from the point of view of eastern management, favorable changes in government policy came too slowly. As Alfred Perlman of the New York Central later pointed out, the blame lay not with the I.C.C., which was "singularly concerned" with the revenue-cost squeeze which the eastern roads experienced, but with the state legislatures and the Congress. The gravity of the revenue-cost squeeze felt by the eastern roads was evident in the case of New York railroads whose net income from operations fell by one-half between 1942 and the mid-1950's. This was much greater than the decline in net operating income reported by all American railroads, which amounted to about 30 percent over the period.

The worsening economic condition of the railroads served in part to justify the capital retrenchment policies begun by the industry during World War II. With encouragement from the A.A.R. and the enthusiastic approval of the I.C.C., American railroads continued to reduce their funded indebtedness by appropriating earned surplus and current earnings. In all, funded debt was reduced by $1,300,000,000 between 1945 and 1955. Meanwhile, the depressed condition of rail stocks virtually eliminated new stock issues as a source for capital funds. As a result, modernization and replacement expenditures after the war were financed exclusively from issuance of low interest equipment obligations, depreciation allowances and retained earnings.

The industry's record with regard to modernization and improvement is difficult to assess during this period. Between 1945 and 1955, American railroads reported gross capital expenditures for transportation property of about $11,000,000,000, only slightly less than allocations made in the twenty-year period after 1920.[68] These expenditures included important developments in the modernization of yards, switching facilities and block signal systems, as well as the purchase of 25,000 diesel units and over 300,000 new freight cars.

The Association of American Railroads opened a central research laboratory in Chicago in 1950, and thereafter most of the important equipment research of the industry was carried on at this central location.[69] Meanwhile, the A.A.R. kept its members informed of new technical changes as well as reported operating cost and efficiency evidence on new equipment. During the late 1940's and early 1950's, the A.A.R. carried on a vigorous campaign to induce the railroads to take advantage of the demonstrated cost and efficiency benefits of such new inventions as diesel locomotives and block signal traffic systems. In particular, railroads in the western and southern states seemed receptive to technological change.[70] Among eastern railroads, economic problems limited technological vision.

In the east, despite the immediate post-war contraction of traffic, rail management had at first remained optimistic. Annual reports to the stockholders usually carried glowing accounts of future earnings to be gained from new diesels, new trains and new traffic systems. The Korean War boom even induced some of the larger eastern roads to make good some of their modernization promises. In 1950, the Erie became the first eastern road to experiment with in-cab radio-phone connections over its mainline, a first step toward the elimination of the old telegraphers craft.[71] The New York Central, through a unique installment-purchase agreement with the Westinghouse Company ordered the first complete block signal system along its mainline.[72] The company noted not only that this would vastly improve safety, but that it might even mean reduced transportation charges.

All of the large systems and even some small roads, such as the Rutland and the New York Ontario and Western, set up ambitious programs for retiring their steam locomotives and replacing them with diesels. In mid-1950, the Lehigh Valley announced that it was the first completely "dieselized" road in the east.[73] At the same time, the New York Central reported that "dieselization was 25 percent complete," and that within the next four years all steam engines would be replaced.[74] However, the Central's modernization plans came to a halt as the Korean War prosperity gave way to recession in late 1953. When railroad operating revenues sagged 15 percent in 1954, the modernization programs of the eastern roads, especially hard hit by the decline in traffic, were replaced by capital expenditure policies which did not even keep pace with the deterioration of equipment.[75] Never especially ambitious by comparison with improvement programs of railroads in the western and southern states, the eastern district's railroads lagged far behind in capital improvements.

During the 1950's, the Association of American Railroads emphasized that the railroads had "scraped the barrel" to provide for modernization and replacement. Usually, Association statements admitted that the new investment was less than what was needed, but as much as the railroads could afford. Although it is difficult to speculate on what effect additional investment might have had upon the downward drift of rail earnings, it is possible that additional outlays, wisely made, might have stemmed the loss of much traffic to trucks and busses.[76] At any rate, the industry's claim that it could not make greater investment allocations is not proved. Railroads' efforts to reduce funded debt alone absorbed more than a billion dollars of earnings, and added to these conservative policies of capital retrenchment was the industry's fairly respectable dividend record. Between 1946 and 1956, rail stocks paying dividends rose from 56.2 to 86.9 percent of all stocks. The average rate of return on those stocks paying some dividends rose from 5.4 to 7.1 percent. Moreover, total dividend payments by the railroads rarely fluctuated according to changes in rail earnings.[77] Therefore, at least from the perspective of aggregate national railroad statistics, it would appear that more investment funds were available to the industry if it had decided to pursue an actively expansionist investment program.

The national statistics, it must be admitted, obscure the fact that eastern railroads showed much poorer earnings and dividend records. In New York, in the depths of the depression in 1935, only three railroads operating in the state were in receivership. However, by 1950, six roads—the New Haven, The New York Ontario and Western, the Rutland, the Long Island, the New Jersey and New York, and the Middletown and Unionville—were in the courts. These roads operated 1145 miles of mainline track in the state, or about 15 percent of the state's trackage.

Between 1946 and 1955, the return of net operating income to investment averaged about 3.75 percent for American railroads; however, only two of the larger railroads operating in

New York exceeded this rate of return. Of special importance, of course, were the depressed earnings of the Central and the Pennsylvania which stood respectively at 2.19 and 2.33 percent return on investment over this period.

The eastern railroads, commensurate with their low rate of return on investment, made only token dividend payments. By 1954, the New York Central and the Baltimore and Ohio, among the trunk roads, ceased dividend payments altogether. After beginning a promising modernization program in the late 1940's and early 1950's, most of the roads slowed down the pace of investment in new equipment. Observing the deteriorated plant, one contemporary study noted: "The eastern district has become the key problem area in the rail industry.... The Eastern Railroads...have raised serious questions about the future of privately-owned railroads and public policy concerning them."[78]

Such concern about the capital position of the eastern roads was somewhat overdrawn. The low rate of return on investment among eastern railroads certainly placed restrictions upon capital improvement programs to be financed from current earnings; however, most roads possessed funds which could have been allocated to investment if management had desired. By the close of World War II, the eastern railroads had greatly improved their capital position over that of the depression years. Practically all eastern roads had accumulated large earned surpluses during the war, and most were able to hold onto their wartime earnings during the drastic losses in traffic of the postwar period. Therefore, even if operating income after 1945 failed to provide new investable funds, most of the roads had sources they could have tapped. The financial policy of most eastern railroads, however, became one of retrenchment. Ambitious modernization programs set up immediately following the war were forgotten by the mid-fifties as the larger systems ceased all but the most essential new investment.

The austerity of the eastern railroads' capital improvement programs drew frequent criticism from shippers and even the I.C.C. In 1950, even while eastern railroads were engaged in what was depicted as a fairly active modernization program and before all of management's postwar optimism was lost, the Commission condemned railroads in the eastern district for retiring inefficient equipment without making provision for its replacement. In particular, the Commission charged that freight cars owned by the district's roads had declined by more than 40,000 since the close of World War II.[79] As the operating situation worsened after the end of the Korean War, the railroads became more reluctant to replace retired equipment. After prodding from eastern shippers, the I.C.C. released a study in 1957 which reported: "Between 1946 and 1955, freight cars owned in the eastern district declined by about 110,000, offset by an increase of about 46,000 in other districts, or a net decline of about 65,000."

Between 1946 and 1953, most eastern railroads completed the replacement of steam locomotives with diesels, but at a slower rate of acquisition than their first modernization plans had called for. For instance, as late as 1957, the New York Central still reported that 15 percent of its locomotives were steam powered.[81] The Central's modernization programs were particularly slow paced, even to the point that the road's conservative management became concerned. With the elevation of President Robert Young to Chairman of the Board in 1954, the Central's board of directors charged the new president, Alfred Perlman, to "refurbish the property" of the railroad.[82] Between 1954 and 1957, Perlman allocated more than $2,000,000,000 for the purchase of new cars and diesels and the modernization of freight yards; however, he was still obliged to report to a Senate Investigating Committee in 1958 that the road was "deteriorated."

Although there is sufficient evidence to show that the railroads of the eastern United States were less than vigorous in their capital improvement programs, it is, of course, difficult to prove that all of their operating problems stemmed from this policy. That a more vigorous improvement program, a different set of investment decisions, or more venturesome expenditures for dealing with competition and shifts in demand might have led to different economic circumstances can only be speculation. Yet, the conservative policies of eastern railroad management, of which austere capital improvement policies were only a partial indication, offered few new ideas for revitalizing the railroads, and railroads badly needed new ideas.

For example, the industry's technique to combat truck competition amounted to little more than pressuring public regulative agencies to maintain competitive rates for all commercial carriers and to object to what it called the unequal subsidy of truck and bus carriers by large public outlays for highways. Not until 1954, did the eastern railroads widely adopt the use of "trailer-on-flatcar," or "piggyback" transportation of truck trailers.[83] This proved to be a very important competitive weapon against the truckers, especially in the east where truck competition was keenest.[84] But, the idea was scarcely new, having been tried by the Baltimore and Ohio with stage coaches in 1833.[85] Even after the idea had been proven profitable, the eastern railroads were slow to exploit it. Between 1954 and 1959, "piggyback" carloadings grew only 35 percent although the advantages of this innovation were widely known.[86] Similar examples of management inertia were evident in the slow adoption of new and more efficient gondolas, coal cars, and box cars.

Railroads, however, have been quick to point out that they were limited in their innovation ability by both regulative authorities and legislators' reluctance to react positively to new transportation developments. The "Full Crew Laws" of most states, for instance, were a special disincentive to seeking economies. Most of these laws stipulating the number of crewmen, length of shift and mileage of a days work had been passed around the turn of the century when trains and rolling stock were smaller, slower, and much less efficient. Nevertheless, railroads charged, wage rates and labor useage was still determined by these outmoded laws.

Similarly, the I.C.C.'s rate setting procedures, it was alleged, were also antiquated and tended to build inefficiency into the rating system. In the case of unit coal trains, railroads were required by the I.C.C. to charge carload rates quite similar to or identical with mixed trains or single carload shipments, the results being that railroads seemed to be pricing themselves out of the coal shipment business. "Slurry," or piped, water-bourne transportation of coal, began to challenge rail movement in the 1950's in the east, precisely at the time when demand for more bituminous coal for electrical generators was rapidly growing. Railroads, it was argued, were prohibited from offering low cost service, competitive with other modes of shipment ("slurry," non-regulated trucks, and even water movement) by the I.C.C. rule that a lower rate per ton on a trainload shipment than on a carload shipment was unlawful. The rule dated from 1897 and was based upon the contention that such reduction in rates for bulk shipment gave an "undue preference" to large shippers.[87]

The railroad contention that such "artificial" regulative procedures worked against the development of cost economies is undeniable but that misses an important point — namely that these procedures had, at one time, been advocated by the very industry that now opposed them. "Full Crew Laws," although the result of labor lobbying, had been acceptable earlier to the railroads because they did set legal maximum limits to train crew size, and therefore this question did not have to be renegotiated periodically in labor-management contract talks. By establishing limits to crew size under law, this issue was eliminated as a contractual question in management-labor dealings, and, for a time, railroad management thought that was to its advantage. On the question of unit train regulations, the railroads were even more clearly the creator of their own problems for they had been among the most ardent supporters of the original I.C.C. opposition to any rate differentiation between varied sizes of shipments. Their position in the 1890's, when the I.C.C. reached its decision on the matter, had been shaped by their experience of being bludgeoned by large shippers, such as Standard Oil or Carnegie Steel, to give reduced rates on bulk shipment. This amounted to rebating and the railroads had lined up on the side of small shippers against this principle for the simple reason that it reduced profits by stimulating competition among rail carriers. Thus, to lay all of the blame for such inefficiency at the feet of the I.C.C. was either to misrepresent the past history of rail corporate policy-making or simply not to understand it.

With regard to passenger services, the railroads did make some effort to innovate. Between 1946 and 1957, American railroads spent $1,131,000,000 for research and purchase of new passenger equipment. Although the figure was impressive, the roads succeeded in replacing only a very small portion of the pre-war passenger coaches. While they experimented here and there with new trains and new coaches, the industry made practically no effort to sell their new services. Total railroad advertising outlays remained about one-sixth of that spent by bus companies and one twenty-fifth of airline outlays; and,

by the mid 1950's, the eastern trunk lines had virtually eliminated advertising budgets for their passenger operations, and had
moved toward a policy of frankly "discouraging" passenger
travel by rail.[88]

The conservative capital improvement policies and the slow
rate of innovation were complemented among eastern railroads
by retrenchment policies aimed at reducing the absolute scale
of the railroad network. As the post-war years became understood as a time of chronic underutilization of the railroad plant,
the reduction of excess capacity more and more came to dominate management decisions. The squeeze caused by dwindling
revenues and rising costs was thus to be solved by attacking
the cost side of the balance sheet. For nearly half a century,
railroads had periodically undertaken a variety of policies to
to mitigate the effects of excess capacity, now they finally
accepted the principle of reducing the physical size of the
network.

The Railroads Press for Solutions to Excess Capacity

Reduction of railroad operating facilities was sought in a
number of ways: the continued curtailment of the physical
network through the outright abandonment of unprofitable lines,
the reduction of freight and passenger service over operated
trackage, and the closing of freight facilities dealing with "less-
than-carload" service as well as the abandoning of other passenger and freight agency services. Under the Transportation Act
of 1920, outright abandonment of trackage had been placed
under I.C.C. control, and, generally, the Commission had served
as a sympathetic respondent to petitions of "convenience and
necessity." However, reductions and abandonment of passenger
operations and the abandonment of allied freight services remained under state regulative control.

In New York, the Public Service Commission failed to emu-
late the I.C.C.'s sympathy for the railroads' professed operating
problems. This is not to say that the Public Service Commission was especially "anti-railroad." By comparison with
other state railroad commissions, the New York commission
appears to have been quite willing to understand the railroads'
economic difficulties. However, during the 1950's, the Public
Service Commission and New York railroads became engaged

in a number of protracted battles over the railroads' attempts to reduce the scale and intensity of operations. Not infrequently these struggles boiled out of the hearing rooms of the Commission and into the courts. As a rule, the Commission's decisions emphasized the effect of changes in rail service on regional economic development in the state. Not without some justification the railroads charged that state regulation rarely showed a comprehension of the operating troubles faced by the roads and instead showed a biased concern for the shipper or the commuter.

The industry's proposals to reduce freight and passenger service usually stemmed from losses due to dwindling demand. Especially in the case of freight service over short hauls or service which depended upon products with declining demand, such as coal, the pressure for reduction in service was a function of falling revenues. However, many proposed service reductions originated from improvements in rail technology. Larger engines and bigger cars, it was argued, reduced the need for frequent service over some lines. Where declining revenues could not be explained as the basis for service reductions, the railroads offered improved technology as justifications.

To the New York Public Service Commission neither justification was sufficient, by itself, to merit regulative approval. The Commission applied its own yardstick to discontinuance petitions, at least publically, arguing that "public service" was the chief determinant for approval or disapproval. The "public service" rule was determined according to three criteria: 1) the effect of lost service upon the regions affected, 2) the "real dollars" loss to the operators if such service was continued, and 3) the overall ability of the railroad to absorb such losses with regard to its net profit position.[89] Such an approach naturally conflicted with the railroads' own philosophy. Their view was, as it had always been, that profit and loss from the companies' operating statistics should be the sole measure for regulative decision-making. As the struggle between the railroads and the commission intensified, the railroads moved to seek the aid of their traditional "friend," the I.C.C., on matters affecting excess capacity.[90]

Among New York railroads, losses in revenue from passenger operations instigated active efforts to reduce passenger service. The passenger losses were of two types — losses due to dwindling long distance travel and losses from high cost commuter service. Between 1944 and 1958, passengers of all types carried by New York railroads declined from 515,000,000 to 243,000,000.[91] As noted earlier, this produced a staggering "passenger deficit."

The response of the Public Service Commission to the increasing number of discontinuance petitions was deliberate. Decision was often not reached until after six to eight months of inquiry. However, until 1956, the Commission responded quite favorably to the railroads' discontinuance requests. Between 1951 and 1956, it approved 51 train discontinuances and denied only 3. Small roads, with extremely depressed overall operating situations and with small-scale passenger operations, received the most favorable treatment. The New York Ontario and Western, its Catskill and southern New York commuter and tourist services destroyed by auto and bus competition was permitted to abandon all passenger service in 1954.[92] Similarly, the bankrupt Rutland, with revenues from milk service twice as great as passenger revenues, was allowed to cease passenger service in 1953.[93] However, the larger, more profitable roads found the Commission less inclined to be swayed by evidence of passenger losses over particular lines.

In 1954, in the largest single service discontinuance proposal received by the Public Service Commission, the New York Central petitioned to abandon its entire Hudson River (or West Shore) Division passenger service. It was not altogether clear if the company actually desired or thought it possible to close the entire line, and, probably, many of the Commission members believed that the requested discontinuance was simply a ploy by the road to obtain permission for at least partial dismemberment of West Shore passenger service. After a year of study, in which the Commission spent considerable time listening to New York City commuters and representatives of communities affected by the proposed service reduction, it denied the petition, noting: "The West Shore has become a vital and important artery in the commerce of New York State. It is accordingly clear that the proposal to abandon all passenger service affects substantial interest of the people of this state."[94]

Similarly, the Public Service Commission announced the denial of the Delaware and Hudson's request to discontinue the "Laurentian," running between Albany and Montreal. Again, the

Commission stated that abandonment of this passenger train would leave large areas of the state without adequate commercial passenger facilities. However, the Commission reluctantly approved the Baltimore and Ohio's plan to discontinue passenger service from Buffalo to East Salmanca and the Pennsylvania's petition to drop service from Canandaigua to Williamsport, Pennsylvania. In these cases, the commissioners noted that approval was practically required since abandonments and discontinuances permitted by the I.C.C. and the Pennsylvania Public Utilities Commission had eliminated the usefulness of these services in New York.[95]

Typical of the industry's hardening opposition to the actions of the state regulatory commissions, the New York Central requested a new hearing on its West Shore petition in early 1956. The Public Service Commission permitted the Central to drop ten trains, but ordered it to retain thirty-nine others. The Central management rejected the order and obtained a court order enjoining the Public Service Commission from interfering with the road's decision to halt service altogether.[96] The P.S.C. countered with a State Supreme Court restraining action against the Central. By late 1956, the Central and the Commission had temporarily resolved their differences by agreeing to await the outcome of a pending I.C.C. decision on the proposed abandonment of the Central's New York to Weehawken ferries.[97] The agreement proposed by the Public Service Commission was that, if these ferries were abandoned and the usefulness of West Shore passenger service then ceased to exist, the state commission would grant the railroad's request. In 1957, the I.C.C. found in favor of the New York Central.[98] With the cessation of ferry service to move commuters from the west shore of the Hudson to New York City, it was presumed by the company that the Public Service Commission would permit abandonment of all Hudson River Division passenger service.

The Public Service Commission first sought assistance in the courts and then in Congress, to set aside the I.C.C. decision. However, the Commission's attempt to reverse the I.C.C. action was not sustained by the courts, and Congress neglected to act on the Commission's suggestions to change the Transportation Act of 1958, which had been passed during the West Shore controversy and which had gone a long way in giving the I.C.C. complete authority over interstate passenger discontinuances.[99] Defeated, the Public Service Commission finally permitted the abandonment of all West Shore passenger service in 1959.[100]

The West Shore case was representative of the growing industry persistence to reduce passenger operations in the east as passenger revenues continued to sag after 1956. In late 1956, in a case which was similar to the West Shore, the New York Central wryly announced to the newspapers that it would request Public Service Commission approval to abandon its Putnam Division commuter service in Westchester County rather than ask for a 360 percent fare increase to offset falling revenues.[101] During 1957, the Erie, the Lackawanna, and the New Haven all announced plans to curtail their New York commuter operations. The New Haven proposed the largest reduction, the elimination of one-third of all of its New York commuter service.[102]

The railroads, meanwhile, experimented with attempts to shift the commuter problem onto local or state governments. In 1956, Erie president, William Johnston, proposed that a regional public authority be created to run all commuter service into New York, "contracting at no profit with the railroads for service."[103] Within three years, a variation on Johnston's proposal had been developed in New York with the New York Port Authority subsidizing essential commuter operations.[104]

The New York Public Service Commission continued to fight delaying actions with each new proposal for service discontinuance. Believing that complete abandonment of any passenger operation would not arrest the economic trend in passenger service and would make later resuscitation of service impossible, the Commission allowed railroads to dismantle their passenger operations only on a painfully slow, train-by-train, basis.

As a means to halt the passenger discontinuances, the state agency remained fairly agreeable to proposals for fare hikes. However, most of the railroads still held that the fare raises were generally inadequate. After the Commission approved a 15 percent hike for all New York commuter roads, the New York Central again turned to the courts demanding an increase of at least 40 percent so that the road could earn "the fair return of six percent" on its commuter operations. [105]

Long distance or inter-city passenger losses produced slightly different tactics from the industry. At first, rather than seeking abandonment of loss-producing service, they sought drastic fare increases. Among the large eastern carriers, the "passenger deficit" led the I.C.C. to open special hearings in May 1956.[106] While the hearings were in progress and the railroads were offering evidence about their passenger losses, the New York Central, the Pennsylvania, the Chesapeake and Ohio, the Pennsylvania-Reading, the Norfolk and Western, the Seashore, and the Pittsburgh and Lake Erie announced that they would seek drastic increases in inter-city passenger fares.[107] Since this came only five months after a 10 percent fare hike, and at the time of the I.C.C. hearings, it was apparent that the eastern carriers were trying to dramatize their operating problems. With only the Baltimore and Ohio among the large eastern passenger carriers failing to join in the request, the petition called for a 45 percent increase in Pullman fares and a 5 percent hike in coach fares.

Critics of the railroads' passenger operations quickly pointed out that this was simply a new method to cease Pullman operations altogether and probably the beginning of a similar effort to price all passenger service from the market. The increase in Pullman fares would have made service between New York and Chicago more expensive than air service. By pricing themselves out of the luxury carrier business, the railroads would have cut off an important loss-producing segment to their passenger operations. The I.C.C. refused to yield immediately to this pressure. Its studies of the "Passenger Deficit," however, generally supported the industry's claim that passenger operations could only be a loss-producing service in the east. Although rail passenger operations had been reduced between 1939 and 1956 by a third, losses for the railroads had doubled. According to the I.C.C., American railroads lost $2.16 for every mile of passenger service which they provided.[108] Later, Alfred Perlman of the New York Central maintained that, for his road, losses amounted to "almost half a billion dollars" between 1948 and 1957.[109] The railroads' passenger problems continued to dominate discussion of rail matters until the passage of the 1958 Transportation Act provided for I.C.C. intervention in cases where state commissions were slow to react to industry requests for abandonment.

The reduction of freight operations during this period can be measured in several ways — reduction in the frequency of service and reduction in allied freight service agencies. Between 1951 and 1956, more than 300 agency operations were closed in New York. For the most part, these were less-than-carload services which the railroads had been losing to trucks since the 1930's and which, due to rising labor costs, were decidedly unprofitable.[110] As noted earlier, most of these abandonments affected only rural freight service which like the economic activity of the surrounding regions would have continued to dwindle regardless of competition from trucks. The Public Service Commission generally responded favorably to close less-than-carload freight services. Although in some cases if other truck operations were not thought to be adequate in the immediate region, the railroads were obliged to replace rail service with their own truck facilities.

The outright abandonment of trackage accounted for an aggregate loss of about 16,000 miles of American railroad mileage between 1940 and 1959. About a fifth of all abandonments took place in nine northeastern states in which only about 12 percent of the American railroad network was operated. For the most part, these abandonments represented attempts by roads to trim off duplicating long distance routes and loss-producing spurs. In New York, the abandonment of the entire New York Ontario and Western system was the only total abandonment of a Class I railroad during this period. However, not reported in the following figures was the abandonment of large segments of parallel second and third tracks. For instance, the New York Central alone pulled up more than four hundred miles of second track along its mainlines in New York between 1946 and 1957.

To some observers, the railroads' eagerness to abandon low revenue routes appeared to be unjustified. The New York Public Service Commission, under the chairmanship of Benjamin Feinberg from 1951 to 1959, continued to berate the I.C.C. for its "undue concern" for railroad operating problems and its neglect of the economic difficulties that abandonment caused local communities. The state commission's concern over I.C.C. actions was certainly heightened by the fact that more

TABLE 13

OPERATED MAINLINE MILEAGE IN U.S.A. AND SELECTED
EASTERN STATES, 1920-1959[a]

State	1920	1940	1959
Connecticut	1,001	887	829
Maine	2,295	1,882	1,786
Massachusetts	2,106	1,793	1,694
New Hampshire	1,252	1,002	869
New Jersey	2,352	2,108	1,915
New York	8,390	7,739	6,541
Pennsylvania	11,551	10,328	9,126
Rhode Island	211	194	181
Vermont	1,077	919	811
Total:			
Eastern States	30,235	26,852	23,710
National	252,845	233,670	217,565

[a]Taken from John F. Stover, *American Railroads* (Chicago: University of Chicago Press, 1961), pp. 223-4.

trackage was abandoned in New York in the twelve years after World War II than had been abandoned in all the years before.

The steady accumulation of branch line abandonments throughout the nation led the *Railway Age* to sermonize about the defeatist attitude of rail management. The magazine editorialized: "it is better business to revive losing operations than to give up — which is especially true in railroading because of the importance of branch lines or feeders to the rest of the operation."[111]

The railroad brotherhoods were probably the most vigorous opponents of abandonments or discontinuances in the post-war period, for these posed a greater threat of employment dislocation than the merger activities of the 1920's and 1930's. Under the Emergency Act of 1933, the unions had obtained some job protection in the case of mergers, but no similar guarantee had been extended to abandonments. Beginning in the early 1940's, the unions, especially the Brotherhood of

Locomotive and Fire and Engineermen, began to press for legislative action to protect their jobs in cases of abandonment and discontinuance. By 1945, all of the Brotherhoods were pressuring for job protection, but the Congresses of the post-war years refused to take up the issue.[112]

The Interstate Commerce Commission remained reluctant to deal with job dislocation as a function of abandonment until finally directed by the Supreme Court that it had the authority "to attach terms and conditions for the benefit of employees displaced by railroad abandonments."[113] The I.C.C. accepted four years of service, or the employees actual service, whichever was least, as severance pay. Actual job losses due to partial abandonments were probably not great, as many workers were shifted to other jobs and the railroads let their overall employment decline through natural attrition due to retirement, death and resignation. In the case where a complete system was abandoned, the I.C.C. claimed that it could take no action on behalf of the displaced employees.[114]

In response to criticism that it acted too frequently in the interest of the carriers, the I.C.C. began, during the fifties, to develop more systematic criteria for deciding upon abandonment petitions. Still, the yardstick for approval or denial accepted the fact that no road could be forced to operate at an overall loss and that compelling any road to offer service which produced aggregate losses was a violation of "due process." Roads were obliged to show, in abandoning a part of their operations that there was insufficient traffic, "now or in prospect" to justify continued operation and that major economies would be gained for the whole system through a partial abandonment. In other words, the I.C.C. was willing to accept the industry's rationale for abandonment — that profitable service would be improved if unprofitable service could be halted.

While the effect of abandonments on regional economic activity remained, theoretically, an important "public interest" criteria in approving abandonments, the due process stipulation naturally took precedence in the Commission's decision. In some cases, the I.C.C. did require loss-producing portions of a line to operate if certain industries or communities could prove the absence of other transportation means and if the losses to the railroad were offset by other earnings.[115]   However, there were frequent charges by shippers, labor unions, and state regulative authorities that many railroads frankly attempted to discourage traffic on routes they sought to close, and, having driven much traffic from the line, they took impressive evidence of little traffic "now or in prospect" to the I.C.C.

Accounting for the I.C.C.'s generally favorable disposition toward the railroads really requires greater study than can be offered here; but a few observations are necessary. First of all, the commission was acting in its usual manner, that is, it remained committed to the overriding obligation of "keeping the railroads going." Second, the I.C.C. had never shown much sympathy for accepting a role as national transportation planner and had persistently held to a fairly narrow constructionist view of its own power. Therefore, it readily evaded the "social planning" question that the state commissions and the shippers constantly raised. The effect, of course, was to make it either a witting or an unwitting supporter of railroad corporate policy. This meant that the burning questions of national transportation policy remained, as they had always been, largely functions of private corporate policy-making.

The Abandonment of the New York Ontario and Western

On October 10, 1957, after extensive hearings, the Interstate Commerce Commission reported approval of the abandonment of the New York Ontario and Western.[116]   This action marked the first complete abandonment of a large American railroad, for the 545-mile Ontario and Western, with its developed port and terminal facilities at Oswego and Hoboken, was quite unlike the hundreds of little spur roads or the miscellaneous bits and pieces of trackage which the I.C.C. had permitted closing in the past. For about 100 towns and villages in the midlands of New York State, the New York Ontario and Western was the only available rail connection. Its closing meant the end of rail service for these areas.

The death throes of the Ontario and Western revealed the degree of economic deterioration which had come to characterize the operating situation of a number of intermediate-sized eastern railroads. The end of the Ontario and Western had, in fact, been a long time coming. Most of the mainline of the railroad had originally been built as the New York and Oswego Midland, one of the speculative constructions of the 1860's.[117] Rather than being laid out according to demonstrated traffic needs, the Oswego Midland had been put together for promotional gain, built with inferior materials and generally poor engineering. After the Oswego Midland was reorganized as the New York Ontario and Western, its new president even questioned why the road had been built at all and why, after it had fallen into bankruptcy in 1879, it had not been allowed to die.[118] However, in the Morgan-inspired peace in the anthracite coal fields, the Ontario and Western, controlled by Morgan's affiliate, the New Haven, obtained about 4 percent of the anthracite traffic.[119] As the demand for anthracite increased in the early twentieth century, the Ontario and Western briefly enjoyed a measure of prosperity. Coal plus the tourist traffic to the Catskill resort areas near Ellenville and Monticello and income from agricultural shipments permitted the road to at least cover its fixed costs until the 1930's.

With the depression, however, the Ontario and Western began to suffer catastrophic revenue losses. The passenger traffic was lost to busses and autos. Coal shipment, declining absolutely for all the anthracite coal carriers, fell quite sharply on the Ontario and Western due to its generally poor connections with the coal producers.[120] Agricultural commodities and other freight shipment over its rights of way sagged as the rural counties of New York continued to suffer population and economic declines. Moreover, much of what was left of the agricultural business, such as milk shipment, which once provided the Ontario and Western with about 11 percent of its earnings, was lost to trucks. In 1937, the Ontario and Western went into receivership.[121]

During the next two decades a number of reorganization plans were drawn up by the court-appointed trustees to raise the road from bankruptcy. On these occasions, the I.C.C. rejected plans submitted to it for approval, arguing that the plans could not possibly assure that the new corporation would produce any improvement in earnings. During the early 1950's, local "booster" committees were organized in the small towns along the Ontario and Western's rights of way to encourage use of the railroad and the location of new plants along its route. However, the uncertain future of the road was little inducement for location along its route and the booster activity seemed to have little impact on railroad earnings. Meanwhile, after making attempts to modernize the line by putting diesels in service, cutting back some trackage and abandoning passenger service, the receivers were sued by the Federal Government in March of 1956 for $7,000,000 in unpaid withholding taxes.[122] In fact, the government suit pointed out, the railroad had not paid its regular contributions to the Railroad Retirement Fund since 1943.

In September of 1956, the Interstate Commerce Commission rejected another reorganization plan submitted by the receivers and practically concluded that the only solution for the Ontario and Western was abandonment, with its property to be sold to other railroads.[123] A bid of $4,600,000 by S.A. Pinsley Associates for the entire road, or $1,425,000 for the 100-mile Oswego to Norwich line, was rejected by the I.C.C. as inadequate for the protection of the existing shareholders and bond holder's interests.[124]

In January of 1957, the Ontario and Western was returned to the courts and new receivers were appointed. Presiding Judge Sylvester Ryan required that the new receivers, John Kilsheimer and Jacob Grumet, raise $250,000 within sixty days to cover operating expenses or the road would be liquidated.[125] During the next month, a number of efforts were undertaken to keep the Ontario and Western operating. Governor Harriman appointed a special investigating committee. The New York State Commerce Department organized a drive to raise the $250,000 by subscription. Local groups which had actively worked to increase Ontario and Western business for the past four or five years renewed their efforts. Meanwhile, New York State dropped a $1,000,000 tax claim against the road and the United States Treasury dropped another $250,000 claim. On March 15, despite the collection of $217,000 from 366 New York State citizens to cover the railroads' operating expenses, Judge Ryan ordered that the road cease operating within fifteen days.[126] The judge pointed out that there had been no improvement in the road's economy since January. A last minute attempt to declare the road essential to the State's civil defense and to loan it $1,000,000 in Civil Defense Funds passed the Legislature and Assembly and was signed by Governor Harriman on March 30, 1957. However, the State Civil Defense Commission publicly announced that the road was not essential, and thus, the close of operations on March 29, 1957, marked the end of the Ontario and Western.[127]   On June 28, 1957, Judge Ryan auctioned off the property of the Ontario and Western in twenty-one lots of assets for $10,631,820.[128]   The I.C.C.'s final approval of the abandonment and destruction of the property, although bitterly contested by the shippers, communities, and labor unions affected, was really little more than a formality.

Apart from the impact of its abandonment of the communities along its mainline, the passing of the New York Ontario and Western was also significant in that it presaged a new period of railroad abandonment. Within the next five years, four other large American railroad systems ceased operation. These were the Chicago Aurora and Elgin (53 miles, approved 1961), the Lehigh and New England (177 miles, approved 1961), the Chicago North Shore and Milwaukee (106 miles, approved 1962), and the Rutland (331 miles, approved 1962). These abandonments combined with the continued reduction of segments of larger systems and the discontinuance of freight and passenger service over operating routes identified the late 1950's and early 1960's as a time of accelerated reduction in the railroad network.

VI

THE TRANSPORTATION ACT OF 1958 AND AFTER, 1958-1966

The 1958 Crisis

The general business recession of 1957-1958 fell particularly heavily upon railroads, and, fed a seemingly inexhaustible supply of depressing facts and statistical data by the Association of American Railroads, business and trade publications and newspapers succeeded in creating a crisis atmosphere surrounding any discussion of railroad operations. Characteristic of most declines in business activity, the recession began earlier, was more acute, and lasted longer for the railroads than for most other industries. From its peak in June of 1957 through April of 1958, the nation's gross national product fell 3.7 percent, or approximately $16,500,000,000.[1] However, railroad earnings alone fell by $1,000,000,000, or 10 percent, over the same period, and their improvement immediately after the recession was disappointing. At the same time, net income fell $135,000,000, or about 17 percent. While dividend payments declined very little as an immediate repercussion of the recession, one-third of all outstanding railroad stocks paid no fourth quarter dividends in 1958.[2] Testifying before a Senate subcommittee in the spring of 1958, Daniel Loomis, the new president of the Association of American Railroads, calculated that the decline was the greatest in railroad history.[3]

Loomis' appearance before a Senate committee in itself marked the degree of official concern for the railroads in 1958, and to a large extent, this concern had been nurtured and maintained by the railroads themselves. Throughout 1956 and 1957, the eastern railroads in particular, in news releases and legal briefs, had alluded to the impending economic crisis. Practically all of the roads offering commuter service into New York City had taken the same position on persistent commuter losses — that without direct subsidy, tax relief, or even public operation, these services would cease.

There had been similar unity and similar depictions of economic hardship in attempts to obtain rate increases. In fact, the Interstate Commerce Commission complained that there seemed to be no end to the railroad petitions for raising rates to offset falling revenue and rising costs. Two months after requesting a 15 percent general increase in September of 1956, eastern and western railroads, feeling the early phases of recession, requested an additional 7 percent general increase.[4] Both of these petitions were in addition to a general raise of 6 percent which the Commission had granted in March, 1956.[5]

Although the railroads and the A.A.R. at first criticized the I.C.C. for its slowness in granting "reasonable rate requests," the Commission, also caught up in the crisis surrounding railroad operations, generally acquiesced to rail demands. In December of 1956 it approved a 7 percent increase, and, in August of 1957, it approved an additional 7 percent hike, for eastern railroads.[6] Although noting that further rate hikes might divert traffic from the railroads, another 2 percent increase was given in February of 1958.[7] In less than two years, the I.C.C. had approved rate increases for eastern railroads of 22 percent.

Whatever the past public posture of the railroads with regard to the actions of the Interstate Commerce Commission and to federal regulation in general, the railroads now began to press publicly for federal intervention to aid rail transportation. By late 1957, the line of attack was clear — laws affecting railroad regulation by the I.C.C. and the state regulatory authorities should be rewritten to fit the new economic problems of the railroads. In an interview in November of 1957, President Perlman of the New York Central announced that the industry was not opposed to regulation, but only to "haphazard regulation."[8] Rather than attacking the Interstate Commerce Commission, Perlman suggested that inadequacies in regulatory laws, which, for example, permitted too much state regulatory intervention, prohibited the I.C.C. from regulating effectively. He suggested, as an alternative, the "modernizing" of I.C.C. regulations. Given the Interstate Commerce Commission's response to the industry's recent rate requests, it must have been clear to even the bitterest industry critics of the I.C.C. that the regulatory agency was not "anti-railroad." At any rate, during late 1957, the Association of American Railroads kept up pressure to renovate interstate commerce law. Most industry proposals, as we shall see, called for the centralizing of regulation under the Interstate Commerce Commission.

In early 1958, the Committee on Interstate and Foreign Commerce of the United States Senate appointed a special subcommittee, headed by Senator George Smathers of Florida, to investigate and make recommendations upon the state of surface transportation in the United States. Although all modes of transportation were to be examined, the subcommittee soon became preoccupied with railroad problems.

Between January 13 and April 3, 1958, the subcommitee collected over 2000 pages of testimony from 103 witnesses. Twenty-seven of those appearing before the subcommittee represented railroad management, thirty represented interests in air, motor or water transportation, thirty-six could be classified as economists, finance experts or government commissioners, and seven shippers and three labor leaders were heard from. From the beginning, the hearings were directed to the current problems of the railroads, and, unlike many of the Senate investigating committees of the thirties, the railroad witnesses found the committee members sympathetic listeners. Most of the committee's response showed a predisposition to accept the industry's claim that American railroads were faced with imminent collapse, and those witnesses who suggested that the railroads' claims of economic crisis were exaggerated often suffered at the hands of the committee members.

Senator Smathers, Committee Chairman, was particularly sympathetic to the railroad arguments and seemed especially interested in including in the official transcript vast collections of data supporting the railroad claim that federal aid of some kind was needed. There never seemed to be much doubt that anything but highly favorable legislation to the railroads would be recommended by the committee.

Most of the testimony on railroads dealt with the problems of the eastern trunk lines. Five eastern railroad presidents and Daniel Loomis, president of the Association of American Railroads (and a former president of the Delaware and Hudson) appeared as witnesses, and questions from the committee members indicated more concern for their problems than for any difficulties of western and southern roads.

Daniel Loomis appeared as the first witness and attempted to construct a picture of the railroads as the most important of American transportation modes. With a certain pretentiousness that always seemed to characterize official inquiries into the railroad problem, Loomis stated:

> Modern transportation began with railroads, todays transportation depends on railroads — and tomorrow the railroads still will be the very base of the transportation structure. As to other forms of transportation, not one of them, nor all of them together, could move such great and varied quantities of goods over such distances, and between such remote sections as do the railroads, for only in trains of cars running on tracks is it possible to combine the convenience and flexibility of the individually loaded and separately unloaded freight cars with the economy of mass movement in trains between terminals. [9]

Loomis and the next witness, James J. Symes, president of the Pennsylvania Railroad, outlined the industry's analysis of the railroads' problems. They noted that although the railroads were essential to the economy, the railroad industry was sick. To illustrate the dimensions of this sickness, they offered mountains of superfluous and expensive statistical studies on railroad finances, revenues and costs. From this evidence, they concluded that most of the railroads' problems stemmed from over-regulation and underprotection from competing transportation modes; and, as a solution to these problems, both men urged new federal regulation aimed at rebuilding the railroad industry.

Symes proposed an eighteen point program for the resuscitation of the railroads, setting priorities for the development of a National Transportation Policy.[10] He listed as some of the more pressing needs of such a policy: the downward revision or elimination of state and local property taxes and federal excise taxes, the creation of greater management flexibility in meeting changing labor requirements relative to capital uses, new rate making policies respecting the problems of "intermodal" transportation competition, relaxation of regulatory opposition to mergers, abandonments, and discontinuances which would improve the railroads' economic position, immediate financial aid to roads facing difficulties in paying obligations or providing for capital improvements, and the establishment of a federal coordinator of inter-modal transport operations.

Alfred Perlman footnoted Loomis' and Symes' contention that practically all railroad problems were traceable to the enforcement of non-economic regulation, taxes, and procedures which prohibited railroads from making decisions consistent with the best business principles. With regard to the frequent charge that railroads had failed to modernize, Perlman recounted his experience with the New York Central in dealing with the passenger deficit:

> When the new management of the New York Central took office in the summer of 1954, one of our first actions was to see how railroad passenger travel could be stimulated by better service and by improvements in operating technology.... We imported a German diesel passenger locomotive with a new concept of power transmission.... We contracted Pullman-Standard to build a light-weight low center of gravity train.... The results were shown the next year by putting into service the aerotrain of General Motors, the "Xplorer" of Pullman-Standard, the Talgo Train of American Can and Foundry and equipment of the Budd Company. On our first run of the aerotrain between Chicago and Detroit, we were able to transport 250 passengers with an expenditure for fuel less than that which would have been used by two Cadillacs. We thought that now we had the answer for low cost, mass transportation.
>
> Then what happened? About this time began a tremendous spiral of wage inflation...and within fourteen months the nationally negotiated wage increases for railroad labor had added $62 million a year to the payroll of the New York Central. During the same period, our taxes were substantially increased. For example, in the city of New York, the taxes on our passenger bridge over the Harlem River were multiplied 700 percent, from $70,000 to $490,000 a year and the franchise tax for them to use an underground tunnel in Grand Central Terminal jumped

from $1,050,000 to $2,500,000 a year. As a result, when we put the experimental train in service between Cleveland and Cincinnati, we found that the gross revenues were not enough to meet the out-of-pocket cost because of the high terminal charges.

Since 1946, the Central has invested a quarter of a billion dollars in passenger service equipment and facilities; it has spent $14 million promoting and administering its passenger service; and it has lost about half a billion dollars providing this service.[11]

Thus, Perlman contended, modernization had not paid out in improved passenger service due to the changes in demand and more importantly, due to rising labor and tax charges. Even the relatively profitable freight operations were depicted as threatened by these rising costs. With regard to taxes, Perlman testified:

I would just like to point out, Senator, that we pay taxes in the city of New York something in the nature of the amount that would be equivalent to $2-1/2 a share on New York Central stock. Since 1930, when the New York Central was put into a railway system as the New York Central System, in only two peacetime years up until 1954, when I came here, had they paid a dividend to the owners —fifty cents in difficult peacetime years was all the owner got on a $2-1/2 billion investment. This tax that we pay New York City is an example. On the other hand, we have a publicly financed bus terminal in New York City, a publicly financed truck terminal in New York City; we have Idlewild and LaGuardia Airports which are something in the neighborhood of a $200 million investment and I heard talk about taxes yesterday. These airports are taxed at a rate of $450,000. And with the values that are put upon the land out there, if that same tax were applied to us, we would be paying $4,000,000 instead of $450,000; hence, the taxes are frozen in the airports. The same thing applies to the bus terminal and truck terminal.

Let's go a little further. Let's go from Albany to Buffalo on one railroad. On one side is the Erie Canal, built by the State of New York, dredged by the State of New York, maintained by the State of New York. Right next to it is the new superhighway built by the State of New York, and on the other side of it is the St. Lawrence Seaway being built. I would say that if the New York Central

Railroad were given the money that the Seaway is going to cost the taxpayers, we would be very happy, with that money, to carry freight that is going to be carried on the seaway free. So when you say, what is happening in the the other forms of transportation compared to the railroad, there is a picture of the New York Central.[12]

The solution, as seen by Perlman, called for a return to "sound business practice" — freedom to determine rates and service. In his concluding statement, the outspoken executive of the New York Central called for the virtual abrogation of the past forty years of national transportation policy:

We are no longer a monopoly of transportation. We are fighting against subsidized competition just for the right to serve the public free of irrelevant, cumbersome, staggering regulations.

Give us freedom to solve the problem ourselves. Remove all regulation from us in pricing and operation of passenger service trains. This is what the New York Central would be if we had that freedom.

First, we would establish our prices on the basis of what each type of passenger service costs us to operate, including the same reasonable return on investment that other utilities receive. We would have the greatest incentive not to over-price our service because we need to retain whatever profitable service there may be.

Second, where the public declined to patronize one service at compensatory prices, we would be free to experiment, seeking new means of getting business, discounting rail service or substituting other means of getting the public's demand.

Third, any service that gives promise of being a profitable operation, we would promote to the utmost, because our continued existence as a private corporation is dependent solely on our ability to produce profits. In other words, we would like to try to operate the railroad passenger service according to the laws of economics, not have it operated for us according to the dictates of local pressures. Give us that freedom and we will solve the passenger deficit problem. The continuance of the present situation can only lead to disaster for railroad systems and that will be a national disaster . . .[13]

It would be inaccurate to interpret this apparent defense of *laissez faire* as an attempt to return the railroads to the situation which existed before 1887. Perlman's pleas for freedom must be viewed in the context of earlier proposals offered by industry leaders for greater transportation coordination. Governmental coordination of transportation along with greater freedom to set prices and adjust service to changes in demand seemed to Perlman to be no paradox at all. Primarily, Perlman was thinking of state regulative authorities in his presentation, and he desired greater federal coordination as a means to protect the railroads from these agencies. He argued:

> Take the New York Central for example. It operates in eleven different states in addition to Canada. There are eleven regulatory commissions... to advise local interests in each of the eleven states.... Our problem is not with the state commissions or the men who serve on them. It is with obsolete laws under which they must regulate.

Support for the railroads' case came from groups which might have been expected to be antagonistic. Shippers and representatives of other transportation modes more or less concurred that the industry was gravely weakened by existing transportation regulations. Meanwhile, the railroads' request for immediate capital aid for equipment and maintenance received support from bankers. John J. McCloy, appearing for Chase-Manhattan Bank, noted that private funds were not attracted to railroads in their present condition. He called for immediate unsecured and non-specified federal loans of short duration. The amount to be issued was to be up to 50 percent of the railroads' annual maintenance expenditures, and the loans were to provide for equipment and maintenance outlays.[15]

McCloy also appealed for the development of a "National Transportation Policy" aimed at federally directing transportation coordination. He stated:

> In examining the problems we must keep our eyes firmly fixed on the welfare of the public, because all along the way we will be met by the selfish opposition of vested interests in statutory, administrative and court-created privilege. In final analysis, however, it cannot be denied that public welfare will be served through the formulation and execution of National Transportation Policy which gives each mode of transportation an equal chance under the law

to establish and maintain the place to which it is entitled by its own inherent advantages.[16]

Among the critics of the railroads' case, which McCloy might have seen as the "selfish opposition of vested interests" was railroad labor. G.E. Leighty, chairman of the Railway Labor Executives Association, raised a question basic to the unions — Would the proposed National Transportation Policy adequately protect employee rights? Leighty concluded that if the railroads had their way it would not.[17] He noted that most of the railroad testimony was aimed at justifying industry claims that costs, of which labor costs had been particularly singled out, must be radically reduced for the industry to survive. Leighty offered that the capital structure and the physical plant of American railroads were as good as any time in American history. Rates and fares had increased since the war at a phenomenal pace, in fact, much faster than total labor costs. He added that the record of net earnings was as good as any time since the mid-twenties and that, despite the 1957 recession, the future looked bright. Offering his own statistical evidence, Leighty charged that the Association of American Railroads (to elicit government support in radically reducing labor costs) deliberately attempted to misrepresent the facts concerning the economic situation of the railroads. In particular, Leighty charged that Loomis had claimed that added labor costs alone had been $870,000,000 in 1957 when, in fact, according to his statistics, it had been less than $100,000,000. Loomis, he claimed, had purposely distorted these figures. Another opposing witness was Harry Hagerty of the Metropolitan Life Insurance Company and unofficially speaking for the insurance industry which held over $4,000,000,000 in railroad bonds. Primarily, Hagerty opposed the railroad's request for direct federal capital aid, noting:

> Railroad working capital is down and no one is more to blame than management. Let's put the blame where it belongs.... Mr. Symes is spearheading a drive down here for railroad loans, for what I call financial aspirin, when the disease is deep-seated. After they get the loans and the headache is over, the disease will still be there.[18]

Hagerty claimed that the loans would perpetuate certain inept management practices and stall real reformation of the railroads. He especially opposed the capital policies sponsored by the A.A.R. since the early 1940's, which emphasized holding the line on capital improvements and refunding bonds. As a representative of the bond holders, this irritated Hagerty, for he envisioned the advancement of federal funds to the railroads as a method for stimulating debt retirement. Despite his single-minded concern for the interests of the bondholders, Hagerty's testimony offered some new insights to the financial maneuvering of the eastern railroads.

Hagerty pointed out that capital policies bore no relation to operating considerations. He noted that during the years from 1953-1956, the Pennsylvania Railroad had paid "$19, $10, $10, and $20 millions in dividends respectively while working capital during the same years was $38, $43, $29, and $4 million."[19] The same pattern of paying dividends as working capital evaporated prevailed among other eastern railroads, and there appeared to be no end in sight to this policy, for "according to Symes' own statement, there was a deficit in working capital of about $15 million in 1957 and the company paid $16 million in dividends."[20]

Hagerty added:

> Now, that isn't all. They don't tell you that cash was used to retire $64 million — yes, $64 million of bonds that were not due for ten, fifteen, or twenty years. Also retired were some $28 to $30 million of guaranteed stocks with the public. This is a total of $92 million which, if the Pennsylvania railroad hadn't so spent, could have it today and make a down payment for equipment....
>
> Management says it can't make down payments on equipment. Pennsylvania paid out dividends when it didn't have adequate working capital and they bought bonds when they were not due. Now bond investors such as ourselves do not often get a chance to explain things like this. Management represents stock. There hasn't been any stock sold by the Pennsylvania railroad in years and no stockholder has ever put a new dollar into railroad stock to be used for capital additions or a betterment. Railroads have borrowed all the time.
>
> Metropolitan loaned about 100 million dollars to Walter Franklin of the Pennsylvania railroad with no down payment, to buy equipment about seven or eight or nine

years ago. We also loaned, I think, $60 million to the New York Central.

The savings were great. In the initial stages, they said they could save thirty percent with the new equipment. Where are those savings? Now they will tell you that they can't afford to sell equipment obligations as the rate of interest is too high. Loomis testified that interest rate has climbed from three to five percent, with industry now earning only three percent. Mr. Loomis must know as any boy out of business school would, that interest is a tax deduction. When he speaks of five to six percent, he is really saying two and a half to three percent.

So I would say that he or anyone else who says the same thing is fifty-two percent wrong.[21]

Hagerty's opposition to direct federal aid, however, should not be interpreted as opposition to increased federal-corporate collaboration. Speaking in the interests of bond holders, he argued that management should have greater rate-making freedom and, like McCloy, he suggested the development of a broad national transportation policy. Such a policy should recognize, he maintained, that the long range survival of the railroads depended upon intelligent consolidations. The consolidations should be publicly planned "so as to avoid the driving up of prices" of securities and to assure the inclusion of the weaker roads.[22]

The overall effect of the testimony of the witnesses was possibly confusing and contradictory to the members of the committee; however, it was, nevertheless, clear that no substantial division existed among the witnesses on the question of whether there *should be* coordination between private carriers and public regulators. Only the degree and direction of such coordination varied among the witnesses. The proposal that some sort of publicly directed national transportation policy be devised had near unanimous approval, even among critics of the railroads. The expressions of Perlman and other rail leaders for greater freedom from regulation were not taken too literally. Since the beginning of the century, eastern railroads had sought refuge from *laissez faire* market tendencies. First, through privately initiated mergers, consolidations and intercorporate agreements; then, through utilization of I.C.C. protection, the railroads had rejected competition. Perlman, to be sure, recognized

these facts in his argument, and he was calling for a new kind
of public-private collaboration in regulation which recognized
the threat of intermodal competition and which responded to
the economic necessities of the railroads' balance sheet problems. His wish was little more than a modern-day variation on
J.P. Morgan's plans.

During and after the Senate hearings and Congressional debate on transportation legislation, the eastern railroads maintained pressure for immediate aid. In an apparent common front
action, they concentrated attention on the problem of commuter
operations. In March, 1958, the New York Central received
permission to close its Putnam (Westchester County) Division.
The Central noted that the $400,000 annually saved by closing
this service was just a beginning, with more abandonments and
discontinuances to follow.[23] On July 3, while the railroad aid
bill was pending before Congress, the Lehigh Valley asked
permission of the I.C.C. to cease all of its passenger and
commutation services.[24] Meanwhile, the Association of American Railroads disclosed that first quarter net earnings for
American railroads was a scant $30,000,000, 82 percent below
1957.[25] In April, as an economy move, with the effect of
heightening the feeling of economic crisis, the Pennsylvania and
the Erie announced that executives' salaries would be slashed
by 10 percent. However, these cuts were quickly restored after
the railroad aid bill, known as the Transportation Act of 1958,
was passed in August.[26]

The Transportation Act of 1958

On the surface it appeared that the industry's requests received only disappointing consideration in the passage of the
Transportation Act of 1958.[27] Public Law 625 was at best
a "slap-dash" effort to deal with the most immediate railroad problems. Unlike the earlier Transportation Acts of 1920
and 1940, or the Motor Carrier Act of 1935, legislative committee work in the drafting of the law was hurried. Real questions
of national transportation policy were deferred to future study.
The railroads had requested the development of a clear national
policy for the resuscitation of the industry, and, as never before,
they had mobilized an ambitious public relations program to
sell their program to the public as well as the Congress. The

act in this regard failed to live up to advance expectations.

The provisions of Public Law 625 included: 1) the abolition of the 3 percent excise tax on freight charges (the 10 percent levy on passenger fares remained), 2) the establishment of government guaranteed loans for railroad borrowing in private money markets, 3) greater rate-making flexibility in respect to intermodal competition, stating in effect that no form of transportation shall be required by law to maintain rates higher than necessary in order to protect the traffic of other modes of transportation, 4) the extension of I.C.C. regulation over all "for hire" transportation, except for a few specific exceptions, 5) the addition of and the removal of certain commodities from the rate regulation list, 6) the extension of I.C.C. authority to review and decide upon intra-state rates and, 7) the granting of new authority to the I.C.C. to review and act upon state regulatory decisions on the discontinuance of intra-state services.

Although the substantive provisions of the Transportation Act of 1958 fell short of management's requests, the act stood as a significant victory for the railroads. Proposals that the railroads be virtually free to carry on their own rate making, that the passenger excise tax be removed, that protection be afforded the railroads from "confiscatory" state taxes, and that a "national transportation policy" be developed were lost. However, the extension of I.C.C. authority over intra-state rate making and service discontinuances was an important gain. The loosening of rate making procedures and guaranteeing of railroad loans were, to the railroads, heartening signs of redirection of government policy, even if they were inadequate in themselves.

Keeping up the momentum, the A.A.R. spoke more confidently and more frequently after the passage of the Transportation Act of an emerging "railroad position" on national transportation policy. While priorities in this policy were not altogether clear, the new tactical approach of the industry included: the increased use of mergers and abandonments to deal with the problems of excess capacity, the use of discontinuance of freight and passenger services for the same purpose, a persistent attack on certain cost problems — especially labor and tax charges, maintaining pressure for greater industry freedom in rate making, and advocating the ending of "unfair" subsidies to other transport modes.

An important outgrowth of the efforts of the railroads to
change public policy in 1958 was the establishment through the
Association of American Railroads of an energetic public relations program, and the gains obtained in Public Law 625
encouraged the Association to broaden this activity. In the past,
the industry had usually employed the better known tactics of
political lobbying in Congress and in state legislatures to obtain
favorable legislation, and, in the distant past, it had employed
outright bribery; however, public relations work after 1958 was
directed toward the general public. For the first time, the
A.A.R. purchased radio and newspaper space to broadcast the
policy goals of the industry. In 1959, over 150,000 copies of
a pamphlet titled *The Urgent Six,* outlining six legislative
enactments sought by the industry from Congress, were distributed to important interest groups. Meanwhile, circulation of
the Association's monthly magazine, *Railway Digest,* climbed
to 25,000, More than 235,000 copies of Daniel Loomis' attack
on work rules, which introduced the appellation "featherbedding," were reported distributed in 1959.[28] Concerned about
what effect these efforts were having on the public, to whom
the industry was looking for support, the A.A.R. employed
Opinion Research Corporation to study public opinion immediately following the passage of the Transportation Act. As
vindication for their public relations activity, the A.A.R. reported that three of every four respondents favored additional
Congressional action to help the railroads.[29]

Railroad Policy after the Transportation Act of 1958

Perhaps the major accomplishment of the Transportation Act
of 1958, from the point of view of rail management, was the
new freedom the act provided for dealing with the industry's
chronic problem of excess capacity. Clearly, the act had accepted
the industry's position on this problem, namely that the continued elimation of duplicating or loss-producing portions of
the rail network would lower both fixed costs and variable costs
of operation so that net income might rise even as revenues
held steady or declined. The act aided the railroads in their
attack upon operating costs by easing regulatory restrictions
to merger and to service abandonment and discontinuance.
    The Senate hearings had scarcely closed when the Associa-
tion of American Railroads set to work on a new policy state-

ment on merger and consolidation within the industry, and, in February, 1960, it released its "Doyle Committee Report."[30] After surveying public and management policy toward mergers up to 1958, the A.A.R. concluded that merger regulation in the past had been inconsistent and unfair; however, they admitted there were recent signs for hope. In particular, the Doyle Report cited a recent I.C.C. decision that the "lessening of competition will not be a factor of controlling importance" in allowing or disallowing mergers.[31] The A.A.R. noted the apparent change in Commission policy since the passage of the Transportation Act of 1958 and concluded:

> These...decisions by the Commission foreshadow the effectuation of sound economic railroad mergers under Section 5(2) of the Interstate Commerce Act at an accelerated pace. We are convinced that Section 5 (2) as written constitutes adequate legislative machinery to accomplish necessary mergers between railroad companies. Administered with an eye to the transportation facts of life, it will encourage consolidation and serve the industry well.[32]

The merger mood of the A.A.R. was supported by the industry's actions. Between 1958 and 1963, eight major mergers were accomplished;[33] and by 1963, four more merger applications were pending before the I.C.C. and at least twelve others were under discussion within the industry.[34] This compared with only seven mergers of Class I railroads between 1931 and 1958.[35]

From the railroads' view, mergers were the only "long run" solution to their difficulties. James Symes, then chairman of the board of the Pennsylvania Railroad, stated the industry's case before a 1960 Senate hearing on transportation. Symes pointed out:

> If someone asked me what I consider the most important single thing the railroads can do to get the industry back to its healthy vigorous status of 30 years ago and ready to take a progressive place in the transportation of tomorrow, you have been talking about, I would answer in one word — *merge*.[36]

The testimony of Symes and others must have been convincing, for the legislative study concluded:

> To the railroads and to the nation as a whole, the issue

of consolidation no longer has as its primary objective the
equalization of rate returns between weak and strong railroads, the exercise of control to assure participation in
the inter-change of traffic or an alternative to coordination
of activities to reduce waste here and there through isolated activities. The issue is more and more a matter of
survival of privately owned railroad industry which is able
to exploit to the fullest the inherent advantages of railroad
transportation set about as it is with growing competition
from other modes of transportation.[37]

The I.C.C. reacted to the Doyle Report and the Senate
Study on *Transportation Trends* with its own report, *Railroad
Consolidation and the Public Interest.* The study was at once a
rationalization of past actions by the Commission and a blue
print for future policy. In surveying the merger movement, the
Commission noted that it had moved through roughly four
discernible periods, stating these as:

> 1) that prior to the anti-trust acts when rail mergers were
> numerous; 2) the period following these acts, characterized
> by restraint of mergers to prevent undue concentration of
> economic power; 3) the period 1920-40, during which atten-
> tion was focused on government responsibility for promoting
> an overall plan for rail mergers; and 4) the period since
> 1940, when the emphasis was shifted to carrier responsi-
> bility for the initiation of suitable mergers, subject to
> approval by the I.C.C.[38]

Pointing out that the Interstate Commerce Acts made no
mention of the "Public Interest" as a goal of regulation, the
I.C.C. concluded that its experience with consolidation had
led to the development of certain clear "Public Interest" tests
in the evaluation of a merger. Moreover, the Commission assumed that this amounted to a positive accomplishment in the
field of public regulation. The report made no mention of the
Commission's failure to impose its planned mergers in the twenties, nor did it offer any justification for shifting merger initiation from public to industry authorities. Looking at fourteen
major consolidations since 1937, the I.C.C. offered the following
criteria for determining the "Public Interest" in mergers: ade-
quacy of service to the public, economies for the carrier and
for shippers, efficiency of service, inclusion or omission of
regionally related railroads, the interest of the carrier's em-

ployees, and the use to which facilities will be put after the merger.[39] Of lesser importance the I.C.C. study noted: local and regional economic impact, national defense, and intermodal competition.[40]

The report proceeded at some length to defend the Interstate Commerce Commisssion from the criticisms of carriers who argued it acted too slowly and without adequate consideration of the carriers' economic difficulties and from critics who saw the Commission as too willing to acquiesce to economic evidence offered by the roads. However, despite the Commission's maintenance that public interest considerations were crucial to I.C.C. approval, the seven mergers permitted in 1959 and 1960 were based primarily upon economies accruing to the carriers. While this may have been within the bounds of the criteria used by the Commission to determine public interest, it suggested that operating economies were the most important "Public Interest" test. Thus, the balance sheet situations for merging railroads were seemingly the most important evidence in merger hearings.[41]

Between 1959 and 1964, the I.C.C. approved four important mergers in the east — the DL &W — Lackawanna and Wyoming (1959), the Norfolk and Western — Virginia (1959), the Erie — DL & W (1960), and the Seaboard Airline — Atlantic Coastline (1963).[42] The Erie-Lackawanna merger illustrates the use of mergers and resulting abandonments as a means to help weak roads. Both the Erie and the Lackawanna faced falling net earnings through the 1950's, associated for both roads with the decline of anthracite coal traffic and loss-producing commuter operations in the New York-New Jersey metropolitan area.[43]

The 2300 mile Erie directly paralleled the 900 mile Lackawanna for 125 miles through New York.[44] Both had terminals in the New York-New Jersey area and in Buffalo. After listening to the roads' proposal to reduce operating expenses by about 7 percent a year after five years, or by about $13,500,000, the I.C.C. approved the merger. Among the economies gained immediately were the abandonment of seventy-six miles of duplicating trackage and the integration of freight yards and operations in thirteen cities. Additional savings were to be obtained from pooling less-than-carload freight and reducing the number of freight trains.

Although not technically a merger, the purchase of control of the Baltimore and Ohio by the Chesapeake and Ohio had some noteable effects in the east.[45] In particular, this combination, more than the Erie-Lackawanna merger, pushed the New York Central and the Pennsylvania toward consolidation. Both roads were threatened by the possibility that one or the other might be left out of the important mergers which were reshaping eastern trunkline operations. Neither road wished to consider the possibility of operating with the other included by merger with another system. The Central had carefully sought and received I.C.C. protection to traffic it interchanged with the merged Erie and Lackawanna, and the Central also had half-heartedly sought inclusion in the Chesapeake and Ohio's control over the B & O.[46] As the corporate base of railroad operations narrowed through these consolidations, merger offered the Pennsylvania and the Central not only operating savings but protection as well. The merger, however, had been a long time coming.

Late in September of 1957, James Symes, President of the Pennsylvania visited Bob Young of the New York Central at his Waldorf-Astoria Tower apartment. After talking with the Central's board chairmen, he left for Washington to meet with Alfred Perlman, the road's president. To the few insiders who were aware of the meetings, the topic was obvious — a Pennsylvania-New York Central merger. After another month of discussion and exchanging of memorandums, Symes and Perlman announced in a joint news conference that they in fact were "looking forward to a possible merger into a consolidated system."[47] Wall Street's growing gloom with worsening business conditions in the nation temporarily lifted as the financial community savored the possibilities of a super-system merger. Indeed, in the deepening economic crisis, combination seemed an increasingly logical solution to the problem of these two weak giants. Between 1956 and 1958, the Central saw its freight tonnage fall by a quarter and its freight earnings decline from $586 to $435 million. Over the same period Central stock plummeted from 49 1/2 to 13 1/4.[48] Despite the considerable savings promised by merging the Central and the Pennsylvania, a number of difficulties, nevertheless, impeded the consolidation.

Although the two railroads had been drawn together as

co-authors of Morgan's "community of interest" and, except
for some mutual irritation during the merger movement of
the 1920's, had sustained good formal relations, there remained
a latent jealousy which harked back to the 1880's. Among the
Central's management, only Bob Young was an ardent ad-
vocate of mergers. Perlman and others were unconvinced that
merger with the "Pennsy" was the best deal the Central could
get. Perlman believed that his road was basically the stronger
of the two, and, if the recession could be weathered, might
emerge the dominant system in the east.[49] He believed that
his own vigorous efforts at trimming excess capacity by abandonments and service discontinuances would lead to radically lowered operating costs and return the road to a more profitable
position. Without much doubt the position of Perlman on the
merger tended to cool official interest on the part of the Central.

Equally as significant as the attitude of the Central's management in 1957 was the expected reaction of the I.C.C. Decisions by the Commission with regard to mergers indicated
that it still tended to hold as primary in any merger application that competition should not be "substantially lessened."
Merger between the Central and the Pennsylvania in itself
seemed to constitute a very great lessening of competition, and
the inclusion of the Pennsylvania's holdings of the Norfolk and
Western, Lehigh Valley, Wabash, and Detroit and Ironton
would have given the new rail system a network that could
seemingly crush all eastern rail competiton. Despite the considerable progress that had been made in "reeducating" the
I.C.C. on the merger question, most observers were pessimistic
about Commission approval.[50] However, the passage of the
Transportation Act in mid 1958 and the resulting change in
I.C.C. attitudes suddenly improved the possibility of a Penn-
Central combination. Just at this point, with barriers to consolidation falling, the Central broke off negotiation with the
Pennsylvania. Alfred Perlman, more secure in his authority at
the Central since Robert Young's death the year before, announced on January 8, 1959, that merger plans were being
suspended. Asked why, Perlman quipped, "Before we marry
the girl, we want make sure that no other heiress is around
that might fall into our lap."[51]

The decision seemed to amount to a last gasp effort by
the Central's management, probably encouraged by Perlman in

particular, to avoid being suffocated in a merger with the Pennsylvania. With additional encouragement by Allan Kirby of the Allegheny Corporation, which was effectively in control of the New York Central and also a sizeable owner of B & O and C & O stock, the Central's management attempted to gain a last minute inclusion in the B & O-C & O consolidation. Such a merger would, of course, have left the Pennsylvania isolated in the east, certainly a potentially fatal position. It is hard to say if the Central's management viewed this proposal very seriously, for the I.C.C. rejected it almost out of hand. The Commission pointed out that the logical partner for the Central was the Pennsylvania. Perhaps this was the kind of "official" encouragement that the Central had been seeking all along, or, perhaps, it really was reluctant to join the Pennsylvania on the terms that had been discussed up to that time. Whatever the real reason for the Central's action, it had the effect of clearing away the last impediments to consolidation.[53]

In November, 1961, the two roads joined again in merger discussions, engaging the banking houses of First Boston, Glore Forgan, and Morgan Stanley to work out an equitable plan for exchanging Central and Pennsylvania stock in the proposed new corporation. In the eventual adjustment, Central stockholders were to be given 1.3 shares in the new company for each Central share owned and Pennsylvania holders were to exchange on a one-to-one basis. Pennsylvania shareholders would own about 61 percent of the new company and fourteen of the twenty-five directors would come from the Pennsylvania. On March 9, 1962, the two companies filed a formal petition for merger with the I.C.C.[54]

The merging roads were aware that there would be considerable opposition to the merger from a number of economic groups. While shippers had shown at the 1958 hearings that they considered the continued operation of the railroads to be more important than the old fears of railroad monopoly, there was bound to be trouble with railroad labor, state governments and regulative agencies, and affected municipalities. To head this off Symes and Perlman joined to promote a broad educational campaign. The merger, the railroads systematically argued in newspaper advertisements, pamphlets and press releases, would benefit the public, serve the national interest, improve national security, lower costs to shippers, raise wages and increase job possibilities for employees, and heighten competition. Any observer who took even a small part of the claims seriously almost had to believe that the consolidation had divine inspiration at the least.

All of these gains were to be the result of trimming excess capacity from the two roads. In all, $75 million was to be saved annually by reducing duplicating facilities and through coordination of plant and equipment. With finances then improved, the railroads maintained, there was virtually no end to the economic benefits to be provided by the Penn-Central. The logic of "savings through abandonment" was firmly imbedded in the railroads' argument, and there could be no mistaking that the merger meant service reduction.

As any acute observer of American railroad history should have expected, the promised reduction of rail facilities was in no way complemented by a corresponding reduction in book value. Even if some services and trackage were to be operationally useless after merger, they lived on in the new company's balance sheet. The new super-system, operating 20,200 miles of track, would have book assets of $5.3 billion. Its promoters projected annual operating revenues of $1.5 billion.[55]

Despite the obvious operating problems of the two roads and the new sympathy of the I.C.C. to mergers, the merger petition drew a violent storm of criticism. The announcement that merger would mean the immediate loss of about 7,800 jobs, most of them in New York City, Cleveland, Columbus, Syracuse, and Chicago naturally created strong reaction from both the railroad brotherhoods and state and municipal authorities; however the reaction was really somewhat surprising since the two roads had quietly eliminated 32,000 jobs during the 1957-1958 recession.[56] Hearings opened before the I.C.C. examiners on August 20, 1962, and what the railroads had hoped would be a quick decision was not to be reached for nearly four years. The examiners heard testimony of over 300 witnesses for the petitioning railroads, labor, affected communities, and other railroads which sought inclusion in the merger. Forty thousand pages of testimony were collected before the examiners published their own 589-page recommendation to approve the merger.[57]

While the I.C.C. heard evidence on the merger of the Pennsylvania and the Central, the Association of American Railroads encouraged further mergers. Speaking to a conference of state railroad and utilities commissioners, Daniel Loomis noted in 1964 that twenty-five mergers were presently under consideration. To those who advocated that a clear national policy be drawn up governing mergers, Loomis said:

> There is a national policy — and it is a sound policy worked out over a period of at least 40 years of trial and error in this field. This record has varied from outright government attempts in the 1920's to force the railroad structure into a "grand plan"...to the final decision in favor of voluntary initiations of merger within the industry itself....[58]

Condemning the slowness of the I.C.C. to act on the recent merger requests, Loomis noted that mergers were the only solution to the railroads' problems:

> It seems to me that we need to recognize first that to some extent the merger movement is the end product of technological and economic change. *It is the effect not the cause.* Instead of flailing away at the end results, it seems to me that the opponents of mergers would serve themselves, not to mention the national and public interest, far better by devoting their time and talents to solving basic problems of the railroads — massive government spending for competitive transport, coupled with over-taxation and over-regulation of railroads.[59]

In mid 1966, the I.C.C. announced the expected, the approval of the Penn-Central merger. The old era of rail operations in the east was officially ended. The rivalry between the two roads had for a long time set the tone in eastern railroad affairs, but this was now all changed. The two giants were one, and the old fears of "railroad monopoly" were pushed aside by a growing concern over how this new supersystem would survive the crisis in transportation. The I.C.C.'s decision along with its earlier approval of the B&O-C&O and Wabash-Nickel Plate combinations, amounted to a final and irrevocable elimination of intra-industry competition in the east. It, of course, had been a long time coming.

The I.C.C. decision, however, was not yet the end of the matter. A number of problems yet remained, such as the status of the ailing New Haven and the relationship of the D and H,

Lackawanna, Norfolk and Western, and the Boston and Maine
to the new system. A number of suits followed and on October
19, 1967, a federal court finally determined that the I.C.C. had
acted "properly and lawfully" in authorizing the merger. Appeals eventually brought the case to the Supreme Court and
on January 15, 1968, the court unanimously found for the
Pennsylvania and the New York Central, although it did specify
that the merged system must shoulder the burden of keeping
the sick New Haven alive.[60]

Although rail management envisioned drastic reductions in
excess capacity as a result of consolidations, the shrinkage of
the New York network after 1958 owed little to mergers. In
all, mainline trackage declined from 6695 miles in 1958 to 5501
miles in 1967. The Erie-Lackawanna merger of 1960 led to the
direct abandonment of 76 miles of mainline which the I.C.C.
considered "unessential duplication," and over the next half
dozen years, the road closed down an equivalent amount of
trackage.[61] However, most of the abandonments in New York
during this period were accounted for by the New York Central's "piece by piece" dismantling of its loss-producing branches
and the complete abandonment of four separate railroads.[62]

Under Perlman's program of radically reducing operating
costs, the Central abandoned about 300 miles of operating
mainline and reduced second track, terminal and switching trackage by about twice this amount. The focus of Perlman's cost
cutting program was the Central's once highly developed branch
system. Most of these branch or lateral routes into northern
New York and those paralleling the road's trunk route through
the midlands of the state had declined as traffic originators as
truck competition and the comparative economic stagnation of
the regions they serviced reduced revenues.

Prominent among the Central's abandonment programs was
what appeared to be the eventual cessation of all service into
northern New York. In 1959, the road closed the forty-two
mile Malone-Lake Clear route, ending all connections between
the Northern Adirondacks and Canada. Formerly important
mainline tracks between Oswego and Mexico and Richland and
Camden were also closed, marking the end of the historic Rome
and Watertown route.[63] Late in 1963, the Central announced
a plan to abandon all of its North Country operations except
for a single line to Watertown and Ogdensburg and a few spurs.

This meant the dismantling of the entire Adirondack Branch with its 127-mile Prospect Junction-Lake Placid route. The Central similarly requested abandonment of one leg of the Ogdensburg Branch by closing the Utica-Carthage route for thirteen miles between Lowville and Lyons Falls.[64] It also asked abandonment of the old Rutland tracks between Norwood and Malone and the shortening of a number of spurs. The decline of tourists, the dwindling of carload freight, and the high cost of maintenance was bringing to an end rail service in northern New York in much the same way that the disappearance of the New York Ontario and Western had left the Catskill region without railroads. By 1966, the Central had only partly succeeded in this plan. The Little Falls to Lowville petition was allowed, but, largely due to the efforts of the Public Service Commission, the I.C.C. had delayed action on the other petitions.

Not all of the abandonment activities of the Central, however, were concentrated in the elimination of its northern branches. The initiation of a central traffic-control system in 1959 also permitted extensive abandonment as the Central shifted its important overhead freight to one, double tracked mainline. After proving that shippers would not be adversely affected, the Central received permission in 1960 to close 70 miles of West Shore line which paralleled its major trunk route between Syracuse and Rochester and between Byron and Chile Junction. Additional abandonments of this line were permitted along the Syracuse-Auburn-Buffalo branch so that this earlier important freight route was reduced to service as a series of spurs.[65] The Central continued to cut back its old West Shore route during the early sixties, abandoning stretches between Byron and Oakfield and between New York Mills and Vernon. Among the more important closings of once-productive spurs was the Central's abandonment of the old Little Falls and Dolgeville and the shortening of the Ulster and Delaware line by cutting back twenty miles of track between Oneonta and Bloomville.[66]

Aside from some insignificant spur reductions, the remaining loss in rail operations in New York resulted from the total abandonment of four companies — the Prattsburgh, the Unadilla Valley, the Rutland, and the Lehigh and New England. The ten mile long Prattsburgh had traditionally depended on milk, coal and less-than-carload shipments. In 1962, after a decade of annual deficits it ceased operation.[67] The Unadilla Valley operating forty-nine miles of track between Bridgewater and Sidney had attempted to continue operations after the New York Ontario and Western ceased operations; however, it serviced no major industries, and the defunct O & W had been its chief source of traffic. The Unadilla Valley finally sought relief in abandonment in 1958.[68] The abandonment of the Rutland and the Lehigh and New England were more important since they were relatively large interstate carriers. The Lehigh and New England operated 177 miles of road, although only four miles were in New York. The Rutland operated 167 of its 331 miles in the Empire State.

In 1961, the Lehigh and New England appealed to the I.C.C. to cease operations, showing that 97 percent of its freight traffic was served by only forty miles of road. After proving that this portion of the road (all operated within New Jersey) would be sold to the Central Railroad of New Jersey, the I.C.C. approved the application of "convenience and necessity."[69]

The Rutland, like the New York Ontario and Western, had been ailing for many years before it was abandoned. With total revenues of $5,500,000 in 1950, gross earnings fell to under $4,000,000 in 1954, and to $3,000,000 in 1960.[70] The loss of traffic to other modes of transportation and the general economic stagnation of the area it serviced was evident in the decline of freight handled by the road. As late as 1956, the Rutland still moved 56,000 carloads and 18,000 less-than-carloads of freight. In 1960, this had fallen to 29,000 and 2,700 respectively.[71] Until the 1950's, milk shipment had accounted for as much as 15 percent of the road's income, but in 1961, the Rutland earned only $57,000 from milk revenues.[72]

The loss in revenues forced the road to forego capital improvements so that the railroad's chief engineer calculated that at least $1,500,000 in repairs was needed in 1961. Costs were ruthlessly cut. Service was halved between 1956 and 1961, and the labor force was reduced from 1142 to 489. Unable to meet contract-required wage increases, the road was struck in 1960 and again from September 1961 until it was abandoned in 1962.[73]

Despite protests from the Railroad Brotherhoods, who charged that abandonment was simply an attempt at union breaking, and protests from the states of New York and Vermont and local shippers, the I.C.C. applied the same rule of reason it had used in the case of the Ontario and Western abandonment — that no shipper may be compelled to operate at a loss, despite the public inconvenience.[74] Although admitting "it is a well-established fact that there is a need for railroad service in the north country of New York and Vermont," the I.C.C. could find no buyer for the Rutland at its salvage value of $5,765,912. Eventually, the state of Vermont bought the 132-mile segment from Burlington to White Creek, New York, for $1,850,000 and placed it in operation as Vermont Railways in January, 1964.

Under arrangements specified by the I.C.C., the New York Central was obliged to operate the Norwood to Malone Junction portion of the Rutland, over which it had had traffic rights. Nevertheless, the loss of the road meant the elimination of rail service for an area of New York and Vermont with a population of approximately 140,000.[75]

Equally significant as the reduction in the rail network through abandonment was the curtailment of service, which the Transportation Act of 1958 almost completely placed under federal control. Section 13a(1) and 13a(2) of the act gave the Commission original jurisdiction over all interstate passenger trains and appellate jurisdiction over intrastate trains.[76] In the case of interstate trains, the I.C.C. was required to enter an investigation within thirty days of receiving notice from the railroad, or the petition was to be automatically approved. With regard to intrastate trains, railroads were permitted to appeal to the I.C.C. any state decision. The I.C.C., then, was obliged to investigate and reach its own decision.[77]

The Commission's reaction to its new authority was predictable in its accommodating response to the industry. Between 1958 and 1963, the Commission received ninety-five applications under Section 13a(1) to discontinue 286 interstate trains. It permitted forty railroads to drop 189 trains and denied discontinuance to seventeen roads affecting fifty-seven trains.[78] Under Section 13a(2) governing appeals from unfavorable state decisions, the I.C.C. responded even more favorably. With twenty-eight petitions received between 1958 and 1963, the Commission denied discontinuance in only three cases.[79]

By 1963, the New York Public Service Commission had received nineteen petitions to discontinue interstate passenger service. The Commission, its hands tied by the Transportation Act, had acted more or less in favor of the railroads in about half these cases.[80] In only one case was its decision to deny discontinuance sustained by the Interstate Commerce Commission. However, even this I.C.C. order for the Central to continue eight trains on its St. Lawrence division was later modified so that the Central could drop six of them.[81] Assessing such developments, the state commissioners described the Transportation Act of 1958 as "a misguided national policy which would appear to be bent on the destruction, not the preservation, of the country's railroad industry in general, and the passenger portion thereof in particular."[82]

It would be inaccurate to characterize the Public Service Commission's actions as totally obstructive after 1958. While fighting to maintain some limited passenger service in the state, the Commission was still responsive to railroad efforts to close less-than-carload freight operations and to curtail freight and passenger station operations. Between 1959 and 1964, the Public Service Commission received petitions to close 569 separate freight or passenger agency stations. Only fourteen requests were denied, and a few were modified by the Commission — requiring some service to be maintained, but allowing partial abandonment. However, 307 petitions were accepted without changes.[83]

A Change of Attitude in New York State

From the point of view of shippers in the state, as well as Governor Harriman and state legislative leaders, the discussions leading up to the passage of the Transportation Act of 1958 seemed to indicate that the railroads would be given almost unqualified permission to curtail operations at their leisure, with no control vested in state authorities. According to the Public Service Commission, the response of the state government, while debate on the Transportation Act of 1958 was going on, was to enlist "the aid of Senator Javits and other members of the New York delegation to Congress" to amend the Transportation Act to protect regional economic interests.[84] The pressure ultimately brought to bear by New York congressmen and congressmen from other eastern states could not match the engergetic proseletizing which had been carried on by the

Association of American Railroads. Opposition to some of the original proposals, the Public Service Commission reported, "succeeded in causing the elimination of provisions under which the railroads in New York and elsewhere could have closed down commuter lines almost at will."[85] However, the emasculation of most of the Public Service Commission's remaining powers was completed under the act.

Having failed to halt the shrinkage of railroad operation through threats and obdurateness, New York State now resorted to sweetness. In 1958, the state legislature directed the Public Service Commission to investigate the financial condition of New York railroads "...for the purpose of evaluating the need and formulating recommendations for state and local government action pertaining to passenger service problems in general, and the taxation of railroad franchises and property in particular."[86] What the legislature was seeking was a device to sustain loss-producing railroad operations, especially commuter operations, by means of tax relief subsidy.

The new Republican administration of Governor Nelson Rockefeller moved quickly to offer selective aid to the railroads. In February, 1959, the governor convened a meeting between himself, Governor Meyner of New Jersey, and Mayor Wagner of New York City to explore the possibilities of tax relief or direct subsidy to the New York commuter roads.[87] On the basis of a special message by the governor to the state legislature on March 20, 1959, and the Public Service Commission's completed study of railroad finances, the New York Legislature approved several measures in 1959 to subsidize state railroads.[88] Long-run tax relief of up to $15,000,000 per year was obtained for the railroads by gradually scaling down assessment taxes. The legislature provided that communities adversely affected by this tax abatement could receive up to 50 percent of their lost revenue in state assistance. The legislature also approved advancing $20,000,000 to the Port of New York Authority to purchase air conditioned commuter cars for lease to the Long Island, the New Haven and the New York Central. For the purpose of purchasing additional equipment and refunding the state's initial loan, the legislature provided a state guarantee to a New York Authority bond issue of $100,000,000. Other measures approved included authorization for the creation of a State Office of Transportation and a New York-New Jersey Transportation Agency.

In its 1959 study of railroad finances, the New York Public Service Commission conceded that the state's Full Crew Laws, which had become an issue to rail management in its public campaign against "featherbedding," were in need of revision.[89] In particular, the Commission noted that "65 percent of the total operating expense budget of the railroads in New York" were labor costs.[90] On the basis of evidence that labor's share in operating costs in New York was high by comparison with national averages, the legislature directed the Commission to make recommendations with regard to the state's full crew laws. Early in 1960, the Commission released a report urging that the laws be modified, more or less in concurrence with what industry had been proposing.[91]

While the long-run effect of the state legislature's and the governor's actions in 1959 are difficult to calculate, they are illustrative of a drastic change in state government approach to railroad regulation. Quantitatively, the dollar value of the financial subsidies given the railroads by the state in 1959 exceeded the value of all state aid given in the nineteenth century. But, more important than the financial aid, was the tacit admission that it was properly the state's function to sustain the railroads. Significant changes in public and private attitudes had occurred between the creation in 1906 of a powerful Public Service Commission, charged with regulating the monster railroad corporations, and Governor Rockefeller's memorandum to the legislature in 1959. In what must be presumed was the new approach toward state regulation of the railroads, the Governor, in requesting financial aid for the industry, observed:

> The obligation on the state to take action to preserve our transportation system arises from the recognition of the public necessity for rapid, mass transportation into and around metropolitan areas. This public dependence necessarily created a degree of public responsibility. In addition, the importance of our transportation system to the entire economy of the state and to the welfare of our people as a whole increases the responsibility.[92]

After 1959, the philosophy underguiding railroad regulation

in New York took basically the same course as concepts which had longer been applied to national regulation. During the mid and late sixties, the state continued to make periodic loan aid available to the commuter railroads, and, finally, in 1968 assumed control of the badly deteriorated but absolutely essential Long Island Railroad. The parent Pennsylvania cheerfully gave up its problem child to the state and there was not the slightest rumor of "growing socialism" raised by any influential observer. It should be noted, however, that the Pennsylvania retained essential ownership of the rights of way and the real estate of the road and continued to operate all passenger concessions on the route. What the state really received was nothing more than a motley collection of obsolescent commuter cars and engines and a badly run down ribbon of rails.

In other areas, the state provided help by altering the full-crew laws to the railroads' advantage and the Public Service Commission appeared to be somewhat more attentive in listening to railroad demands for service discontinuances. Overall, it appeared by the late 1960's that "public interest" responsibilities were considered discharged by state officials if actions were taken to keep the trains, or at least some of the trains, running.

The New Railroad Policy's Effect on Railroad Balance Sheets

The railroads' decision to press for contraction of the rail network through mergers, abandonments and service discontinuance produced no immediate economic miracles. The American railroad industry continued to stagger through the comparatively poor business conditions of the late fifties and early sixties. In fact, by 1963, five years after the crisis year of 1958, gross earnings stood well below their 1958 levels.

For New York railroads, earnings were about 3 percent, or $65,000,000 lower in 1963 than five years before, and none of the larger roads, with the exception of the Long Island equalled their 1958 earnings. The Long Island's performance was, of course, somewhat unique since it had received large amounts of direct aid from the Long Island Transit Authority and the Port of New York Authority to improve equipment as well as obtaining a number of helpful fare increases from the Public Service Commission. Only the New York Central and the Pennsylvania, of those roads not reporting net losses, were able to improve their net income percentages between 1958 and 1963. This improvement was quite modest and, when compared with more prosperous periods for the industry, would scarcely seem to offer much encouragement to management. For the Central, net income actually fell between 1958 and 1963, but by much less than its $150,000,000 decline in total operating revenue over the period. By 1963, the Pennsylvania, the B&O, and the Central all reported net incomes of less than 2 percent of operating revenue. The Erie-Lackawanna, the New Haven, and the Lehigh Valley, meanwhile, reported deficits.

Even the slight improvement after 1958 in net income by the Pennsylvania and the Central had only been obtained by the most drastic cost cutting.[93] As we have noted earlier, under Perlman, the Central had radically reduced the scale of its operations; however, along with reducing trackage and service, it has also pruned 13,000 full-time employees from its payroll between 1958 and 1960, a cutback of about 22 percent. This alone had given the road an additional $40,000,000 in reduced costs. The Pennsylvania had similarly reduced its employment by about 20 percent, eliminating about 18,000 jobs over the same period.[94]

For both the Central and the Pennsylvania, the existence of even a modest net income was really the result of "non-railroad" business activities rather than rail operation. Both roads were important real estate operators as well as security owners. In 1963, the Central collected over $10,000,000 from office rents and concessions in New York City and obtained another $10,000,000 from its six New York hotels.[95] These and other sources of "non-operating" income netted the road $23,000,000 in 1963, a figure more than three times greater than net income from all other Central business activities. The Pennsylvania similarly reported net earnings from non-railroad enterprises as $29,000,000.[96]

The Erie-Lackawanna merger, earlier heralded as the cure-all to the economic problems of these two weak roads, had not brought a sudden reversal in their operating condition. Net losses from their combined operation in 1963 was more than $8,000,000, half a million dollars more than the total of their separate losses in 1958. Nevertheless, rail leaders remained optimistic about the Erie-Lackawanna's future.[97]

Such general optimism among industry leaders reflected their faith in the ultimate economic benefits of contraction policies. Most understood that the savings they were effecting would not return immediate gains. Mergers and abandonments provided benefits over a much longer period of time than the public assumed. And, as the national economy took off in a protracted period of expansion beginning in 1963, they could point proudly at the temporarily improved performance of the railroads. In the economic boom, largely provided by the Viet Nam War build-up, railroad earnings again soared. By 1966, overall railroad net income to total earnings showed a better record than that of most airlines and trucking firms. A national financial publication proclaimed:

> True, the railroads are no longer the blue chips of the investment world. True, they have lost out to cars and airplanes in the transportation of people. But, as the profit and revenue figures show, the railroad industry is still the backbone of the nation's long haul freight transportation system.[98]

Among New York railroads, freight movement expanded by more than 35 percent between 1961 and 1966. At the same time total revenue grew from about $2.5 billion to $3.1 billion and net income rose from a deficit of $88 million to a surplus of $210.3 million.[99] By reducing their dwindling earned surplus in 1962, the New York railroads had paid a scanty $14 million in dividends, but they were easily able to pay $118 million in 1966.

While the boom in freight movement and the incidental economies of contraction briefly stimulated a new surge of hopefulness among rail leaders, the continued operation of the hated passenger service provided an interesting contrast. Between 1960 and 1966, total passenger volume in New York fell from 205 million to 122 million.[100] By 1966, only the Central provided significant non-commuter passenger functions in New York, and the quite unsubtle thrust of the Central's corporate policy was to waste no money on present service and no time in compelling the I.C.C. to accept its plan for dropping long-distance passenger movement altogether.

The contraction of the rail network, the resultant cost cutting, and the general rise of railroad business, however, had not yet brought a lasting solution to all of the industry's problems. In the east particularly, most roads reported serious cash and capital problems by the late 1960's. These resulted from a number of developments. First, the long post-war downslide of railroad fortunes had greatly reduced their earned surpluses. Second, much of their available cash and considerable amounts of credit had been absorbed in making good the approved mergers. Third, the general inflationary push after 1967 had necessitated action by monetary authorities to tighten credit and dry up sources of loanable funds. As a result of these forces, railroads found themselves owners of enormous book value assets but quite impoverished with regard to ready cash or credit sources. The old policies of capital austerity were continued and with undesireable effects. Equipment and mainline trackage in the east, according to the New York Public Service Commission began to show unmistakable signs of deterioration which could be measured by an alarming rise in derailment and other service breakdowns.

In early June 1970 the Penn-Central super-system, one of the world's largest corporations, with admitted assets of over $7 billion, announced that it was in serious financial trouble. Penn-Central stock, which hit the market at an optimistic high of 86 on February 1, 1968, was down to an embarrassing 10. Management, under Stuart Saunders, former president of the old Pennsy, admitted that it had not yet been able to obtain the sought after savings that merger was to produce. As had been the case with the smaller Erie-Lackawanna merger, the income statement of the merged roads was worse than the separate statements of the two systems before. The Penn-Central admitted losses from its rail operations of $85 million for the eleven months of merged operation in 1968, a deficit of over $120 million for calendar 1969, and a prospective loss of over $150 million for 1970. The company had seen its $275 million contingency fund, set up to cover extraordinary costs after consolidation, vanish, and complete disaster had been avoided only by the average annual earnings of $80 million from its $4 billion of non-railroad investment.[101]

Faced with the immediate problems of covering $100 million in long term debt that would fall due in 1970 and maintaining the decrepit New Haven, as per the merger stipulations, the

Penn-Central followed what by this time was a predictable policy for railroads faced with economic crisis. It again turned to the federal government. Pleading that it could not raise the cash or credit privately and hinting that the essential commuter operations of the railroad were threatened, management appealed to the federal government to indemnify up to $500 million in loans to see the road through its present crisis. While such action demanded special legislation, the Penn-Central asked that an immediate Defense Department guarantee of $50 million be granted under the provisions of the Defense Production Act which provided for government loans to essential private businesses.[102]   As a gesture of its intentions to take its difficulties seriously and to attack the merger problem more vigorously, the road dropped Saunders from his $250,000 a year job as president and replaced him with Paul Gorman, the President of Western Electric. Although without railroad background, Gorman was expected to bring to his new job the experience of running a large, monopolistic public utility and that was, after all, the direction to which rail corporate policy had been pointing for a long time.[103]   In announcing its management change and the loan request, the Penn-Central lost no opportunity to point out that its real difficulties lay in not being able to make good the economies of the merger — especially the court imposed requirements to operate the New Haven and the obligation to keep all of the old Central and Pennsylvania employees or to furlough them at full pay.[104]   It was apparent that management had not given up on "contraction" as its way to prosperity. It simply maintained that it had not yet been able to make good such a policy.

These actions, however, were only a prelude to events that followed as the Penn-Central moved more determinedly toward obtaining emergency relief. Federal officials, especially high cabinet officers voiced concern over the road's financial and operating status, but immediate aid could not be obtained. Faced with the problem of more than $75 million in loans and interest falling due at the end of June, the Penn-Central's management moved to the bankruptcy courts on June 21.

The decision, at least superficially, evoked more public sympathy and concern than was frankly deserved. First of all, the bankruptcy petition only affected the Penn-Central Transportation Company, the railroad subsidiary of the giant Penn-Central Company. While the transportation company did in fact own some attractive non-railroad properties, such as 30 acres of Manhattan offices and hotels, the more profitable railroad and non-railroad facilities of the parent corporation had been carefully separated from the old Central and Pennsylvania operations in the merger. These assets were unaffected by the bankruptcy petition, and since their earnings had for the past two years been wiped out by the railroad's losses, the bankruptcy action actually served to strengthen the parent company's financial position. The "good" investments were now protected from the chronic disease of the vast bulk of the rail operations.

A second noteworthy aspect of the bankruptcy proceedings was that under existing laws such proceedings could be made to work for the management's benefit. Under ordinary business bankruptcies a company's assets could be sold off to pay creditors; however, under Section 77 of the Bankruptcy Act of 1933, railroads were exempted from this procedure. Instead, a court-appointed trusteeship might be created to order the company's debts and generally put the line in order before returning it to its original ownership. While operating under the bankruptcy trusteeship, the road was, of course, free of all tax and interest obligations. Such provisions doubtless made bankruptcy a desireable alternative for a line hard-pressed by a cash squeeze and facing continuing operating losses. In fact, it allows for reorganization with very little in the way of penalties.

The decision to accept bankruptcy must also be seen to have a "political" effect. Railroads had always received the most favorable legislative and regulative attention in times of crisis. The Penn-Central's unhappiness with accepting the New Haven and the employment conditions of the merger were well known, as was its wish to abandon or reduce all of its commuter and passenger operations. Insofar as these uneconomic operations could be cited as causes for the road's difficulties, bankruptcy might only be a prelude to a program of accelerated service contraction. The possibility of the Penn-Central's collapse was a Damocles sword hanging over the State of New York and the federal government. The old, implied blackmail had reappeared and there was little reason to believe that it would not be paid as it had always been paid before. The eventual bill was not altogether clear, but, assuming that there was no sudden and unexpected sentiment for nationalizing the company, observers speculated that it probably amounted to direct financial aid, permission to contract facilities, and, perhaps, government commitment to directly subsidize the hauling of the Penn-Central's 100,000 daily commuters.

Although a detailed study of the long-term prospects for the Penn-Central and other railroad giants remains for another time, the evidence is still certain that the illusion of great success through merger and network contraction, which have become key parts of railroad corporate policy, remains to be realized. After 1958, the railroads had won their battle to attack excess capacity through the abandonment of all marginal services and they had succeeded in enlisting government as their active financial and regulative protector. What this means ultimately for the privately owned railroad industry can, at this point, be only speculative assertion. What it means for New York and other states is the promise of greater corporate concentration and therefore greater contraction in rail operations. For many communities and shippers across the nation, "saving railroad service" would actually mean losing it.

VII

WHAT RAILROAD STRATEGY HAD ACCOMPLISHED
—THE NEW YORK NETWORK IN THE LATE 1960s

The development of railroad corporate policy in the twentieth century, as the foregoing study has endeavored to show, has been dominated by two crucial themes. It has been persistently preoccupied by the problem of excess capacity, first stemming from extensive over-building in the era of construction and then from the rise of competing transportation modes; and, it has steadily moved toward ever greater reliance upon government regulative and legislative action to deal with the railroads' special economic problems. These two themes are, of course, tightly interwoven and completely inseparable.

At first, eastern railroads resorted to a kind of industry leadership under the corporate hegemony of the New York Central and the Pennsylvania. This "community of interest" arrangement attempted to end the destructive competition and rate wars set off by excess capacity, as these two roads tried to acquire financial control of key routes while maintaining close corporate ties between each other. In the 1920's, with consolidation technically granted political approval under the Transportation Act of 1920, the railroads resumed their efforts to develop a high degree of industry integration. However, the depression, the growth of auto, bus, and truck competition, and radical changes in the compostion of commodity movement produced even greater underutilization. For the first time, in the 1930's, outright abandonment of loss-producing rail operations was accepted as the only solution. Meanwhile, the industry obtained long sought after government approval for formal intercorporate cooperation. The formation of the Association of American Railroads as the official railroad policy-making instrument had encouragement from both President Roosevelt and the I.C.C. The trucking industry was brought under federal regulation, railroads were given virtual exemption from anti-trust legislation, and, in the financial crisis posed by the depression, the federal government made available large amounts of loan aid for the industry. By the late 1950's, after more than two decades of continued economic crisis only briefly interrupted by World War II, the railroads succeeded in getting federal approval for accelerated mergers and abandonment activity. For some roads, there was no possible economic solution to their problems, and total abandonment was the only alternative. For the larger lines, consolidation and the resulting trimming of duplicated trackage and services promised the possibility of a brighter economic future. Meanwhile, state regulative agencies, which had long been a thorn in the industry's side, were systematically stripped of their power in favor of the I.C.C., and the federal commission usually proved itself to be a friend of the railroads.

To be accurate and to avoid a too narrow misinterpretation of these developments, it should be understood that not all of the industry's requests were granted out of hand by government authorities. From the railroads' point of view, the I.C.C. always moved too slowly on rating matters and mergers, tax burdens were consistently too heavy, and the great body of regulative law built up by statutes and administrative and court decisions was cumbersome and contradictory. Nevertheless, despite often bitter attacks on the Interstate Commerce Commission by the Association of American Railroads and other spokesmen of the industry, relations between government and the railroads still indicated that if the industry's financial or operating problems became serious enough, some measure of relief would always be obtained through favorable federal regulation or legislation. While the relief may not have been all that was sought by railroads, it was likely to be largely on their terms. Despite the existence of elaborate regulative machinery and their own protestations to the contrary, American railroads have had pretty much their own way in developing and pursuing their own corporate policies in the twentieth century.

However, where has this corporate policy ultimately led? What has been its effect? Clearly from the industry's point of view of profit and loss, it has not yet produced final economic success. While management may maintain, and possibly quite correctly, that this is because the full integration of operations and the contraction of excess facilities has not yet been achieved, that is not really the point, or at least, it is not the whole point. This study has focused almost exclusively on the evolution and maturity of corporate policy, and, while this may indeed be evaluated in terms of its own performance, there have been important external effects which must be considered as well. Such effects are vividly pointed out by looking at what happened to the physical pattern of New York's railroad network.

By the late 1960's, the New York railroad network had contracted to under 5500 miles of mainline trackage, a reduction of more than 25 percent from that operated in 1900 and more than 30 percent from its peak of operations in 1914. Moreover, another 200 miles of trackage was involved in abandonment proceedings before the I.C.C.[1] The reduction in trackage was all the more significant since almost all of it had taken place within the past thirty years. In fact, more than 1500 miles had been eliminated in the decade before 1966.

The decision to abandon trackage had been based upon a number of different operating situations. About one-half of the abandoned trackage was the result of decisions by railroads to discontinue all operations. The other half were partial abandonments. Roughly, half of the latter type resulted from the cutting back of low revenue spurs or loss-producing branch lines. The remainder reflected the closing of duplicating mainline routes, such as the Central's abandonment of segments of the old West Shore route or the Erie-Lackawanna's discontinuance of parallel trackage.

A close examination of the tables and maps in the appendix shows that most of the rail abandonments, whether of complete roads or of branch lines, were along routes which generally ran north and south. Most of these routes had originally been laid out as "feeders" interchanging with the New York Central and the Erie and had been built in the period of highly speculative construction in the seventies and eighties. After their construction, many of these roads lost their initial identity in reorganizations and mergers which often absorbed them into larger systems, although a few, like the Unadilla Valley, had remained small and unattached.[2] However, for many of these speculative feeders, neither merger nor reorganization could overcome their inherent traffic weaknesses.

The feeders rarely serviced large urban areas and depended heavily upon the shipment of coal and agricultural goods. As we have previously noted, the decline of coal traffic, especially anthracite coal, and the steady depopulation and economic decline of agricultural areas in the state meant serious hardship for a number of small feeders and the abandonment of many which earlier had been absorbed as branches of larger systems.

In 1900, coal had accounted for more than 40 percent of the gross freight tonnage carried by railroads operating in New York and probably contributed to as much as 35 percent of total freight revenues. In fact, eight of the larger railroads reported that more than 49 percent of their freight tonnage was derived from coal. By 1966, the formerly important anthracite carriers, the Erie-Lackawanna, the Delaware and Hudson and the Lehigh Valley, carried coal equivalent to only about 15 or 20 percent of their total freight tonnage. In terms of revenue, coal contributed to only 5 percent of the Erie-Lackawanna's income and about 10 percent for the Lehigh Valley and the Delaware and Hudson. The Central, the Pennsylvania, and the Baltimore and Ohio, largely due to their longer routes and to their connections with the bituminous coal fields, still reported that coal amounted to more than 30 percent of their total tonnage. However, all of these roads had lost earlier important anthracite business in New York State.[3] As suggested earlier in the study, the anthracite business had provided much of the impetus to the reorganization of the New York railroad network at the beginning of the century. Thus, the virtual collapse of this industry is critical to understanding the railroads' economic difficulties in the state in the 1960's.

However, the unique role played by coal and other bulk commodities in the railroads' decline has usually been overestimated by the railroads. To be sure, the permanent loss of any intensively transported bulk item presented a serious revenue problem, but only a relatively few lines were absolutely dependent upon a single good and generated no other important traffic. Railroads rarely saw the other types of traffic as sufficient, from an operating point of view, to justify keeping these branch lines going; and, generally, as coal or some other major item dwindled, the railroad began to dismantle other services. The technique that was developed was used widely. On a branch line with declining revenue, the railroad would first begin to cut back frequency of service. Then, it would reduce or eliminate less-than-carload operations. Next, it would petition to abandon parts of the branch, operating it as a spur or even two spurs. Each step, of course, reduced the quality of service and tended to induce shippers along the right of way to seek new modes of transportation. Finally, when traffic demand had been reduced enough, the road would petition the I.C.C. for a "convenience and necessity" certificate to abandon the entire line.

The technique was well developed and, presumably, well-known. Once when the New York Central was applying the procedure to its old Ulster and Delaware line, it was embarrassed by some local railroad buffs' purchase offer on a 20-mile segment running out of Oneonta to Bloomville. The Central had just managed to demonstrate that this portion of the branch line did not pay its way and had received I.C.C. approval to abandon it and run the remainder of the line into Kingston as a spur. The amateur railroad operators hoped to use the trackage for steam excursion runs and even offered to interchange freight with the Central. The Central's management was horrified, for this could clearly delay their plan to eventually abandon the entire U & D route. By pointing out the lack of capital and expertise of the prospective operators and through a rush job of tearing up the old trackage, they succeeded in deterring I.C.C. approval of the purchase offer.

No section of the state was exempt from railroad abandonment; however, the north, the central midlands, and the southeast portions suffered the greatest railroad losses. In the North Country, the abandonment of the Rutland and the New York Central's decision to cut back its once promising St. Lawrence and Adirondack divisions meant the elimination of any kind of rail service for several dozen communities. In the midlands and the southeast portions of the state, the closing of the New York Ontario and Western left over 100 villages without direct rail service.[4]

While a comparison of the Railroad Maps of 1900 and 1966 makes the abandonment of trackage appear quite prodigious, it should be recalled that a large part of the reduction in operations is not shown at all. For instance, the closing of less-than-carload freight agencies had the effect of discontinuing rail service in many communities. Less-than-carload freight had once accounted for as much as 10 percent of the freight traffic of the Central and the Pennsylvania. However, by 1955, after drastic reductions in "L.C.L." operation, the Erie, the New York Central, and the Pennsylvania all reported less-than-carload tonnage to be only slightly more than 4 percent of freight volume, and, by 1963, the Central and the Pennsylvania had reduced "L.C.L." tonnage to less than half of 1 percent of all tonnage. Meanwhile, the non-trunk carriers, which had also moved much "L.C.L." freight in the predominantly rural areas of the state, had similarly reduced this service.

The corporate structure of the New York railroad network also illustrated the constriction of railroad operations. While the rail network in 1900 had been dominated by a few large railroad corporations, seventy-one separately capitalized steam railroad companies operated in the state. By 1966, only twenty-one of these retained their earlier corporate identify; and, of the eighteen roads built after 1900, only seven were more or less unchanged. The routes of forty-three companies that disappeared between 1900 and 1966 had been wholly or almost completely abandoned, and seventeen other properties were identifiable only as parts of larger systems. During this period, six new railroad corporations had been formed by the acquisition or merger of these companies.

The degree of corporate integration of the railroad network, however, is not completely revealed in this comparison. The seven largest railroads alone controlled more than 90 percent of all trackage. Moreover, two of these roads — the Lehigh Valley and the Long Island — were then controlled by the Pennsylvania through majority stock ownership. Six of the small separately capitalized roads were also directly controlled by several of the large roads. The approval of the Penn-Central merger in 1966, of course, meant the elimination of any pretense to competition among the eastern railroads; but, the old fears of "railroad monoply" were no longer viable political levers or an important source of public argument. All that had passed as part of an earlier era.

The modifications in the physical dimensions and the corporate structure of New York's railroads in the twentieth century, however, has much larger significance than that indicated in a mere recitation of abandonments, mergers and operating statistics. For one thing, the changes in the railroad network mirrored an important readjustment of the basic economic organization and business outlook of the industry.

In the nineteenth century, railroad companies, especially those operating in the east, had a primarily regional character to their enterprise. Railroads usually had been built with large amounts of local capital and local speculative genius. Communities with railroads were exceedingly proud of their transportation facilities and, in most cases, were willing to grant the companies certain financial and operational advantages. The railroads, in particular, the smaller roads and, in lesser degrees, the trunk lines, tended to reflect local economic interests on their boards of directors. It was understood by both the railroad's management and the communities serviced that the future of the railroad and the future of the region were intricately connected. Although by the 1890's, as Taylor and Neu have pointed out, the American railroad network had become "national" in its distribution, commodity shipment, and financial structure, most individual railroads still provided very important regional transportation functions.[6] They afforded transportation for important intra-regional shipments while they also tied the little communities along their rights-of-way to other areas.[7]

The abandonment of routes, the discontinuance of certain types of freight and passenger service, and the further integration of the railroads into fewer and fewer large systems marked the decline of the local or regional aspect of railroad operations. By the mid 1960's railroads served almost exclusively an interregional function, and then only between a relatively few large cities or collecting points. Railroads no longer carried less-than-carload freight and, instead, were attempting to exploit their advantages as long distance, bulk carriers. Railroad leaders ceased to view many of the localities through which their mainlines ran as important to the roads' own economic future. Indeed, most of these little terminals, if they were still operated at all, were thought to be economic liabilities. Meanwhile, both large and small communities, after observing the persistent shrinkage of the New York railroad network, could not afford to place so much reliance on the railroads for future economic development. This is not to say that the railroad was no longer an important transportation device or that it obtained no real economic benefits for areas having rail service, but the character of the service was quite different. The regional nature of the network had been replaced by a more national and inter-regional direction. A contemporary map of New York's railroads fails to express the degree of this change, for it only shows the distribution of trackage. However, with the closing of smaller stations and the abandonment of many other services, hundreds of communities along the rights-of-way of operating railroads received no railroad benefits whatsoever.

What happened in New York State, of course, happened to some degree throughout the nation. This was the community's cost for the railroads' policy of eliminating excess capacity through consolidation and contraction. This study has tried to demonstrate that such policies, regardless of their approval and encouragement by government regulative and legislative authorities, had never calculated the community or social costs they created. Although railroads, and indeed all forms of transportation clearly serve a broad public service function private interest remains the key to understanding the historical and present conditions of American transportation.

"Private interest," of course, presumes the primary goal of profit-making while "public interest" supposedly weighs social benefits and costs in other than market profit and loss terms. While private profits and the public interest need not always conflict, they clearly do not always coincide. The dollar gains or losses which a railroad may calculate as the consquence of a particular set of business decisions do not necessarily reflect similar gains or losses measured from the community's point of view, unless it is assumed that profitability is the sole basis for resource allocation. Although very few American corporate leaders of the twentieth century would subscribe to such a literal application of *laissez faire*, it is obvious that, if they have had any notion of public interest, it was always subordinate to private interest.

The Transportation Act of 1920 apparently closed the doors

to the question of public ownership of American railroads. And, although the railroads have long opposed the huge public subsidies paid to other transportation modes, in the building of highways for truckers and payments of grants to airlines and shipping firms, private ownership of these industries similarly prevails. Discussion of a "national transportation policy" has occurred from time to time, but there has been no overall public policy toward transportation resource allocation, nor have there been any attempts at the social planning of transportation use. The general effect of the regulatory acts and their interpretation has been remedial and piecemeal at best, aimed mostly at giving temporary relief of one kind or another to private firms in times of business crisis. No consistent public policy ever emerged to deal with the industry's attack on the problems of excess capacity and competition. Committed to a program of regulating a non-competitive, privately owned industry, public policy toward the railroads has steadfastly supported the principle that profit-seeking is the real organizing force in the operation of the American railroad network. This, of course, did not mean unlimited profits, nor did it always mean, from the railroads' position, enough profit; but, profits were to be sufficient to keep the industry operating, thus providing some kind of public service — even a dwindling service.

The modifications of the rail network in this century, as seen in the corporate structure of the industry, as well as the changes in the intensity and distribution of service, have been, to a large degree, the result of such a public policy. Abandonments, discontinuances, and mergers are technically regulated; however, the regulation is based upon the demonstrated balance sheet conditions of a non-competitive, protected industry rather than upon general transportation needs of the economy. As a result, business and financial decision-making in the railroad industry has enjoyed neither the theoretic efficiency envisioned under purely competitive situations nor has the nation obtained the alleged benefits of social planning.

This corporate and public policy has meant, in the case of New York State, as well as most other eastern states, a serious loss of railroad facilities. Many of the routes abandoned, admittedly, could not have been maintained under any operating condition, "private interest" or "public interest." Of course, neither should some of these routes been built initially. How-

ever, the loss of many services, such as some important freight
spurs and most passenger operations, produced serious economic
consequences for hundreds of communities that could not be
measured by the gains thus obtained in railroad balance sheets
and income statements. Quite as Commissioner Maltbie of the
New York Public Service Commission pointed out before the
I.C.C. in 1945, when railroad regulation in the "public interest"
chiefly means preoccupation with improving the carrier's economic condition, the public's service is reduced. After all the
economic justifications for attempts to reduce the industry's
excess capacity have been recounted, the fact remains that, with
the railroad network of the 1970's, large portions of New
York State have lost a transportation facility upon which they
were earlier utterly dependent. Whether alternative transportation
modes can replace the loss, very much as railroads once replaced   canals, or whether many of those regions without
rail facilities are condemned to economic decay, are questions
which cannot yet be answered. However, the problem is not
just New York State's, for all Americans must ask themselves
if the reduction of the national rail network to a few dozen,
long-distance inter-city routes, which concentrate on bulk product movement and offer virtually no passenger service, is
truly in the national interest. That is, nevertheless, the unmistakable direction of present industry and government policy.
It may ultimately solve the excess capacity problem, and, per-
chance, even the problem of excessive capitalization will be
eliminated along the way, although this is surely less certain.
However, the final cost to the community, to the nation as
a whole, seen in terms of motor vehicle pollution and con-
gestion, urban concentration, and tax and aesthetic burdens for
maintaining highways and airports, may be too great a bill
to pay. It seems to this writer that to ask how secure and
sound a nation can be without railroads, or at least without
many railroads, is not simply a naive and sentimental question.
It is a question that has begged answering for most of this
century and further evasion, for whatever reason, ideological
or economic, may be catastrophic.

NOTES

INTRODUCTION

1. Leland Jenks, "Railroads as an Economic Force In American History," *Journal of Economic History*, IV, No. 1 (May, 1944), pp.1-20. It is difficult to evaluate the real impact of Jenks' article, which was a modification of a paper given at the Mississippi Valley Historical Association meeting in 1938. It would appear that his brief article had special importance to later interpretations as is evidenced by Cootner and Fogel's *(Supra)* obligations to debunk Jenks' thesis in their own introductions. It should be noted that Jenks was not saying anything new. His arguments had been implicity accepted long before the appearance of Schumpeter's books. His application of empirical data to a theoretical structure such as Schumpeter's innovation theories was, however, unique. On this Jenks noted: "This general interpretation of the role of the railroad . . . suggests what might be undertaken in greater detail to apply the innovation theory . . . It is a question of using a theory as a tool to a coherent understanding of the facts. (Jenks, *op. cit.*, p. 18).

2. *Ibid.*, p. 3.

3. For the easiest exposition of Rostow's position, see Walt W. Rostow, *The Stages of Economic Growth* (Cambridge: Harvard University Press, 1962), pp. 49-78.

4. It is not the function of the following paper to debate the merits of what has been called "the indispensability thesis" of American railroads. The view that railroads were indispensable to American economic growth was certainly held by contemporary observers in the nineteenth century. It is implicit in the works of such commentators as William Z. Ripley, Stuart Daggett, and others and is central to most recent railroad history studies. Quite recently, at least two empirical studies have attempted to dent the indispensability thesis. The impact of their argument cannot yet be assessed. See: Paul Cootner, "The Role of Railroads in United States Economic Growth." *Journal of Economic History*, XXIII, No. 4 (December, 1963), 477-521: and Robert Fogel, *Railroads and American Economic Growth.* (Baltimore: John Hopkins Press, 1964).

5. See Table 1.

6. One of the more recent public studies of American Transportation has argued in favor of further substantial reductions in railroad mileage. See: U.S. Congress, Senate, Special Study Group on Transportation Policies in the United States, *Transportation Trends* (Washington: U.S. Government Printing Office, 1961).

7. Statistical information on the reduction of service is frequently offered in the following study. See Chapters VI and VII.

8. See Tables 3 and 43.

9. A survey of textbooks in American economic history upholds this point. The picture produced by most of these surveys is to depict the railroad in the twentieth century as critically essential to our economic organization but technologically surpassed by air and motor transport in many fields. Adversely affected by these new technologies, the contraction and central-ization of American railroad systems is seen as essential. For example, see: Robert R. Russel, *A History of the American Economic System* (New York: Appleton-Century-Crofts, 1964) or G.C. Fite and J.E. Reese, *An Economic History of the United States* (Second Edition), New York: Hough-ton Mifflin, 1965).

10. Among the fairly recent statistical studies produced by economists: Harold Barger, *The Transport Industries, 1889-1946: A Study of Output, Employ-ment, and Productivity* (New York: National Bureau of Economic Research, 1951); Michael Conant, *Railroad Mergers and Abandonments* (Berkeley: University of California Press, 1965); Kent T. Healy, *The Effects of Scale in the Railroad Industry* (New Haven: Yale University Press, 1961); Meyer, et. al., *The Economics of Competition in the Transport Industries* (Cam-bridge: Harvard University Press, 1959); and James C. Nelson, *Railroad Transportation and Public Policy* (Washington, D.C.: The Brookings In-stitution, 1959).

While these are merely representative studies, it should be noted that all are heavily statistical in methodology and none cited above have looked much beyond their collected historical statistics in obtaining a picture of rail operations in this century.

11. The interpretation advancing inadequate government regulation as a causa-tive factor in rail decline is documented in Nelson, *op. cit.* It is not sur-prising that this approach is similar to that advanced by the Association of American Railroads in its occasional publications. Presumably, under this interpretation, the railroads' economic condition would be improved with a more enlightened public policy.

12. For an intelligent and provoking discussion of the role excess capacity played in the nineteenth and twentieth century development of American business institutions, see: Ray Ginger, *The Age of Excess* (New York: The Macmillan Company, 1965), pp. 35-55.

13. Gabriel Kolko, *Railroads and Regulation, 1877-1916* (Princeton: Princeton University Press, 1965).

CHAPTER I

1. *New York Times,* January 1, 1900, p. 10.

2. New York State, Board of Railroad Commissioners, *Eighteenth Annual Report, 1900* (Albany: J.A. Lyons and Co., 1901), Vol. 1, pp. iv-v. Here-after referred to as Railroad Commissioners, *Annual Report* by year of report.

3. *Ibid.,* pp. 57-58.

4. *Ibid.*, Vol. II, pp. 423-451.
5. For an analysis of the Central's operating economics, see: U. S. Interstate Commerce Commission, *In The Matter of Consolidation of the Railway Properties into a Limited Number of Systems,* Docket No. 12964, 63 I.C.C. 455, pp. 485-486 (1921).
6. U.S. Bureau of Census, *Historical Statistics of the United States to 1957* (Washington: U.S. Government Printing Office, 1960), p. 57.
7. Noble E. Whitford, *History of the Canal Systems of the State of New York* (Albany: State Printing Office, 1905), Vol. II, pp. 1062-3. In fact the canal surpassed both railroads in tonnage until the mid 1970's.
8. *Historical Statistics of the United States to 1957*, p. 57.
9. In 1900 the Pennsylvania acquired majority stock control of both the Long Island Railroad and the Western New York and Pennsylvania. In the case of the Western New York and Pennsylvania, formal control was not achieved until 1901. Not until 1926 did the line pay its fixed charges. After 1930, the Pennsylvania operated the road under a fixed rental arrangement with the road's bondholders. The line provided the Pennsylvania access to both Buffalo and Rochester for its bituminous coal shipment. See: George H. Burgess and Miles C. Kennedy, *Centennial History of the Pennsylvania Railroad Company* (Philadelphia, Pennsylvania Railroad Company, 1949), pp. 473-487.
10. The New York Ontario and Western carried less than 3 per cent of the total railroad shipments of anthracite coal. See: William Z. Ripley, *Railroads – Finance and Organization* (New York: Longmans Green and Company, 1915), pp. 534-548.
11. Calculated from annual company reports in *Railroad Commissioners Annual Report, 1900,* Vol. II.
12. For the best study of New York electric interurban and suburban railroads, see: George W. Hilton and John F. Due, *Electric Interurban Railways in America* (Stanford: Stanford University Press, 1960), pp. 309-319. The Erie Railroad ran its Avon-Mount Morris-Rochester branch as an electric road. The New York Central eventually became the chief stockholder in New York State Railways, one of the state's largest interurban operations.
13. Railroad Commissioners, *Annual Report, 1900,* Vol. I, pp. xi and xiii.
14. *Ibid.*, p. v.
15. Calculated from *Ibid.*, pp. 57-59. The calculation, of course, does not perfectly measure New York capitalization per mile since it is reached by dividing all of the mainline trackage of all roads operating any routes in New York into their total capitalization (Capital Stock and Funded Debt).
16. For a contemporary analysis of considerable significance of this problem of capitalization, see: William Z. Ripley, *op. cit.*, pp. 53-97.
17. For example see: *The American Railway Review* (New York), *Railway World* (Philadelphia), *The Railway Age* (Chicago), and *Railway Review* (Chicago). All of these were weeklies published between 1860 and 1900.
18. Carter Goodrich, *Government Promotion of American Canals and Railroads* (New York: Columbia University Press, 1960), p. 175.
19. *Ibid.*, p. 204.
20. See Table 1.
21. J. F. Dewhurst and Associates, *America's Needs and Resources: A New Survey* (New York: 20th Century Fund, Inc., 1955), pp. 40-41.
22. Ripley, *op. cit.*, pp. 227-228.
23. See Harry H. Pierce, *Railroads of New York – A Study of Government Aid, 1826-1875* (Cambridge: Harvard University Press, 1953), pp. 26-40.

24. *Ibid.*, taken from Chart 1, pp. 178-192.

25. *Ibid.*, p. 193.

26. For a fairly good description of the state of New York agriculture at the turn of the century, see: Elmer O. Flippin, *Rural New York* (New York: Macmillan, 1921), pp. 22-55.

27. *The Railway News* (London), January 5, 1884.

28. *The Bankers Magazine* (New York), XXXVII, January, 1883, No. 7, pp. 481-2.

29. *Poor's Manual of the Railroads of the United States for 1885* (New York: H.V. and H.W. Poor, 1885), p. v.

30. *Ibid.*, pp. v-vi.

31. For a standard interpretation of this period of consolidation see: E. G. Campbell, *The Reorganization of the American Railroad System, 1893-1900* (New York: Columbia University Press, 1938).

32. For an interesting account of this reorganization and the role played by J.P. Morgan see Lewis Corey, *The House of Morgan* (New York: Grosset and Dunlap, 1930), pp. 148-151.
    Lewis Corey notes: "Morgan's railroad reorganization developed three decisive aspects:
    Financial Reorganization. The insolvent railroad was financially rehabilitated and put on a paying basis.
    Consolidation and Community of Interest. Morgan's reorganizations always lessened competition . . .
    Control. By a variety of means — the Voting Trust, stock purchase and interlocking directors — the House of Morgan retained control of reorganized railroads, originally to insure fulfillment of reorganization agreements and later as an expression of deliberate Morganization (Corey, *op.cit.*, p. 157.)

33. Interstate Commerce Commission, *Eighth Annual Report, 1894* (Washington: U.S. Government Printing Office, 1895), p. 10.

34. For another study on Morgan see: N.S.B. Gras and H.M. Larson, "J. Pierpont Morgan," *Casebook in American Business History* (New York: Crofts and Company, 1939), pp. 550-559.

35. For a discussion of the building of a national railroad network in the post-Civil War period, see: George H. Taylor and Irene D. New, *The American Railroad Network, 1861-1890* (Cambridge: Harvard University Press, 1956).

36. Ripley, *Railroads: Finance and Organization,* pp. 54-87.

37. U.S. Congress, Senate, Committee on Interstate Commerce, *Railroad Combination in the Eastern Region,* Senate Report No. 1182, Part 1, 76th Cong. 3rd Session, 1940, p. 6. Hereafter this will be referred to as *Railroad Combination.*

38. Ripley, *Railroads-Finance and Organization,* pp. 374-376.

39. Kolko, *op.cit.,* pp. 30-44. At first glance this argument seems quite spurious; however, as Kolko points out, the general effect of the Commerce Act of 1887 was to reduce competition and this had been also the goal of rail management. While the intent of the act and the intent of management, as seen in the creation of "traffic associations," certainly diverged, this does not prove that the act, *per se,* was inimicable with rail interests.

40. As Kolko points out the original membership of the commission was noteworthy in its sympathy for railroads. *Ibid.*, pp. 47-49.

41. Ripley, *Railroads: Finance and Organization.* p. 591. For Morgan's role see: Corey, *op.cit.,* pp. 176-180.

42. Ripley, *Railroads: Finance and Organizations.* p. 592.

43. *Ibid.,* pp. 553-554.

44. *Railroad Combination...*, Part 1, Exhibit C-3.
45. *Ibid.*, pp. 124-5.
46. *Ibid.*, Exhibit C-4.
47. *Ibid.*
48. Ripley, *op.cit.*, p. 554.
49. *Railroad Combination...*, Part 1, pp. 18-19.
50. *U.S. v. Joint Traffic Association,* 171 U. S. 505 (1898).
51. See Chapter II.
52. For the conventional analysis of this development of Banker control, see: Harold U. Faulkner, *The Decline of Laissez Faire* (New York: Holt, Rinehart and Winston, 1962), pp. 191-202.
53. For a study of Morgan's activities, see: E. G. Campbell, *The Reorganization of the American Railroad System* (New York: Columbia University Press, 1938), pp. 149-189. For a lighter and highly biased view of Morgan's railroad activities at this time, see: Corey, *op. cit.,* pp. 140-151.
54. *Railroad Combination...*, Part 1, p. 16.
55. *Ibid.*, pp. 17-18.
56. Corey, *op.cit.*, pp. 144-147.
57. Frederick L. Allen, *The Great Pierpont Morgan* (New York: Harper and Brothers Company, 1948), pp. 37-40.
58. *Ibid.*, pp. 41-43.

CHAPTER II

1. *Railroad Combination...* Part 1, pp. 18-20.
2. For the best discussion on techniques of combination, 1899-1901, see: Ripley, *op.cit.,* pp. 412-455.
3. Corey, *op.cit.,* pp. 145-148.
4. Ripley, *Railroads-Finance and Organization,* p. 426. By 1912, in the east, fourteen men held 67 directorships in 27 different roads, virtually controlling eastern railroad affairs.
5. *Railroad Combinations...*, Part 1, Exhibit C-5.
6. *Ibid.*, Part 1, C-8.
7. *Ibid.*, p. 20, and Burgess and Kennedy, *op.cit.,* pp. 458-460.
8. *Railroad Combinations,* Part 1, Appendix 1, pp. 73-76.
   The division of the eastern region between the Pennsylvania and the Central worked fairly amicably for the next half-dozen years. The best records on the operations of these roads in acquiring joint control in the east is found in *Ibid.,* Appendices 1-8, pp. 73-108. These summaries were put together as part of the statistical exhibits used in the Senate Report and are based upon company records.
9. *Ibid.,* Appendix 2, pp. 79-84.
10. *Ibid.,* Appendix 3, pp. 85-92 and p. 23.
11. Burgess and Kennedy, *op.cit.,* pp. 459-60.
12. *Railroad Combination...*, Part 1, Exhibit C-138.
13. Burgess and Kennedy, *op.cit.,* p. 460. The expenditures for stock were:

Chesapeake and Ohio	...$ 5,569,000
Norfolk and Western	... 17,894,000
Baltimore and Ohio	... 65,042,000
Reading (through B&O)	... 21,563,000
	$110,068,000

14. Burgess and Kennedy, *op.cit.,* pp. 463-471.
15. *Ibid.,* pp. 473-481.

16. *Ibid.,* pp. 482-487.
17. *Ibid.*
18. Ripley, *Railroads-Finance and Organization,* pp. 473-476.
19. *Railroad Combination* ..., Part 1, p. 26. The Central promised to pay $2,000,000 per year in fixed charges amounting to an 8 percent return on B. & A. stock.
20. *Ibid.,* Appendix 5, pp. 97-100.
21. *Ibid.,* Appendix 4, pp. 93-96.
22. On this very point, the *New York Times* editorialized on January 10, 1903 that the anthracite roads were "pivotal" to Morgan's domination over eastern railroads.
23. For a good study on the coal situation, see: Ripley, *op.cit.,* pp. 540-547.
24. *The Financial Review,* 1912 (New York: William B. Dana Company, 1912), p. 60.
25. The Hepburn Act eventually was to include a section covering this matter. It declared that railroads could not own properties whose goods they shipped.
26. *Annual Report of the Pennsylvania Railroad Company,* 1873, in Burgess and Kennedy, *op. cit.,* p. 195.
27. *Railroad Combination* ..., Part 1, pp. 43-45 and Appendix 4, pp. 93-96.
28. Campbell, *op.cit.,* pp. 187-189.
29. Ripley, *Railroads-Finance and Organizations,* p. 538.
30. *Ibid.,* pp. 545-548. Note in Table that the division of traffic remains fairly stable during the dozen years noted.
31. *New York Times,* January 10, 1903.
32. Philadelphia *Press,* January 9, 1903. Cited in *Railroad Combination* ..., Part 1, Exhibit C-387.
33. Railroad Commissioners, *18th Annual Report, 1900,* p. ix.
34. For a fine detailed discussion of the Gould plan see: *Railroad Combination* ..., Part 1, pp. 27-59.
35. Burgess and Kennedy, *op.cit.,* pp. 513-514, and *Railroad Combination* ..., Part 1, pp. 27-36.
36. *Ibid.,* Part 1, p. 40.
37. Burgess and Kennedy, *op.cit.,* pp. 515-516.
38. *Ibid.,* p. 515 and *Railroad Combination* ..., Part 1, pp. 51-55.
39. Taken from: *Financial Review, 1903,* (New York: William B. Dana Company, 1903), pp. 106-120 and *Financial Review, 1912,* (New York: William B. Dana Company, 1912), pp. 123-135.
40. U.S., Interstate Commerce Commission, *Intercorporate Relationships of Railways in the United States, as of June 30, 1906.* (Washington: U.S. Government Printing Office, 1908), p. 40.
41. I.L. Sharfman, *The Interstate Commerce Commission* (New York: Fund for the Republic, 1931), p. 35.
42. Burgess and Kennedy, *op.cit.,* p. 461.
43. Kolko, *op.cit.,* pp. 95-100. Among the Interstate Commerce Commissioners, Martin Knapp was particularly vocal in his support of pooling.
44. *Baltimore Herald,* January 9, 1903.
45. Kolko, *op.cit.,* pp. 127-137.
46. *Wall Street Journal,* December 28, 1904.
47. *New York Times,* March 8, 1906.
48. *Ibid.,* June 14, 1906.
49. U.S., Interstate Commerce Commission, *Activities of the Interstate Commerce Commission, 1887-1937* (Washington: U.S. Government Printing Office, 1937) p. 36.

50. Ripley, *Railroads-Finance and Organizations*. p. 287.
51. *Ibid.*, p. 286.
52. *Railroad Combination* . . Part 1, Exhibits C-93, C-95, and C-101.
53. *Ibid.*, p. 63.
54. *Ibid.*, Appendix 1, pp. 73-78.
55. *Ibid.*, Appendix 3, pp. 85-92.
56. *Ibid.*, Appendix 2, pp. 79-84.
57. *Ibid.*, Appendix 4, pp. 93-96.
58. *Ibid.*, Appendix 7, pp. 103-104 and p. 68.
59. Burgess and Kennedy, *op.cit.*, p. 516.
60. It is difficult to evaluate the true role played by Cassatt among eastern railroad leaders and bankers. From letters and memorandums collected in *Railroad Combination* . . . it appears that Cassatt through the strength of the Pennsylvania Railroad and his own prestige had done much to reconcile the initial antagonism between the railroads and the Interstate Commerce Commission.
61. *Financial Review, 1912* (New York: William B. Dana and Company, 1912), p. 11.
62. See also: Kolko, *op.cit.*, pp. 195-197.
63. *Financial Review*, 1912, p. 11.
64. See Kolko, *op.cit.*, pp. 202-207. Kolko argues persuasively that railroad support for public regulation was not at all diminished.
65. Samuel Rea, "Pressing Need of a Constructive Railroad Policy," Address before New York Chamber of Commerce, December 3, 1914, in Slason Thompson, *The Railway Library, 1914* (Chicago: Stromberg and Company, 1915), p. 38.
66. *Railroad Combination* . . . , Part II, pp, 562-564, 606-618.
67. Johnson and Van Metre, *op.cit.*, p. 91.
68. Interstate Commerce Commission, *Intercorporate Relationships of Railways in the United States, as of June 30, 1906*, p. 66.
69. Ripley, *Railroads: Finance and Organization*, p. 430.
70. U.S., Congress, Senate, *The Interstate Commerce Act, Revised to November 1, 1951*, Senate Document No. 72, 82nd Cong. 1st Sess., 1951, pp. 8-9. Hereafter this will be cited as: *The Interstate Commerce Act* (1951).
71. See: Ripley, *Rates and Regulation*, pp. 552-556.
72. See *Railroad Combination* . . . , Part I, Exhibits C-130-145.
73. *Ibid.*, Exhibit C-138.
74. *Ibid.*, pp. 26-7.
75. *Ibid.*, pp. 24-27.
76. Dewhurst and Associates, *America's Needs and Resources*, pp. 40-41, 51.
77. *Financial Review*, 1912, p. 88.
78. Calculated from: State of New York, *Public Service Commission, Annual Report, 1909, Second District*, (Albany: J.B. Lyon and Company 1910), Vol. II, Hereafter these reports will be referred to as: *Public Service Commission, Annual Report* and year of report and district.
79. *Financial Review*, 1912, p. 86.
80. *Ibid.*, p. 87.
81. For a study of the financial developments of this period, see Ripley, *op.cit.*, pp. 124-127. For an analysis of the use of Collateral Trust Bonds in financing see H.C. Guthmann and H.E. Dougall, *Corporate Financial Policy*. 4th edition (New York: Prentice Hall, 1961), pp. 191-196.
82. Burgess and Kennedy, *op.cit.*, p. 520.
83. *Ibid.*, p. 521.
84. *Ibid.* p. 543.

85. *Railroad Combination . . .* , Part II, pp. 529-30.
86. Ripley, *Railroads-Finance and Organization*, pp. 418-420.
87. See: *Public Service Commission, Annual Report, 1915,* Second District, Vol. II, pp. 378 ff. The depressed condition of the Central and other eastern roads, with regard to the equipment and maintenance, became painfully apparent with the coming of World War I.
88. Ripley, *Railroad-Finance and Organization*, p. 169.
89. *Railroad Combination . . .* , Part II, p. 530.
90. *Ibid.,* p. 531.
91. Interstate Commerce Commission, *Intercorporate Relationships of Railways in the United States as of June 30, 1906,* p. 25.
92. New York State, *Public Service Commission Annual Report, 1913,* Second District, Vol. II, p. 100.
93. Ripley, *Railroads-Finance and Organization*, p. 288.
94. *Ibid.*
95. Ripley, *Railroads-Finance and Organization*, pp. 289-290.
96. *Financial Review,* 1912, p. 11.
97. *Ibid.,* pp. 11-12.
98. U.S., Interstate Commerce Commission, *Interstate Commerce Commission Activities, 1887-1937,* p. 141-3.
99. *Ibid.,* p. 141.
100. *Ibid.,* p. 147.
101. *Ibid.,* pp. 147-149.
102. The enforcement of the recapture provisions of the Transportation Act of 1920 was dependent upon the Interstate Commerce Commission revaluing rail properties. In 1933, the recapture provisions were rescinded by Congress and the Interstate Commerce Commission felt that its valuation studies importance had been greatly weakened. See *Ibid.,* pp. 148-149.
103. U.S., Interstate Commerce Commission, *Twenty-fifth Annual Report, 1911* (Washington: U.S. Government Printing Office, 1912), pp. 111-115.
104. Thompson, *op.cit.,* pp. 390-391.
105. *Ibid.,* p. 443.
106. Samuel B. Rea, "The Pressing Need of a Constructive Railway Policy," in *Ibid.,* pp. 31-38. At first the commission refused to approve the rate advance for eastern railroads, but eventually granted an increase equal to 2-1/2 or 3 percent.

CHAPTER III

1. Walker D. Hines, *War History of American Railroads* (New Haven: Yale University Press, 1928) is the "official" government source on this period of operation.
2. Interstate Commerce Commission, *Activities of Interstate Commerce Commission, 1887-1937,* p. 43.
3. Hines, *op.cit.,* pp. 12-19.
4. Interstate Commerce Commission, *Activities of Interstate Commerce Commission,* 1887-1937, p. 45.
5. Hines, *op.cit.,* p. 19.
6. *Ibid.,* p. 1.
7. *Ibid.,* p. 2.
8. Burgess and Kennedy, *op. cit.,* p. 562. On the B&O, see: Edward Hungerford, *The Story of the Baltimore and Ohio* (New York: Putnam and Company, 1928), Vol. II, p. 300-310.

9. Hines, *op. cit.*, p. 4.
10. The Delaware and Hudson Company, *A Century of Progress, A History of the Delaware and Hudson* (Albany, 1929), 1. 392.
11. *Ibid.*, p. 374-5.
12. Public Service Commission, *Annual Report, 1919, Second District,* Vol. II, pp. 334, 382-3.
13. Hines, *op. cit.*, pp. 53-55.
14. Burgess and Kennedy, *op. cit.*, p. 563-4.
15. Hines, *op. cit.*, p. 253.
16. *Ibid.*, p. 55.
17. Burgess and Kennedy, *op. cit.*, p. 664.
18. Delaware & Hudson Co., *op. cit.*, p. 430.
19. *Ibid.*, pp. 434-440.
20. Hines, *op. cit.*, p. 63.
21. *Ibid.*, p. 71 and 95.
22. *Ibid.*, p. 216.
23. *Ibid.*, p. 120.
24. *Ibid.*, p. 137.
27. Public Service Commission, *Annual Report, 1919, Second District,* Vol. II, pp. 386-403, and Delaware and Hudson Company, *op. cit.*, p. 444.
26. Hines, *op. cit.*, p. 125.
27. *Ibid.*, p. 155-171.
28. Interstate Commerce Commission, *Activities of the Interstate Commerce Commission, 1887-1937,* p. 175-6.
29. For discussion, see: William N. Leonard, *Railroad Consolidation under the Transportation Act of 1920* (New York: Columbia University Press, 1946), pp. 40-63.
30. Frank Haigh Dixon, *Railroads and Government* (New York: Macmillan and Company, 1922), pp. 343-344.
31. Hines, *op. cit.*, p. 91.
32. See: Leonard, *op. cit.*, pp. 44-52.
33. The Interstate Commerce Commission had recommended to Congress in December 1917 that operation of the railroads as a "unit" was necessary. U.S. Interstate Commerce Commission, *Thirty-Second Annual Report of Interstate Commerce Commission, 1918,* (Washington: U. S. Government Printing Office, 1918), p. 5.
34. *Railroad Combination . . . ,* Part II, pp. 515-529.
35. U.S., *Statutes at Large,* XLI, p. 478-486.
36. Interstate Commerce Commission, *Activities of Interstate Commerce Commission, 1887-1937,* p. 191-2.
37. From the beginning the Commission appeared to have had doubts that this type of planning would work. Leonard, *op. cit.*, pp. 54-63.
38. 63 Interstate Commerce Commission (1921), p. 485.
39. Ripley cited the Ontario and Western as an example of weak roads which he reluctantly had to assign to someone. 63 Interstate Commerce Commission (1921), pp. 495-496.
40. *Ibid.*, pp. 479-480.
41. *Railroad Combination . . . ,* Part II, pp. 530-532.
42. *Ibid.*, pp. 541-555.
43. *Railroad Combination . . . ,* Part II, Exhibit C-703 and C-704.
44. *Ibid.*, p. 546.
45. *Ibid.*
46. *Ibid.*, Exhibit C-728.
47. *Ibid.*, Exhibit C-727.

48. *Ibid.*, pp. 545-6.
49. *Ibid.*, pp. 571-626.
50. *Ibid.*, Exhibits C-702 and C-703, and pp. 533-4.
51. For extended discussion see: Leonard, *op. cit.*, pp. 87-118.
52. *Railroad Combination* . . . , Part II, p. 565.
53. U.S., Interstate Commerce Commission, *Thirty-Ninth Annual Report, 1925* (Washington: U. S. Government Printing Office, 1925), pp. 10-13.
54. *Ibid.*, p. 13.
55. Leonard, *op. cit.*, p. 127.
56. *Railroad Combination* . . . , Part III, p. 1178-1181.
57. Leonard, *op. cit.*, pp. 129-132, 135-145, and 149-155.
58. *Railroad Combination* . . . , Part I, p. 68.
59. *Ibid.*, Part II, p. 547 and 571-578.
60. *Ibid.*, Part III, p. 1219-1228, and *Nickel Plate Unification,* 105 Interstate Commerce Commission 425 (1926).
61. *Railroad Combination* . . . , Part III, p. 1227 and Part IV, pp. 1955-6.
62. *Ibid.*, Part III, pp. 1228-1238 and Appendix 10, pp. 1271-76.
63. *Ibid.*, Appendix II, pp. 1277-1278.
64. *Ibid.*, p. 1261.
65. Burgess & Kennedy, *op. cit.*, p. 577.
66. *Philadelphia Enquirer,* Sept. 13, 1923.
67. Burgess and Kennedy, *op. cit.*, p. 580-581. The Pennsylvania was especially concerned about the B & O's acquisition of the Reading.
68. *Railroad Combination* . . . , Part III, pp. 1191-1192, and 1197-2010.
69. *Ibid.*, pp. 1243-1245.
70. *Control of the Buffalo Rochester and Pittsburgh,* 133 Interstate Commerce Commission 750 (1927).
71. *Railroad Combination* . . . , Part IV, pp. 2057-2064.
72. *Interstate Commerce Commission vs. Pennsylvania Railroad Co.,* 169 Interstate Commerce Commission 618 (1930).
73. *Railroad Combination* . . . , Part IV, p. 2073.
74. *Ibid.*, Part V, p. 2837.
75. *Ibid.*, Part IV, pp. 2073-2103.
76. The New England railroads were to suffer quite heavily during the depression and the Pennsylvania's investment amounted to a considerable loss.
77. *Ibid.*, Part IV, Exhibit 3056.
78. *Ibid.*, pp. 2129-31, 2161.
79. *Ibid.*, pp. 2139-49. Terminal facilities were particularly inadequate for this system.
80. *Ibid.*, Part V, p. 2837.
81. *Ibid.*, Part IV, Appendix 16, pp. 2186-88.
82. *Ibid.*, Part V, p. 2853.
83. *Ibid.*, pp. 2965-67.
84. *Ibid.*, pp. 2971-2991.
85. *Ibid.*, pp. 2968-2969.
86. *Ibid.*, p. 2993.
87. *Ibid.*, pp. 3002-3.
88. *Ibid.*, p. 2878.
89. *Ibid.*, p. 2876.
90. *Ibid.*, p. 2878.
91. "The Vans Hold On," *Business Week,* March 24, 1934, p. 14. However, news of their failure provided lurid reading later. See: D. Dodge, "Empire in Hock," *American Mercury,* Vol. 34, February, 1955, pp. 160-174.

92. *Railroad Combination . . .* , Part V, p. 3003.
93. Frank D. Dixon, *op. cit.,* pp. 4-5.
94. See: I. L. Sharfman, *The Interstate Commerce Commission,* 4 Vols., (New York: Twentieth Century Fund, 1931-7).
95. *Ibid.,* Vol. I, 11. 3-5.
96. *Ibid.,* p. 5.
97. See: Introduction and long note on Kolko, *Regulation and Railroads.* See also: Lee Benson, *Merchants, Farmers and Railroads: Railroad Regulation and New York Politics, 1850-1887* (Cambridge: Harvard University Press, 1955), pp. 210-213.
98. Sharfman, *op. cit.,* Vol. III A, p. 332.
99. Charles R. Cherington, *The Regulation of Railroad Abandonments* (Cambridge: Harvard University Press, 1948), pp. 100-101.
100. Interstate Commerce Commission, *Activities of the Interstate Commerce Commission, 1887-1937,* p. 147.
101. For two years after the Transportation Act, the fair return was to be 5-1/2 per cent with Interstate Commerce Commission authority to then raise this one-half per cent.
102. D. Philip Locklin, *Railroad Regulation Since 1920* (New York: A. W. Shaw Company, 1928), pp. 33-4.
103. See: Kolko, *op. cit.,* pp. 228-230.

CHAPTER IV

1. Interstate Commerce Commission, *Forty-eighth Annual Report, 1934,* pp. 134-5.
2. "The New York Central Chooses," *Fortune Magazine,* VII, February, 1932, pp. 70, 112-145.
3. *Ibid.,* p. 70.
4. *Ibid.*
5. Leonard, *op. cit.,* p. 193.
6. Calculated from, Public Service Commission, *Annual Report, 1935, 2nd District,* Vol. 1, p. 134.
7. This figure is based upon applying the Central employment cut proportionately to New York rail employment.
8. Burgess and Kennedy, *op. cit.,* p. 808.
9. Public Service Commission, *Annual Report, 1935, 2nd District,* Vol. 1, p. 138.
10. *Ibid.*
11. *Ibid.,* Vol. II, pp. 578-584.
12. *Ibid.,* Calculated from annual reports.
13. *Ibid.,* pp. 570-590.
14. For a study of the Erie, see Edward Hungerford, *Men of Erie* (New York: Random House, 1946), pp. 248-9, and *New York Times,* January 19, 20, 1938.
15. Burgess and Kennedy, *op. cit.,* p. 678.
16. U. S. Congress, House, Committee on Interstate and Foreign Commerce, *Hearings on the Omnibus Transportation Bill, January 24, 1938* (Washington: U. S. Government Printing Office: 1939), pp. 24-5.
17. Burgess and Kennedy, *op. cit.,* p. 808.
18. *Ibid.,* p. 678.
19. Association of American Railroads, *Railroads and Railroad Wages,* (Washington: Association of American Railroads, 1938), p. 4.

20. *Ibid.*, p. 1.
21. *Ibid.*, p. 11.
22. *Ibid.*, p. 9.
23. Public Service Commission, *Annual Report, 1945,* Vol. II, pp. 563-573.
24. *New York Times,* January 19, 1938.
25. *Wall Street Journal,* September 3, 1938.
26. *New York Times,* July 15, 1932 and December 14, 1929.
27. *Ibid.*, August 23, 1943, and December 12, 1940.
28. U. S., Congress, House of Representatives, Interstate and Foreign Com-
    merce Committee, *Regulation of Stock Ownership in Railroads,* House
    Report No. 2789, 71st U. S. Cong. 3rd Sess., 1931.
29. U.S., *Statutes at Large,* XLVIII, 211.
30. Burgess and Kennedy, *op. cit.*, pp. 642-3.
31. National Resources Committee, *The Structure of the American Economy,
    Part I* (Washington: June, 1935), p. 162 (pull out diagram).
32. *Ibid.*
33. *Regulation of Stock Ownership in Railroads,* H.R. No. 2789, p. xvi-xx.
34. Harry Laidler, *Concentration in American Industry* (New York: Crowell
    and Company, 1931), p. 132.
35. *New York Times,* March 1, 1931.
36. *Ibid.*
37. *Hearing on the Omnibus Transportation Bill,* p. 1423.
38. *Ibid.*, p. 1425.
39. New York *Evening Post,* September 18, 1932, cited in Leonard, *op. cit.*,
    pp. 220-1.
40. Passed on June 16, 1934. U. S., *Statutes at Large,* XLVIII, 211.
41. Burgess and Kennedy, *op. cit.*, p. 660-1.
42. A. J. County, *A Plan of Unification of the Eastern Railroads,* (Philadelphia:
    May 19, 1934), pamphlet in files of Association of American Railroads.
43. *New York Times,* September 23, 1934.
44. *Ibid.*, September 21, 1934.
45. Association of American Railroads, *Plan of Organization,* Mimeo copy
    in files of Association of American Railroads, p. 1.
46. *Ibid.*
47. *Ibid.*, p. 4.
48. *Ibid.*, p. 5.
49. *Plan of Organization,* p. 5.
50. *Ibid.*, p. 4.
51. Leonard, *op. cit.*, pp. 288-290.
52. U. S., Congress, Senate, Committee on Interstate and Commerce, *Some
    Educational, Legislative, and Self-Regulatory Activities of United States
    Railroads,* Additional Report No. 26, Part 2, 77th Cong., 1st Sess., 1940,
    p. 49.
53. John G. Shott, *The Railroad Monopoly* (Washington: Public Affairs In-
    stitute, 1950), p. 85.
54. *Some Educational, Legislative and Self-Regulatory Activities of United States
    Railroads,* Additional Report No. 26, Part 2, p. 1.
55. *Ibid.*, pp. 44. For a rather biased opposition to the Transportation Associa-
    tion and the American Enterprise Association which grew from it, see
    Shott, *op. cit.*, pp. 112-126.
56. "Brief of State of Georgia versus Pennsylvania Railroad Company, *et.
    al.,*" Appendix C, in Shott, *op. cit.*, 195.
57. "Brief for the Federal Government in the Western Railroad Case," Appen-
    dix B, in Shott, *op. cit.*, pp. 171-193.

58. "The Central Chooses," *Fortune Magazine*, Feb., 1932, p. 70.

59. Burgess and Kennedy, *op. cit.*, p. 645.

60. U.S., Office of the Federal Coordinator, *Public Aids to Transportation* (Washington: U.S. Government Printing Office, 1937), Vol. II, Part 1, p. 101. Hereafter this will be cited as *Public Aids to Transportation* by appropriate volume and part.

61. Schumpeter, *Business Cycles* (New York: McGray-Hill and Company, 1964), p. 348.

62. *Public Aids to Transportation*, Vol. II, Part I, pp. 170-171.

63. *Ibid.*, p. 171.

64. *Ibid.*, p. 171.

65. *Ibid.*, p. 172. F.E.A. loans to eastern railroads were distributed accordingly.

66. Interstate Commerce Commission, *Activities of the Interstate Commerce Commission, 1937-62*, p. 90.

67. Nelson, *op. cit.*, pp. 112-116 and Ernest R. Williams, *The Regulation of Rail-Motor Rate Competition*, (New York: 1958), p. 21.

68. See Joseph D. Eastman, "The Economic Adjustment of Rates between Competing Forms of Transportation," *American Economic Review, Papers and Proceedings*, Vol. XXX (March, 1940), pp. 124-129.

69. *New York Times*, April 16, 1935.

70. Joseph B. Eastman, "Public Ownership and Operation of Railroads in the United States," *Annuals of the American Academy of Political Science*, Vol. 187 (September, 1936), p. 108-9.

71. *Ibid.*, p. 110.

72. *Ibid.*, p. 107.

73. *Ibid.*

74. John J. Pelley, "The Case for Private Ownership and Operation of the Railroads in the United States," *Annuals*, 187, p. 122.

75. *New York Times*, October 14, 1939.

76. *Ibid.*, December 18, 1939.

77. *Ibid.*, January 9, 1940.

78. *Ibid.*, March 2, 1939.

79. *Ibid.*, May 11, 1939.

80. *Ibid.*, May 13, 1939.

81. *Ibid.*, July 29, 1939.

82. *Ibid.*, November 15, 1945.

83. *The Interstate Commerce Act* (1951), p. 1.

84. For the opinion of the Association of American Railroads on the Act see *New York Times*, September 19, 1940.

85. On Interstate Commerce Commission reorganization plans, see Sharfman, *op. cit.*, Vol. IV, pp. 314-15.

86. Public Service Commission, *Annual Report, 1945*, Vol. I, 1. 176.

87. Leonard, *op. cit.*, p. 225.

88. *Ibid.*, pp. 221-227.

89. *Ibid.*, p. 226.

90. Eastman himself promised to look at each proposed rail merger on its own merits and seemed uninterested in enforcing a general plan in 1934.

91. *New York Times*, July 27, 1933.

92. *Ibid.*, June 5, 1934.

93. U.S., Interstate Commerce Commission, *Railroad Consolidation and the Public Interest* (Washington: U. S. Government Printing Office, 1962), pp. 33-34.

94. "Socrates Among the Railroads," *Fortune Magazine*, VII, February, 1932, pp. 71-3, 102-104.

95. *Ibid.*, p. 73.
96. U. S., Office of Federal Coodinator, *Fourth Report of the Federal Co-ordinator of Transportation*, House Document 394 (Washington: U. S. Government Printing Office, 1936), p. 36.
97. Interstate Commerce Commission, *The Activities of the Interstate Commerce Commission, 1937-62*, pp. 230-234. See Leonard, *op. cit.*, pp. 247-255.
98. Interstate Commerce Commission, *Activities. . . . 1937-62*, p. 234.
99. *The Interstate Commerce Act* (1951), p. 27.
100. Association of American Railroads, *Consolidations and Mergers in the Transportation Industry* (Washington: Association of American Railroads, 1960), p. 11. This report was known as the "Doyle Report."
101. Cherington, *op. cit.*, pp. 105-6.
102. *New York Evening Post*, April 4, 1922.
103. *Washington Post*, August 1, 1923.
104. American Short Line Railroad Association (Pamphlet), 1926.
105. *Railway Age*, January 3, 1919, Vol. 66, pp. 57-8.
106. *The Interstate Commerce Act* (1951), p. 14.
107. Cherington, *op. cit.*, pp. 20-22.
108. *Ibid.*, p. 24.
109. Sharfman, *op. cit.*, Vol I, p. 240.
110. Cherington, *op. cit.*, pp. 100 and 105.
111. 221 Interstate Commerce Commission 133-144 (1937) and 212 Interstate Commerce Commission 406-6 (1936).
112. Public Service Commission, *Annual Report, 1935, 2nd District*, Vol. I, pp. 578-590.
113. *Wall Street Journal*, September 3, 1938.
114. *New York Central Abandonment*, 221 Interstate Commerce Commission 133-144 (1937).
115. *New York Central Abandonment*, 330 Interstate Commerce Commission 351 (1938). See also on *New York Central Abandonments*, 224 Interstate Commerce Commission 190-1 (1937), 233 Interstate Commerce Commission 700-702 (1939), and 166 Interstate Commerce Commission 373 (1939).
116. *Lehigh Valley Abandonment*, 228 Interstate Commerce Commission 449-453 (1938).
117. *New York and Pennsylvania Abandonment of Entire Road*, 212 Interstate Commerce Commission 406-408 (1936).
118. 207 Interstate Commerce Commission 603 (1935).
119. Public Service Commission, *Annual Report, 1945*, Vol. I, p. 177.
120. *Ibid.*, p. 178.
121. *Ibid.*, p. 176.

CHAPTER V

1. *The Annals*, Vol. 230, November 1943, p. 22.
2. Interstate Commerce Commission, *Sixty-Second Annual Report, 1948*, p. 157.
3. The Office of Defense Transportation was created by Executive Order No. 8989 (6 F.R. 6721) 1941.
4. Stover, *op. cit.*, pp. 202-209.
5. *New York Times*, January 21, 1944.
6. Average rail wages rose 33 percent between 1941 and 1945 while the industry pointed out that prices rose only 19 percent. See Stover, *op. cit.*, pp. 206-207.

7. *Ibid.*, p. 215.
8. "What Railroad Made Money in 1938," *Business Week*, March 11, 1939, p. 44. Half of the roads not meeting fixed charges were in the east—the Central, the B & O, the Erie, the DL & W, the D & H, the Lehigh Valley, the New Haven, and the Long Island.
9. *New York Times*, May 11, 1939.
10. Interstate Commerce Commission, *Forty-Seventh Annual Report*, 1933, p. 26.
11. Calculated from Interstate Commerce Commission, *Statistics of Railways in the United States, 1940-45* (annal).
12. *Ibid.*
13. Interstate Commerce Commission, *Sixty-Second Annual Report, 1948*, pp. 152-3.
14. John J. Pelley, "American Railroads in and after the War," *The Annals*, Vol. 230, November, 1943, p. 26.
15. *Ibid.*, p. 27.
16. Interstate Commerce Commission, *Sixty-Eighth Annual Report, 1954*, p. 154.
17. *Ibid.*
18. H. G. Guthmann and H. E. Dougall, *Corporate Financial Policy* (Englewood Cliffs: Prentice-Hall, Inc., 1962), p. 339.
19. M. W. Clement, *One Hundred Years, 1846-1946* (Philadelphia: The Pennsylvania Railroad Company, 1946), p. 1.
20. Interstate Commerce Commission, *Sixty-Seventh Annual Report, 1953*, p. 155.
21. Association of American Railroads, *Transportation in America* (Washington: Association of American Railroads, 1947), pp. 12-21. "Fair Return," of course, meant a 6 percent return on invested capital.
22. *Ibid.*, pp. 12-13.
23. *Ibid.*, p. 7.
24. See Nelson, *op. cit.*, for a recent exhaustive economic study completed by the Brookings Institution which supports this A.A.R. concept.
25. See Interstate Commerce Commission, *Activities of the Interstate Commerce Commission, 1937-1962*, p. 233, for a report on a 1960 National Academy of Science Conference on Transportation Research.
26. *Ibid.*, p. 10.
27. *Ibid.*, p. 11.
28. *Ibid.*, p. 11.
29. *Ibid.*, p. 10.
30. *Ibid.*, p. 9.
31. In *State of Georgia v. Pennsylvania Railroad Col*, 324 U. S. 439 (1945) the courts had held that Interstate Commerce Commission approval for combined rate setting did not constitute anti-trust exemption.
32. Public Law 662, 80th Congress, (1948).
33. William Norton, *Modern Transportation Economics* (Columbus: Charles E. Merrill, 1963), p. 246.
34. Interstate Commerce Commission, *Activities of Interstate Commerce Commission, 1937-62*, pp. 52-3.
35. Among the approved mergers up to 1958, there were no important ones in the East. An important denial in the East, however, was the 1947 attempt by the C&O through its parent holding company, The Allegheny Corporation, to exercise its voting rights of 400,000 shares of New York Central stock. The petition was denied because it would weaken competition, See Conant, *op. cit.*, pp. 60-61.
36. Clement, *One Hundred Years, 1846-1946*, p. 1.

37. United States President, *Economic Report of the President, 1965* (Washington: United States Government Printing Office, 1965), p. 189.
38. E. F. Dennison, *The Sources of Economic Growth in the United States* (New York: Council for Economic Development, 1962), p. 16.
39. Calculated from Interstate Commerce Commission *Annual Reports, 1945 and 1958.*
40. Association of American Railroads, *Transportation in America,* p. 42.
41. *Ibid.,* p. 42.
42. See Table 28.
43. *New York State Legislative Manual, 1941,* pp. 243-44.
44. Unimproved meant unsurfaced. Improved, however, did not mean that the road was necessarily in good condition, only that it had once been paved.
45. The peak was reached in 1916 with total mileage of 15,580, See Due and Hilton, *Electric Interurban Railroads in America,* pp. 186-7. In New York, suburban and interurban electric railroads operated about 1800 miles of track.
46. By 1921, the total investment in American interurbans was a very substantial $1,500,000,000.
47. Public Service Commission, *Annual Report, 1910,* Second District, Vol. II, p. 220.
4. Public Service Commission, *Annual Report, 1920,* Second District, Vol. II, pp. 438-444.
49. Interstate Commerce Commission, *Seventy-Eighth Annual Report, 1964,* p. 130.
50. Burgess and Kennedy, *op. cit.,* p. 602.
51. Public Service Commission, *Annual Report, 1920,* Second District, Vol. II, pp. 386-391.
52. *Ibid.* These roads were: Ulster and Delaware, Central New York Southern, Schoharie Valley, Delaware and Northern, Arcade and Attica, Middletown and Unionville, and Lowville and Beaver River.
53. Public Service Commission, *Annual Report, 1949,* Vol. kk, pp. 442-445.
54. State of New York, Department of Public Works, *Highway Needs* (Albany: 1950), pp. 151-157 and 162.
55. *Ibid.,* p. 16.
56. United States Senate Subcommittee on Surface Transportation of the Committee on Interstate and Foreign Commerce, *Problems of the Railroads,* 85th Congress, Second Session (1958), P.I., p. 289. Hereafter, this will be cited as *Problems of the Railroads.*
57. The decline of anthracite is evident in that in 1929 it accounted for 89 percent of all heating fuel consumed, but by 1962 it accounted for only 21 percent. See: United States., Bureau of Mines, *Mineral Facts and Problems,* Bulletin 556 (Washington: United States Government Printing Office, 1963), p. 43.
58. Harvey Perloff, *Regions, Resources and Economic Growth* (New York: Resources for the Future, 1958), pp. 75-76.
59. *Ibid.*
60. Nelson, *op. cit.,* pp. 209-210.
61. E. Hoover and R. Vernon, *Anatomy of a Metropolis* (Cambridge: Harvard University Press, 1960), p. 205.
62. The Pennsylvania, the New York Central and the Long Island, all operating in New York State, carried more than 65 percent of all of the nation's commuters.
63. United States, Bureau of Census, *Statistical Abstract of the United States, 1964* (eighty-fifth edition), p. 356.

64. Interstate Commerce Commission, *Activities of the Interstate Commerce Commission, 1937-1962*, p. 90.
65. Interstate Commerce Commission, *Sixty-Eighth Report, 1954*, p. 155.
66. Interstate Commerce Commission, *Seventy-Eighth Annual Report, 1964*, p. 143.
67. In all 10,191 government units taxed railroads in New York State in 1958, Local units accounted for from 90 to 95 percent of all taxes collected within the state. See: *Problems of the Railroads*, Part II, p. 1848.
68. Nelson, *op. cit.*,
69. *New York Times*, May 27, 1950.
70. Stover, *op. cit.*, pp. 235-251.
71. *Ibid.*, June 25, 1950.
72. *Ibid.*, August 2, 1950.
73. *Ibid.*, June 21, 1950.
74. *Ibid.*, April 17, 1950. However, the Central had not completed replacement of its steam equipment in 1957.
75. Interstate Commerce Commission, *Seventy-Eighth Annual Report, 1954*, p. 141.
76. For a discussion of this problem see Nelson, *op. cit.*, pp. 374-435.
77. Figures are taken from Interstate Commerce Commission, *Annual Reports 1964*, pp. 142-148. In 1958, rail gross earnings fell 10 percent. Allowing for the fact that dividend payments usually lag by a year, 1959 dividend payments were less than 3 percent below the preceeding year.
78. Nelson, *op. cit.*, p. 210
79. *New York Times*, July 16, 1950.
80. 300 I.C.C. 633, 649 (1957).
81. In fact, the Central operated one-third of all the steam engines still used in the country.
82. *Problems of the Railroads*, Part I, p. 281.
83. Stover, *op. cit.*, pp. 228-9.
84. By 1964, the eastern district accounted for 46 percent of all "Piggyback" carloadings, Interstate Commerce Commission, *Seventy-Eighth Annual Report, 1964*, p. 137.
85. Stover, *op. cit.*, p. 228.
86. *Transportation Trends*, p. 657.
87. See Paul W. MacAvoy and James Sloss, *Regulation of Transport Innovation* (New York: Random House, 1967), pp. 1-35.
88. *Ibid.*, p. 329.
89. See Public Service Commission, *Annual Report 1959*, pp. 62-64.
90. It was in response to railroad complaints to such matters as state regulation that the Smathers Committee opened its hearings in 1958.
91. See Table 10.
92. Public Service Commission, *Annual Report, 1954*, p. 67.
93. However, milk service, too, was declining on the Rutland. Abandonment of passenger service did cause some hardship for some north country communities, but the Public Service Commission felt that there was no way to make such service pay.
94. Public Service Commission, *Annual Report, 1955*, p. 85.
95. *Ibid.*, p. 86.
96. *New York Times*, November 16, 1956.
97. *Ibid.*, November 17, 1956.
98. For discussion of this case see Conant, *op. cit.*, pp. 152-3.
99. Public Service Commission, *Annual Report 1959*, p. 248.
100. *Ibid.*, pp. 58-9.

101. *New York Times,* September 11, 1956. The Public Service Commission allowed reduction of Putnam service, but the last commuter train was not discontinued on this line until 1959.
102. *New York Times,* December 21, 1957.
103. *Ibid.,* October 9, 1956.
104. See Chapter VII for discussion of changes in state attitudes toward the railroads.
105. *New York Times,* December 3, 1957. President Perlman argued that pricing of commuter operations should be based upon the same procedure used in pricing "any public utility" to guarantee a fair return to the operator.
106. *Ibid.,* March 23, 1956.
107. *Ibid.,* August 11, 1956.
108. 229 I.C.C. 429, 436 (1956), See also Nelson, *op. cit.,* pp. 472-492.
109. *Problems of the Railroads,* Part I, p. 229.
110. *Ibid.,* pp. 221-4.
111. *Railway Age,* Vol. 135, no. 17, October 26, 1953, p. 23.
112. *Brotherhood of Locomotive, Fire and Engineermen Magazine,* Vol. 110.
113. Interstate Commerce Commission, *Activities of the Interstate Commerce Commission, 1937-1962.* p. 52.
114. *Ibid.*
115. A considerable body of administrative and judicial precedent exists with regard to criteria for Interstate Commerce Commission approval and denial of abandonments. Generally, however, it is conflicting and obscure. For a more detailed study of abandonment decision see Cherington, *op. cit.,* pp. 17-79, and Conant, *op. cit.,* pp. 113-131.
116. New York Ontario and Western Co. Receivers Abandonment (F.D. 19861), 295 Interstate Commerce Commission 831 (1957). For a general study of fair quality see: William F. Helmer, O & W (Berkeley: Howell-North and Company, 1959).
117. Helmer, *O and W.* pp. 1-30.
118. Alvin Harlow, *The Road of the Century* (New York: Creative Age Press, 1947), pp. 319-320.
119. *New York Ontario and Western Railway Co. Reorganization,* 295, I.C.C. 346, 361 (1956).
120. See Table 4, for study of the road's share of anthracite traffic.
121. 295 I.C.C. 831 (1957).
122. *New York Times,* March 10, 1956.
123. *Ibid.,* September 5, 1956.
124. *Ibid.,* November 9, 1956.
125. *Ibid.,* January 13, 1957.
126. *Ibid.,* March 15, 1957.
127. *Ibid.,* March 30, 1957.
128. *Ibid.,* June 28, 1957.

CHAPTER VI

1. Alvin Hansen, *The Post-War American Economy* (New York: Norton and Company, 1964), pp. 1-9.
2. Interstate Commerce Commission, *Annual Report, 1964,* p. 140.
3. Loomis pointed out that carloading had declined 5 percent in 1957 and he anticipated a 10 percent loss in 1958. In fact, carloading declined 15 percent in 1958. See: *Problems of the Railroads,* Part I, pp. 116-118.

4. *New York Times*, September 19, 1956, and November 6, 1956.
5. *Ibid.*, March 3, 1956.
6. *Ibid.*, December 18, 1956 and August 7, 1958. Western railroads received 6 percent in March, but only 5 percent in December.
7. *Ibid.*, February 13, 1958.
8. *U.S. News and World Report*, November 15, 1957, pp. 92-94.
9. *Problems of the Railroads*, Part I, p. 16.
10. *Ibid.*, pp. 37-48.
11. *Ibid.*, p. 229-230.
12. *Ibid.*, pp. 295-296.
13. *Ibid.*, p. 232-233.
14. *Ibid.*, p. 233.
15. The amount would have been 50 percent of approximately $1,400,000,000 then allocated to maintenance annually.
16. *Ibid.*, p. 1960.
17. *Ibid.*, Part IV, pp. 1987-1993.
18. *Ibid.*, p. 1934-1935.
19. *Ibid.*, p. 1936.
20. *Ibid.*, p. 1937.
21. *Ibid.*, pp. 1935-1936.
22. *Ibid.*, p. 1938.
23. *New York Times*, March 13, 1958.
24. *Ibid.*, July 3, 1958.
25. *Ibid.*, May 3, 1958.
26. *Ibid.*, April 2, 1958, and April 9, 1958.
27. Public Law 85-625 (1958).
28. Charles O. Morgret, "Role of Basic Materials," a speech delivered at University of Minnesota Public Relations Forum, May 19, 1959, reprinted in Arthur M. Johnson, *Government-Business Relations* (Columbus: Charles E. Merrill Books, Inc., 1965), pp. 42-46.
29. J. Handly Wright, "Public Relations of the American Railroads," a speech delivered at the University of Minnesota Public Relations Forum, May 19, 1959, reprinted in Johnson, *op. cit.*, pp. 39-72. According to Wright, who was Vice-President in Charge of Public Relations for the A.A.R., the study also revealed what the public felt were the basic economic problems confronting the roads. According to the study, labor costs were thought to be most important and the industry accordingly decided to attack this issue first with its campaign against "featherbedding."
30. See: Association of American Railroads, *Consolidations and Mergers in the Transportation Industry, Report of the Association of American Railroads to Transportation Study Group of U. S. Senate Resolution 29*, February 1, 1960 (mineo).
31. *Ibid.*, p. 27.
32. *Ibid.*, pp. 27-28.
33. U. S. Interstate Commerce Commission, *Railroad Consolidation and the Public Interest*, Statement # 6201 (Washington: U. S. Government Printing Office, 1962), pp. 83-87.
34. Daniel P. Loomis, "Merger Spooks and Spitballs," Speech delivered at Great Lakes Conference of Railroad and Utilities Commissioners, White Sulphur Springs, West Virginia, June 2, 1963.
35. Interstate Commerce Commission, *Railroad Consolidations and the Public Interest*, pp. 80-83.
36. *Transportation Trends*, p. 229.
37. *Ibid.*

38. Interstate Commerce Commission, *Railroad Consolidation and the Public Interest*, p. 4.
39. *Ibid.*, pp. 63-71.
40. *Ibid.*, pp. 72-76.
41. Despite continued complaints by shippers and state authorities that the Commission was too willing to accept evidence supplied by the railroads, the Interstate Commerce Commission continued to accept the railroads' economic studies.
42. See Conant, *op. cit.*, pp. 66-90 and Interstate Commerce Commission *Railroad Consolidation and the Public Interest*, appendices (pages unnumbered).
43. The Interstate Commerce Commission allowed both roads to reduce their passenger service immediately.
44. *Erie Railroad Company Merger*, 312 I.C.C. 185 (1960).
45. *Chesapeake and Ohio Railroad Company Control*, 317 I.C.C. 261 (1962).
46. 312 I.C.C. 185 (1960) and see below.
47. *Wall Street Journal*, November 3, 1957.
48. Gilbert Burck, "The World's Biggest Merger," *Fortune*, June, 1965, p. 179.
49. Practically the only source for this judgment is the two-part series in *Fortune* in June and July, 1965; however, the story's analysis fits well with the known facts.
50. *Ibid.*, p. 178.
51. The death of Robert Young in January, 1958 provided Perlman with the opportunity to scuttle the merger plans which Young had been promoting. After the announcement of the withdrawal of the Central, Symes of the Pennsylvania announced that it would cost the two roads $100,000,000 a year. See *Wall Street Journal*, January 9, 1958.
52. Conant, *op. cit.*, p. 79.
53. Gilbert Burck, *op. cit.*, p. 204.
54. *New York Times*, March 10, 1962.
55. *Ibid.*, August 12, 1962.
56. Gilbert Burck, *op. cit.*, p. 202.
57. Gilbert Burck, "The Worlds Biggest Merger—Part II," *Fortune*, July, 1965, p. 209.
58. Daniel P. Loomis, "Merger Spooks and Spitballs," speech delivered at Great Lakes Conference of Railroad Utilities Commissioners, White Sulphur Springs, West Virginia, June 22, 1963.
59. *Ibid.*
60. *New York Times*, January 16, 1968, p. 54.
61. 312 I.C.C. 185 (1960).
62. These branch abandonments included: Bath to Kanona (3.3 miles), Wayland to Groveland (14 miles), Ray to Elana (20.5 miles), Avon to Livonia (13.3 miles), North Alexander to Ray (3.8 miles), and Howells to Otisville (6.3 miles).
63. This had been the first rail line into the Adirondacks and Northern New York.
64. Public Service Commission, *Annual Report, 1963*, pp. 81-82, and *Annual Report, 1964*, pp. 88-89.
65. Public Service Commission, *Annual Report, 1959*, pp. 61-62. This route had earlier been an important secondary freight connection between Syracuse and Buffalo. By 1963, abandonments had fractured it between Caledonia and Holcomb, Pittsford and Canandaigua, and Seneca Falls and Auburn.

66. Public Service Commission, *Annual Report, 1964*, pp. 88-89.
67. Gross Revenues on the road amounted to only about $25,000.
68. The Unadilla Valley had taken up operation of 20 miles of the abandoned NYO & W's tracks from New Berlin to Sidney.
69. *Lehigh and New England Abandonment*, 312 I.C.C. 645, 652 (1961).
70. Interstate Commerce Commission, Finance Docket 21820, (1961), p. 10.
71. *Ibid.*, pp. 12-13.
72. *Ibid.*, p. 14.
73. In the case of the complete abandonment, the Interstate Commerce Commission was not obliged to protect the employees. Interstate Commerce Commission, *Activities of the Interstate Commerce Commission*, 1937-62, p. 52.
74. *Ibid.*, p. 52-53.
75. *Ibid.*, p. 53.
76. 72 Stat. 571, 49 U. S. C. (1958).
77. For a fine survey of Interstate Commerce Commission action under Section 13a(1) see: Conant *op. cit.*, pp. 149-161.
78. Calculated from Interstate Commerce Commission, *Annual Reports, 1959-1963*.
79. *Ibid.* The three cases did affect 61 trains, but 51 of these were the result of the Pennsylvania Railroad's and the Reading-Seashore's attempt to virtually discontinue commuter service at Pittsburgh and in southern New Jersey.
80. Public Service Commission, *Annual Report, 1963*, p. 79.
81. *New York Central Railroad Company*, 312 I.C.C. 4 (1960).
82. Public Service Commission, *Annual Report, 1959*, p. 15.
83. Calculated from Public Service Commission, *Annual Reports, 1959-1964*.
84. Public Service Commission, *Annual Report, 1959*, p. 5.
85. *Ibid.*
86. *New York Times*, March 26, 1958.
87. Public Service Commission, *Annual Report, 1959*, p. 16.
88. *New York Times*, March 21, 1959. See Public Service Commission, *Report of Investigation by the Public Service Commission of the Financial Condition of the Railroads Operating in the State of New York*. (mimeo, January 26, 1958).
89. The Full Crew Laws had been passed in 1913, with slight modification in 1921, 1936, and 1937. Under these laws trains operating in New York State required: 1) six man crews on all freight trains of more than 25 cars; 2) five man crews on all switching operations; 3) five man crews on all trains other than freights (a baggageman was added in 1921); and 4) three man crews on any light engine without cars. See: Public Service Commission, *Annual Report, 1959*, pp. 19-20.
90. Public Service Commission, *Report of Investigation . . . p.* 23.
91. Public Service Commission, *Annual Report, 1959*, p. 22.
92. *Ibid.*, p. 19.
93. See: Appendix 3.
94. *Moody's Transportation Manual* (New York: Moody's Investors Service Incorporated, 1966), pp. 497 and 624. In 1963, Central employment was 48,527 and Pennsylvania employment was 62,905.
95. *Ibid.*, p. 494-5.
96. *Ibid.*, p. 627.
97. Loomis, *op. cit.*
98. *Forbes*, January 1966, p. 121.
99. Public Service Commission, *Annual Reports*, 1961 and 1966.
100. *Ibid.*

101. New York *Times,* June 14, 1970, Section 3, p. 1.
102. *Ibid,* June 10, 1970, p. 1.
103. *Ibid,* June 9, 1970, p. 1 and June 10, 1970, p. 53.

CHAPTER VII

1. Public Service Commission, *Annual Report,* 1967, pp. 81-82.
2. The Unadilla Valley was finally abandoned in 1959.
3. For statistics on correct freight movement, see *Moody's Manual of Transportation, 1967.* For earlier data on coal movement, see Chapter 1.
4. Helmer, *op. cit.,* p. 94.
5. *Moody's Manual of Transportation Industries, 1965,* pp.
6. Taylor and Neu, *op. cit.,* pp. 75-91.
7. Less-than-carload service was, of course, the bulk of the freight service provided for small villages and hamlets having rail service.

APPENDICES

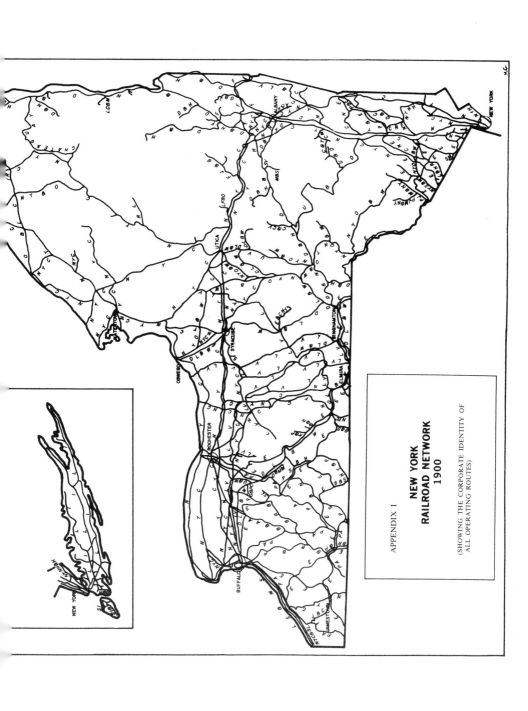

APPENDIX I

**NEW YORK
RAILROAD NETWORK
1900**

(SHOWING THE CORPORATE IDENTITY OF
ALL OPERATING ROUTES)

APPENDIX I

ABBREVIATIONS AND MILEAGE
OF NEW YORK RAILROADS, 1900

Abbreviation	Road	Mainline Mileage in New York
A & H	Albany and Hudson	16
B & H	Bath and Hammondsport	10
B & R	Brooklyn and Rockaway	3
BA & A	Buffalo Attica and Arcade	28
BRP	Buffalo Rochester and Pittsburgh	180
B & S	Buffalo and Susquehanna	21
CM	Catskill Mountain	19
C & T	Catskill and Tannersville	6
CNE	Central New England	113
CHAT	Chateauguay	83
C & LV	Chatham and Lebanon Valley	51
C & CV	Cooperstown and Charlotte Valley	24
D & H	Delaware and Hudson	568
D & MM	Dansville and Mt. Morris	12
DL & W	Delaware Lackawanna and Western	475
E	Erie	887
E & CNY	Erie and Central New York	18
F	Fitchburg	102
FJ & G	Fonda Johnstown and Gloversville	32
G & W	Genesee and Wyoming	16
GT	Grand Trunk	23
G & J	Greenwich and Johnsonville	15
J & C	Jamestown and Chataqua	27
K & P	Kanona and Prattsburg	11
K & AC	Keeseville and Ausable Chasm	6
LC & M	Lake Champlain and Moriah	8
LS & MS	Lake Shore and Michigan Southern	71
L & H	Lehigh and Hudson	25
L & NE	Lehigh and New England	7
LV	Lehigh Valley	618
LF & D	Little Falls and Dolgeville	10
LI	Long Island	379
M & S	Middleburgh and Schoharie	5
ND & C	Newburgh Dutchess and Connecticut	59
NYC	New York Central	2535
NYC & SL	New York Chicago and St. Louis	68
NYNH	New York New Haven and Hartford	56

ABBREVIATIONS AND MILEAGE
OF NEW YORK RAILROADS, 1900

NYO & W	New York Ontario and Western	376
NY & O	New York and Ottawa	71
NY & P	New York and Pennsylvania	21
NYS & W	New York Susquehanna and Western	13
NC	Northern Central of Pennsylvania	166
O & LC	Ogdensburgh and Lake Champlain	118
PS & N	Pittsburgh Shawmut and Northern	63
PJM & NY	Port Jervis Monticello and New York	41
PA	Pennsylvania	316
P & E	Poughkeepsie and Eastern	35
RL	Raquette Lake	18
SV	Schoharie Valley	4
SL	Silver Lake	7
S	Skaneatles	5
SI	Staten Island	13
SIRT	Staten Island Rapid Transit	11
SM	Sterling Mountain	7
U & D	Ulster and Delaware	110
UV	Unadilla Valley	19

ROADS NOT SHOWN OR NOT LABELED

Road	Mainline Mileage in New York
Boston and Albany (Shown as part of NYC)	57.0
Buffalo Creek	6.0
Connecting Terminal	1.0
Island	.1
Jerome Park	2.0
Marine	.4
Milford and Matamoras	.2
New Jersey and New York	20.0
New York Central and Fort Orange (Shown as part of NYC)	1.0
Otis	1.0
Owasco River	.5
South Brooklyn	1.0
St. Lawrence and Adirondak (Shown as part of NYC)	10.0

APPENDIX II

CONTROL AND BANKING CONNECTIONS OF MAJOR EASTERN RAILROADS IN 1920[a]

Railroad	Large or Controlling Stock Ownership	Established Banking Connections
1 — *Trunk Lines*		
New York Central	Union Pacific (8.4%)	J.P. Morgan and Co.
	Vanderbilt Family (4.8%)	First National Bank
	Baker Family (4.1%)	of N.Y.
Pennsylvania	None	Kuhn, Loeb & Co.
Baltimore & Ohio	Union Pacific (2.5%)	Kuhn, Loeb & Co.
Erie	George F. Baker (9.4%)	J.P. Morgan and Co.
		First National Bank
		of N.Y.
2 — *Pocahontas Coal Region*		
Chesapeake & O	H.E. Huntington	Kuhn, Loeb & Co.
Norfolk and Western	Pennsylvania Railroad	None
Virginian	H.H. Rogers Family	National City Bank
		of N.Y.
3 — *New England*		
Bangor and Aroostock	Aroostock Const. Co.	Brown Brothers & Co.
Maine Central	None	Kidder, Peabody & Co.
Boston & Maine	New Haven	Kidder, Peabody & Co.
Boston & Albany	Leased to New York Central	Kidder, Peabody & Co.
New Haven	Pennsylvania Railroad (3.4%)	J.P. Morgan and Co.
Rutland	New Haven, New York Central	None
Central Vermont	Canadian National	None
4 — *Pennsylvania Anthracite*		
Lehigh Valley	George F. Baker (2.6%)	J.P. Morgan and Co.
		First National Bank
		of N.Y.
Reading	New York Central Baltimore and Ohio	J.P. Morgan and Co.

CONTROL AND BANKING CONNECTIONS OF
MAJOR EASTERN RAILROADS IN 1920 [a]

Railroad	Large or Controlling Stock Ownership	Established Banking Connections
Delaware & Hudson	None	Kuhn, Loeb & Co. First National Bank of N.Y.
Delaware Lackawanna & Western	George F. Baker (10.6%)	J.P. Morgan and Co.
New York Ontario & Western	New Haven	None
Lehigh and New England	Lehigh Coal Co.	None
Lehigh and Hudson	Lehigh Coal Co.	None

[a] *Railroad Combination* ..., Part II, pp. 537-39 and determined from Report of House Committee on Interstate Commerce, House Rept. 2789. 71st Cong., 2nd Sess., p. 471.

APPENDIX III

SELECTED DATA ON EASTERN RAILROAD OPERATING PERFORMANCE, 1900-1963

Operating Revenues, 1900-1963 (000 omitted) [a]

Road	1900	1910	1920	1930	1940	1950	1958	1960	1963
Pa.	$88,539	$160,457	$378,091	$570,465	$477,598	$930,141	$844,232	$843,705	$840,111
N.Y.C.	66,333	99,908	311,032	478,918	370,545	759,685	858,985	759,824	705,533
B & O					179,175	402,542	382,540	389,402	371,660
Erie	39,102	56,649	91,797	95,372	86,606	166,190	152,746	220,419	169,091
DL & W	20,887	36,052	71,824	69,661	51,891	76,279	(Erie-Lackawanna after 1960)		
New Haven	39,920		106,545	118,885	85,604	150,756	149,551	134,044	122,781
D & H	11,485	20,431	64,528	37,900	26,775	54,835	46,453	43,287	41,125
Lehigh Valley	23,009	37,687	34,749	60,664	47,479	71,236	57,787	51,309	45,471

[a] Calculated from New York State, *Public Service Commission Reports* (selected years).

Net Income as a Percent of Operating Revenue [a]

Road	1920	1930	1940	1950	1958	1960	1963
Pa.	13.6%	12.0%	9.6%	4.1%	.4%	Deficit	1.0%
N.Y.C.	23.5%	8.3%	3.0%	2.4%	.6%	.6%	1.9%
B & O			3.0%	3.7%	4.2%	.6%	1.4%
Erie (Erie-Lack)	8.7%	4.3%	0.0%	8.0%	Deficit	Deficit	Deficit
DL & W	38.8%	8.7%	.3%	4.6%	5.1%	(Erie-Lackawanna after 1960)	
New Haven	8.7%	13.3%	Deficit	4.9%	Deficit	Deficit	Deficit
D & H	12.3%	5.7%	2.8%	6.2%	7.1%	13.1%	7.4%
L.V.	22.3%	4.1%	Deficit	5.0%	Deficit	Deficit	Deficit

[a] Calculated from New York State, *Public Service Commission Reports* (selected years).

APPENDIX IV

CHANGES IN MAINLINE MILEAGE OPERATED BY MAJOR RAILROADS IN NEW YORK, 1900-1966 [a]

Road	1900	1914 (Peak year)	1920	1930	1940	1950	1966
New York C.	2535	2556	2819	2871	2836	2811	2221
Erie	887	948	950	1003	969	947	1149
(Showing Erie-Lackawanna in 1966)							
DL & W	475	495	494	493	493	493	—
Lehigh V.	618	653	659	651	601	601	534
D & H	568	706	718	721	714	668	609
Long Island	379	399	398	404	378	364	339
Balt. & Ohio	180	191	189	209	209	209	166
(Buff. Roch. & Pitt. to 1940)							
Boston & Me.	—	122	122	122	122	97	94
New Haven	56	79	47	232	131	130	129

[a] Calculated from New York State, *Railroad Commission Reports* and New York State, Public Service Commission, *Annual Reports* (selected years).

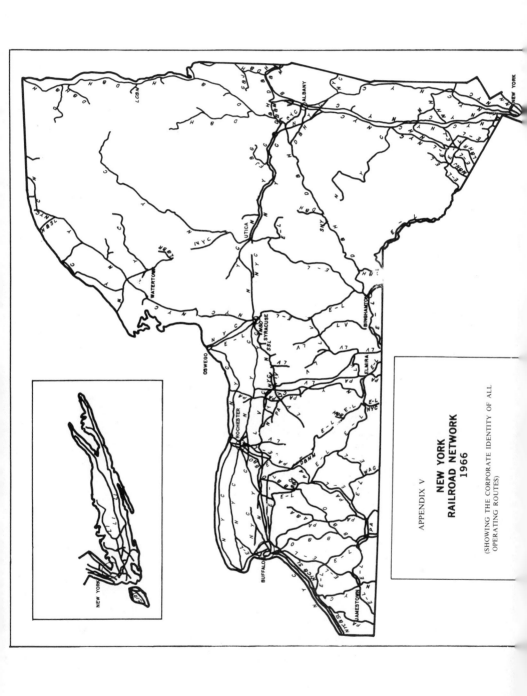

APPENDIX V

**NEW YORK
RAILROAD NETWORK
1966**

(SHOWING THE CORPORATE IDENTITY OF ALL
OPERATING ROUTES)

APPENDIX V

ABBREVIATIONS AND MILEAGE OF NEW YORK RAILROADS, 1966

Abbreviation	Road	Mainline Mileage in New York
A & A	Arcade and Attica	28
B & O	Baltimore and Ohio	166
B & H	Bath and Hammondsport	9
B & M	Boston and Maine	94
CN	Canadian National	22
D & MM	Dansville and Mount Morris	7
D & H	Delaware and Hudson	609
E-L	Erie-Lackawanna	1149
FJ & G	Fonda Johnstown and Gloversville	17
G & J	Greenwich and Johnsonville	15
LC & M	Lake Champlain and Moriah	7
L & H	Lehigh and Hudson	13
LV	Lehigh Valley	456
LI	Long Island	339
L & BR	Lowville and Beaver River	12
M & O	Marcellus and Otisco	3
M & MJ	Middletown and New Jersey	14
NH	New Haven	130
NYC	New York Central	2221
NYC & SL	New York Chicago and St. Louis	70
N & SL	Norwood and St. Lawrence	18
P	Pennsylvania	382
SSL	Skaneatles Short Line	5
SNY	Southern New York	1
SIRT	Staten Island Rapid Transit	15
WAG	Wellsville Addison and Galeton	32

ROADS NOT SHOWN

Road	Mainline Mileage in New York
Buffalo Creek	31
Massena Terminal	2
New Jersey and New York	1
New York Connecting	12
Niagara Junction	44
Owasco River	3
South Buffalo	2
Troy Union	2

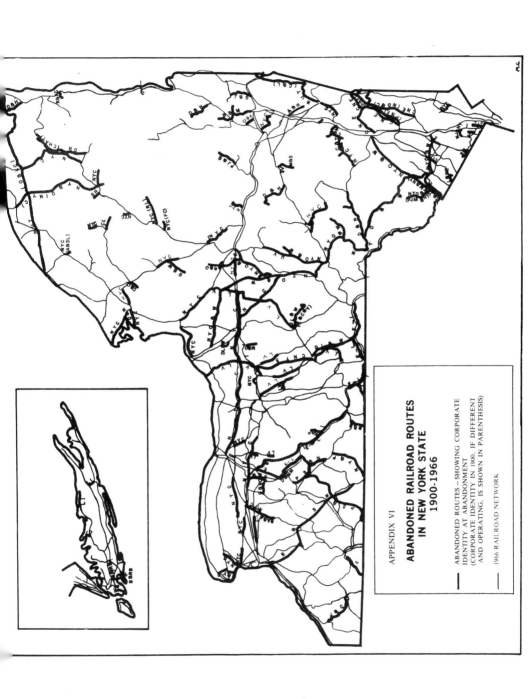

APPENDIX VI

ABANDONED RAILROAD ROUTES
IN NEW YORK STATE
1900-1966

—————   ABANDONED ROUTES – SHOWING CORPORATE
        IDENTITY AT ABANDONMENT
        (CORPORATE IDENTITY IN 1900, IF DIFFERENT
        AND OPERATING, IS SHOWN IN PARENTHESIS)

————   1966 RAILROAD NETWORK

APPENDIX VI
KEY TO ABANDONED RAIL ROUTES

Abbreviation	Road
A & H	Albany and Hudson
B & M	Boston and Maine
B & RB	Brooklyn and Rockaway Beach
BA & A	Buffalo Attica and Arcade
B & S	Buffalo and Susquehanna
CM	Catskill Mountain
C & T	Catskill and Tannersville
CNE	Central New England
CNY & S	Central New York and Southern
C & C	Copenhagen and Carthage
CL	Cranberry Lake
D & MM	Dansville and Mt. Morris
D & H	Delaware and Hudson
DL & W	Delaware Lackawanna and Western
D & N	Delaware and Northern
E	Erie
E-L	Erie-Lackawanna
FJ & G	Fonda Johnstown and Gloversville
G & W	Genesee and Wyoming
GW	Glenfield and Western
G & PC	Greigsville and Pearl Creek
GR	Grass River
G & J	Greenwich and Johnsonville
J & C	Jamestown and Chataqua
K & P	Kanona and Prattsburg
K & AC	Keeseville and Ausable Chasm
L & NE	Lehigh and New England
LV	Lehigh Valley
LI	Long Island
M & S	Middleburg and Schoharie
M & O	Marcellus and Otisco
NJ & NY	New Jersey and New York
NYC	New York Central
NYO & W	New York Ontario and Western
NY & P	New York and Pennsylvania
PS & N	Pittsburgh Shawmut and Northern
R & O	Rome and Osceola
RUT	Rutland
SV	Schoharie Valley
SM	Sterling Mountain
UV	Unadilla Valley

APPENDIX VII

RAILROADS OPERATING OR ORGANIZED 1900-1963 WITH CORPORATE IDENTITY LOST THROUGH MERGER OR REORGANIZATION[a]

Railroad	Operating Road (1963)
1. Boston and Albany	NYC
2. Buffalo Rochester and Pittsburgh	B & O
3. Buffalo and Susquehanna	WAG
4. Cooperstown and Charlotte Valley	D & H
5. Delaware Lackawanna and Western	E-L
6. Erie	E-L
7. Fitchburg	B & M
8. Grand Trunk	Canadian National
9. Lake Shore and Mich. Central	NYC
10. Little Falls and Dolgeville	NYC
11. Northern Central of Pennsylvania	Pa.
12. Marion	Pa.
13. Silver Lake	B & O
14. Ulster and Delaware	NYC
15. Western New York and Pennsylvania	Pa.
16. Staten Island	SIRT
17. St. Lawrence and Adirondack	NYC

[a] New York State, Public Service Commission, *Annual Reports* and miscellaneous Commission records.

BIBLIOGRAPHY

Books

Allen, Frederick L. *The Great Pierpont Morgan.* New York: Harper and Brothers Company, 1948.

Barger, Harold. *The Transport Industries. 1889-1946: A Study of Output, Employment, and Productivity.* New York: National Bureau of Economic Research, 1951.

Benson, Lee. *Merchants, Farmers and Railroads: Railroad Regulation and New York Politics, 1850-1887.* Cambridge: Harvard University Press, 1955.

Bernstein, Marver H. *Regulating Business by Independent Commission.* Princeton: Princeton University Press, 1955.

Burgess, George H. and Kennedy, Miles C. *Centennial History of the Pennsylvania Railroad Company.* Philadelphia: Pennsylvania Railroad Company, 1949.

Campbell, E. G. *Reorganization of the American Railroads, 1893-1900.* New York: Columbia University Press, 1938.

Cherington, Charles R. *The Regulation of Railroad Abandonments.* Cambridge: Harvard University Press, 1948.

Clement, M.W. *One Hundred Years, 1846-1946.* Philadelphia: The Pennsylvania Railroad Company, 1946.

Cleveland, F. A. and Powell, F. W. *Railroad Finance.* New York: Appleton and Company, 1922.

Conant, Michael. *Railroad Mergers and Abandonments.* Berkeley: University of California Press, 1965.

Corey, Lewis. *The House of Morgan.* New York: Grosset and Dunlap, 1930.

Daggett, Stuart. *Principles of Inland Transportation.* (3rd ed.). New York: Harpers, 1941.

——. *Railroad Reorganization.* Boston: Houghton, Mifflin Company, 1908.

Delaware and Hudson Company. *A Century of Progress: A History of the Delaware and Hudson.* Albany: 1929.

Dennison, E. F. *The Sources of Economic Growth in the United States.* New York: Council for Economic Development, 1965.

Dewhurst, J. F., and Associates. *America's Needs and Resources: A New Survey.* New York: Twentieth Century Fund, Inc., 1955.

Dixon, F. H. *Railroads and Government.* New York: Scribners, 1922.

Faulkner, Harold U. *The Decline of Laissez Faire.* New York: Holt, Rinehart and Winston, 1962.

Fite, C. C. and Reese, J. F. *An Economic History of the United States.* Second edition. New York: Houghton Mifflin, 1965.

Flippin, Elmer O. *Rural New York.* New York: Macmillan and Company, 1921.

Fogel, Robert. *Railroads and American Economic Growth.* Baltimore: Johns Hopkins Press, 1964.

Ginger, Ray. *The Age of Excess.* New York: The Macmillan Company, 1965.

Goodrich, Carter, *Government Promotion of American Canals and Railroads.* New York: Columbia University Press, 1960.

Gras, N.S.B. and Larson, H.M. *Casebook in American History.* New York: Crofts and Company, 1939.

Guthmann, H. G. and Dougall, H. E. *Corporate Financial Policy.* Englewood Cliffs: Prentice-Hall, Inc., 1962.

Hadley, A. T. *Railroad Transportation.* New York: G.P. Putnam, 1885.

Hanson, Alvin. *The Post-War American Economy.* New York: Norton and Company, 1964.

Harlow, Alvin. *The Road of the Century.* New York: Creative Age Press, 1947.

Healy, Kent T. *The Effects of Scale in the Railroad Industry.* New Haven: Yale University Press, 1961.

Helmer, William F. *O and W.* Berkeley: Howell-North and Company, 1959.

Herring, James Morton. *The Problem of Weak Railroads.* Philadelphia: University of Pennsylvania Press, 1929.

Hilton, George W. and Due, John F. *Electric Interurban Railways in America.* Stanford: Stanford University Press, 1960.

Hines, Walker D. *War History of American Railroads.* New Haven: Yale University Press, 1928.

Hoover, E. and Vernon, R. *Anatomy of a Metropolis.* Cambridge: Harvard University Press, 1960.

Hungerford, Edward. *The Story of the Baltimore and Ohio Railroad, 1827-1927.* New York: G. P. Putnams and Sons, 1928.

————. *Men and Iron: The Story of the New York Central.* New York: Crowell Co., 1938.

————. *Men of Erie.* New York: Randon House Inc., 1946.

Johnson, Arthur H. *Government-Business Relations.* Columbus: Charles E. Merrill Books, 1965.

Johnson, E.R. and Van Metre, T.W. *Principles of Railroad Transportation.* New York: Appleton and Company, 1917.

Kolko, Gabriel. *Railroads and Regulation. 1877-1916.* Princeton: Princeton University Press, 1965.

Latham, Earl. *The Politics of Railroad Coordination, 1933-1936.* Cambridge: Harvard University Press, 1959.

Laidler, Harry. *Concentration in American Industry.* New York: Crowell and Company, 1931.

Leonard, William Norris. *Railrad Consolidation Under the Transportation Act of 1920.* New York: Columbia University Press, 1946.

Locklin, D. Philip. *Economics of Transportation* (Rev.). Chicago: Business Publications, 1938.

———. *Railroad Regulations Since 1920.* New York: A.W. Shaw Company, 1928.

Meyer, John R., *et. al. The Economics of Competition in the Transport Industries.* Cambridge: Harvard University Press, 1959.

Moody, John. *The Truth About the Trusts.* New York: Moody Publishing Co., 1904.

Moulton, H.G. *The American Transportation Problem.* Washington: Brookings Institution, 1933.

Myers, Gustavus. *History of the Great American Fortunes.* Chicago: Kerr, 1908.

Nelson, James C. *Railroad Transportation and Public Policy.* Washington, D.C.: The Brookings Institution, 1959.

Norton, William. *Modern Transportation Economics.* Columbus: Charles E. Merrill Books, Inc., 1963.

Perloff, Harvey. *Regions, Resources and Economic Growth.* New York: Resources for the Future, 1958.

Pierce, Harry H. *Railroads of New York — A Study of Government Aid, 1826-1875.* Cambridge: Harvard University Press, 1953.

Prince, Frederick H. "A Plan for Coordinating the Operations of Railroads in the United States." Mimeographed, March 15, 1933, Revised September, 1933.

Ripley, William Z. *Railroads: Finance and Organization.* New York: Longmans, Green and Co., 1915.

———. *Railroads: Rates and Regulations.* New York: Longmans, Green and Co., 1912.

Rostow, Walt W. *The Stages of Economic Growth.* Cambridge: Harvard University Press, 1962.

Russel, Robert R. *A History of the American Economic System.* New York: Appleton-Century-Crofts, 1964.

Sharfman, I.L. *The Interstate Commerce Commission,* 4 Vols. New York: Twentieth Century Fund, 1931-7.

Shott, John G. *The Railroad Monopoly.* Washington, D.C.: Public Affairs Institute, 1950.

Splawn, W.M.W. *Consolidation of Railroads.* New York: Macmillan, 1924.

Taylor, George R. *The Transportation Revolution.* New York: Holt, Rinehart and Winston Company, 1951.

———., and Neu, Irene D. *The American Railroad Network, 1861-1890.* Cambridge: Harvard University Press, 1956.

Thompson, Slason. *A Short History of American Railroads*. New York: Appleton and Co., 1925.

Whitford, Noble, E. *History of the Canal Systems of the State of New York*. Albany: State Printing Office, 1905.

Articles

Atterbury, W.W. "Railroad Consolidation," *Annals of the Academy of Political Science*, Vol. 71 (September,1934), 56-71.

Bunck, Gilbert, "The World's Biggest Merger," *Fortune*, June, 1965, 176-179, 200-208 and *Fortune*, July, 1965, 128-131, 202-215.

Cootner, Paul. "The Role of Railroads in United States Economic Growth," *Journal of Economic History*, Vol. XXIII (December, 1963), 477-521.

Dodge, D. "Empire in Hock," *American Mercury*, Vol. 34, February, 1935. 160-174.

Eastman, Joseph B. "Public Ownership and Operation of Railroads in the United States," *The Annals of the American Academy of Political Science*, Vol. 187 (September, 1936), 106-114.

———. "Transportation Problems and Suggestions Toward a Constructive Solution," *Academy of Political Science Proceedings*, Vol. 17 (January, 1937). 239-249.

———. "The Economic Adjustment of Rates between Competing Forms of Transportation," *American Economic Review*, Vol. XXX (March, 1940), 124-129.

Esch, John J. "Advantages and Disadvantages of Consolidation," *American Academy of Political Science Proceedings*, Vol. 13 (June, 1929), 383-395.

Jenks, Leland. "Railroads as an Economic Force in American History," *Journal of Economic History*, Vol. IV (May, 1944), 1-20.

Lewis, Ben. W. "Ambivalence in Public Policy Toward Regulated Industries," *American Economic Review*, *Supplement*, Vol. 53 (May, 1963), 38-52.

"The New York Central Chooses," *Fortune*. February, 1932, 70, 112-145.

Pelley, John J. "The Case for Public Ownership and Operation of Railroads in the United States," *The Annals of the American Academy of Political Science*. Vol. 187 (September, 1936), 120-131.

———. "American Railroads in and after the War," *The Annals of the American Academy of Political Science*, Vol. 230 (November, 1943), 23-31.

"The Railroads' Problems," *U.S. News and World Report*. November 15, 1957.

"Socrates Among the Railroads," *Fortune*. February, 1932, 71-3, 102-104.

Ullman, Edward A. "The Railroad Pattern of the U.S.," *Geographical Review*, Vol. 39 (1949), 242-256.

"The Van's Hold On," *Business Week*, March 24, 1934, 14-15.

"What Railroads Made Money in 1938," *Business Week*, March 11, 1939, 44-45.

Government Documents

New York State. Board of Railroad Commissioners. *Annual Reports,* 1899-1906.

———. Department of Public Works. *Highway Needs.* Albany: 1950.

———. *New York State Legislative Manual,* 1933-1954.

———. Public Service Commission. *Annual Reports.* 1906-1967.

———. ———. *Report of Investigation of the Public Service Commission of the Financial Condition of the Railroads Operating in the State of New York.* Mimeographed: January 26, 1958.

U. S. Bureau of Census. *Historical Statistics of the United States to 1957.* Washington: U.S. Government Printing Office, 1960.

———. *Statistical Abstract of the United States, 1964.*

U.S. Bureau of Mines. *Mineral Facts and Problems.* Washington: U.S. Government Printing Office, 1963.

U.S. Congress. *United States Statutes at Large,* Vols. 1-71.

———. House of Representatives. Committee on Interstate and Foreign Commerce. *Railroad Consolidation.* Hearings on H.R. 11212, 69th Congress, 1st Session, 1928; H.R. 5641, 70th Congress, 1st Session, 1928.

———. ———. ———. *Regulation of Stock Ownership in Railroads* (by W.M.W. Splawn). House Report No. 2789, 71st Congress, 2nd Session, 1931.

———. ———. ———. *Omnibus Transportation Bill.* Hearings on H.R. 2531, 76th Congress, 2nd Session, 1939.

———. Senate, Committee on Interstate Commerce. *Railroad Combination in the Eastern Region.* Senate Report No. 1182, 76th Congress, 3rd Session, 1940.

———. ———. ———. *Some Educational, Legislative and Self-Regulatory Activities of United States Railroads.* 77th Congress, 1st Session, 1940.

———. ———. ———. *Problems of the Railroads* Hearings, 85th Congress, 2nd Session, 1958.

———. ———. Special Study Group on Transportation Policies in the United States. *Transportation Trends.* 86th Congress, 2nd Session, 1960.

———. ———. *The Interstate Commerce Act, Revised to November 1, 1951.* Senate Document No. 72. 82nd Congress, 1st Session, 1951.

———. ———. Temporary National Economic Committee. *Investigation of Concentration of Economic Power.* Washington: U.S. Government Printing Office, 1940.

U.S. Interstate Commerce Commission. *Activities of the Interstate Commerce Commission, 1887-1937.* Washington: U.S. Government Printing Office, 1937.

———. *Activities of the Interstate Commerce Commission, 1937-1962.* Washington: U.S. Government Printing Office, 1962.

————. *Annual Reports,* 1887-1969.

————. *Intercorporate Relationships of Railways in the United States as of June 30, 1906.* Washington: U.S. Government Printing Office, 1908.

————. *Proceedings,* 1900-1962.

————. *Railroad Abandonments, 1920-1943.* Washington: U.S. Government Printing Office, 1945.

————. *Railroad Consolidation and the Public Interest.* Washington: U.S. Government Printing Office, 1962.

————. *Statistics of Railways in the United States,* 1888-1953.

————. *Transportation Statistics in the United States.* 1954-1964.

U.S. National Resources Planning Board. *Transportation and National Policy.* House Document No. 883, 77th Congress, 2nd Session, 1942.

U.S. Office of Federal Coordinator. *Public Aids to Transportation,* 4 Vols., Washington: U.S. Government Printing Office, 1938-40.

————. *Report of Economic Possibilities of Regional Coordination Projects.* Washington. U.S. Government Prining Office, 1935.

————. *Fourth Annual Report of the Coordinator.* Washington: U.S. Government Printing Office, 1938.

U.S. President. *Economic Report of the President.* Washington: U.S. Government Printing Office, 1965.

Manuals and Reports

Association of American Railroads. *Railroads and Railroad Wages.* Washington: Mimeographed, 1937.

————. *Report on Coordination.* Washington: Association of American Railroads, 1942.

————. *American Railroads and the War.* Washington: Association of American Railroads, 1943.

————. *A Chronology of American Railroads.* Washington: Association of American Railroads, 1945.

————. *Consolidation of Railroads.* Washington: Association of American Railroads, 1945.

————. *Transportation in America.* Washington: Association of American Railroads, 1947.

————. *Consolidations and Mergers in the Transportation Industry, Report of the Association of American Railroads to Transportation Study Group of U. S. Senate.* Washington: Mimeographed, 1960.

Bituminous Coal Facts, 1950. Washington: National Coal Association, 1950.

Bituminous Coal Facts, 1958. Washington: National Coal Association, 1958.

Moody's Transportation Manual. New York: Moody's Investors Service, 1950-1969.

National Resource Committee. *The Structure of the American Economy.* Washington: Privately Printed, 1935.

Poor, H.V. and H.W. *Manual of the Railroads of the United States for 1885.* New York: Little and Company, 1885.

Newspapers

New York Times, 1899-1970.

Wall Street Journal, 1904-1964.

Journals

The Bankers Magazine (New York), Vol. XXXVIII (January, 1883).

Financial Review (New York), 1900-1912.

Railway Age, Vols. 72-131 (1900-1960).

The Railway News (London), January 5, 1884.

Pamphlets

American Shortline Railroad Association. Washington: 1926.

Committee on Public Relations of the Eastern Railroads. *A Yearbook of Railroad Information.* Washington: 1929.

P.R.R. plus N.Y.C. Spells Economic Ruin for Pennsylvania. Philadelphia: 1963.

Unpublished Sources

Association of American Railroads. Miscellaneous records and correspondence on open file at Association headquarters in Washington, D.C.

County, A.J. "A Plan of Unification of the Eastern Railroads." A speech given before Philadelphia Chamber of Commerce, May 19, 1934. Mimeographed.

Loomis, Daniel P. "Merger Spooks and Spitballs," A speech delivered at Great Lakes Conference of Railroad and Utilities Commissioners, White Sulphur Springs, West Virginia, June 22, 1963. Mimeographed.

INDEX